Transnational Evidence and Multicultural Inquiries in Europe

Stefano Ruggeri

Editor

Transnational Evidence and Multicultural Inquiries in Europe

Developments in EU Legislation and New Challenges for Human Rights-Oriented Criminal Investigations in Cross-border Cases

 Springer

Editor
Stefano Ruggeri
Department of Law
University of Messina
Messina
Italy

ISBN 978-3-319-02569-8   ISBN 978-3-319-02570-4 (eBook)
DOI 10.1007/978-3-319-02570-4
Springer Cham Heidelberg New York Dordrecht London

Library of Congress Control Number: 2013957063

Printed on acid-free paper

Springer is part of Springer Science+Business Media (www.springer.com)

Acknowledgements

This book contains the results of a conference organized at the University of Messina, Sicily, in June 2012, on the developments in EU legislation in the area of transnational evidence gathering and the new challenges for a human rights-oriented model of transborder criminal investigations in the EU. This conference was organised by my chair of Italian and European criminal procedure at the Department of Law of the University of Messina and was founded by the University of Messina, the *Assemblea Regionale Siciliana* (ARS) and the Bar Council of Messina, which I sincerely wish to thank for their financial support to this initiative.

Above all, I am very grateful to my colleagues for their contributions to this book. A particular thanks goes, again, to Springer Verlag and especially to Dr. Brigitte Reschke for her constant interest in our initiatives. Of course this research could be completed through the help of my chair team. Moreover, this book constitutes the first step of a project undertaken by my chair, aimed at promoting both young scholars and students of our *Corsi di laurea* to research activities. In this light I am very proud that some students and chair assistants of mine—namely Simona Arasi, Alessandro Arena, Diego Foti and Alessandra Grio—have therefore taken part actively in this research and their papers appear in this book.

Last but not least, I would like to thank, as always, my family, my wife Norma and my two little daughters, Anna Lucia and Maria Isabel, who constantly accompany and enlighten my researches with their love.

Thank you all very much!

Messina   Stefano Ruggeri
25 August 2013

Abbreviations

AFSJ	Area of Freedom, Security and Justice
CCP	Code of Criminal Procedure
CISA	Convention Implementing de Schengen Agreement
EAW	European Arrest Warrant
ECHR	European Convention on Human Rights
ECJ	European Court of Justice
ECMACM	European Convention on Mutual Legal Assistance in Criminal Matters
EEW	European Evidence Warrant
EIO	European Investigation Order
EJN	European Judicial Network
EPPO	European Public Prosecutor's Office
EU	European Union
EUCMACM	Convention on Mutual Assistance in Criminal Matters between the Member States of the European Union
EU FRA	European Union's Agency for Fundamental Rights
EU FRCh	Charter of Fundamental Rights of the European Union
FD	Framework Decision
FD EAW	Framework Decision on the European Arrest Warrant
FD EEW	Framework Decision on the European Evidence Warrant
FD OFPE	Framework Decision on the Execution in the EU of Orders Freezing Property or Evidence
IACMACM	Inter-American Convention on Mutual Assistance in Criminal Matters
JIT	Joint Investigation Teams
OCTA	Organized Crime Threat Assessment
PD EIO	Proposal for a Directive on a European Investigation Order

SAP ECMACM	Second Additional Protocol to European Convention on Mutual Legal Assistance in Criminal Matters
TEU	Treaty on the European Union
TFEU	Treaty on the Functioning of the European Union
UN CTOC	United Nations Convention against Transnational Organised Crime
UN MTMACM	United Nations Model Treaty on Mutual Assistance in Criminal Matters

Contents

**Part I   Current Perspectives in EU Legislation. The European
Investigation Order: Towards a European Cross-Border
Investigative Procedure?**

**Introduction to the Proposal of a European Investigation Order:
Due Process Concerns and Open Issues**   3
Stefano Ruggeri

Part II   Critical Analysis of the EIO Proposal: General Issues

**The European Investigation Order: A Rush into the
Wrong Direction**   29
Bernd Schünemann

General Considerations on the European Investigation Order   37
Tommaso Rafaraci

The European Investigation Order: Fundamental Rights at Risk?   45
Richard Vogler

**Collecting Criminal Evidence Across the European Union:
The European Investigation Order Between Flexibility and
Proportionality**   51
Silvia Allegrezza

Part III   Critical Analysis of the EIO Proposal: Specific Issues

**The Proposal for a Directive on the European Investigation
Order and the Grounds for Refusal: A Critical Assessment**   71
Lorena Bachmaier Winter

**Critical Remarks on the Proposal for a European Investigation
Order and Some Considerations on the Issue of Mutual
Admissibility of Evidence**   91
Rosanna Belfiore

European Investigation Order: The Defence Rights Perspective   107
Laura Autru Ryolo

**The Rules on Legal Remedies: Legal Lacunas and Risks
for Individual Rights**   111
Alessandro Arena

The Defendant's Rights in the Hearing by Videoconference   119
Alessandra Grio

**The EIO Proposal and the Rules on Interception of
Telecommunications**   127
Simona Arasi

**The EIO Proposal for a Directive and Mafia Trials:
Striving for Balance Between Efficiency and Procedural
Guarantees**   139
Paola Maggio

**European Investigation Orders and Non-repeatability
of Evidence in Cross-Border Cases: The Italian Perspective**   151
Diego Foti

**Part IV   Cross-Border Criminal Inquiries in Europe: Solution Models
and Human Rights Challenges**

**Solution Models and Principles Governing the Transnational
Evidence-Gathering in the EU**   161
Bernd Schünemann

**Criminal Evidence and Respect for Fair Trial Guarantees in the
Dialogue Between the European Court of Human Rights and
National Courts**   181
Richard Vogler

**Transnational Investigations and Prosecution of Cross-Border
Cases in Europe: Guidelines for a Model of Fair Multicultural
Criminal Justice**   193
Stefano Ruggeri

Annex   229

Contributors

Silvia Allegrezza University of Bologna, Bologna, Italy

Simona Arasi Department of Law, University of Messina, Messina, Italy

Alessandro Arena Department of Law, University of Messina, Messina, Italy

Laura Autru-Ryolo Criminal Law Committee of Council of Bars and Law Societies in Europe, Advisory Board of European Criminal Bar Association, Bar Council of Messina, Messina, Italy

Lorena Bachmaier Winter University Complutense of Madrid, Madrid, Spain

Rosanna Belfiore University of Catania, Catania, Italy

Diego Foti Department of Law, University of Messina, Messina, Italy

Alessandra Grio Department of Law, University of Messina, Messina, Italy

Paola Maggio University of Palermo, Palermo, Italy

Tommaso Rafaraci University of Catania, Catania, Italy

Stefano Ruggeri University of Messina, Messina, Italy

Bernd Schünemann Juristische Fakultät, Ludwig-Maximilians-Universität München, Munich, Germany

Richard Vogler University of Sussex, Falmer, UK

Part I
Current Perspectives in EU Legislation. The European Investigation Order: Towards a European Cross-Border Investigative Procedure?

Introduction to the Proposal of a European Investigation Order: Due Process Concerns and Open Issues

Stefano Ruggeri

Abstract The draft Directive on a European Investigation Order, launched by eight Member States in 2010, constitutes the last step in a long path towards the creation of a European regulation on the collection of evidence abroad. The complex structure of the proposed instrument, aimed both at conducting investigations overseas and obtaining evidence which is already in the possession of the executing State, reveals a new way of providing mutual recognition, combined with the flexibility of the MLA system. Despite its ambitious goals and the announced innovations, this instrument provides a complicated combination of fairly old solutions, which does not allow a proper balance to be achieved between the efficiency of transnational prosecution and the protection of human rights, and therefore does not satisfy the need for a fair investigative procedure in transnational cases. This introductory study provides a critical view of the main general and specific issues of the draft proposal, focusing on some due process concerns and unresolved issues of the new instrument.

Keywords Cross-border investigations • European investigation order • Transnational evidence

Contents

1 Introductory Remarks. The Long Path Towards a European Transnational Investigative
  Procedure 4
2 The European Investigation Order. General Issues 6
  2.1 Subject of the Proposed Directive: A New Legislative Action Aimed at Providing a
      Single Instrument for Gathering Evidence in Other EU Member States 6
  2.2 Approach and Goals of the Draft Proposal Instrument: A New Way of Providing
      Mutual Recognition 9

S. Ruggeri (✉)
Department of Law, University of Messina, Piazza Pugliatti No. 1, Messina, Italy
e-mail: steruggeri@unime.it

S. Ruggeri (ed.), *Transnational Evidence and Multicultural Inquiries in Europe*,
DOI 10.1007/978-3-319-02570-4_1, © Springer International Publishing Switzerland 2014

3   The European Investigation Order. Specific Issues 10
    3.1   Defining the Investigative Activity to Be Conducted 10
    3.2   Proportionality and Admissibility of the Investigation Abroad 12
    3.3   Methods of Obtaining Evidence Abroad and Defence Rights 14
    3.4   The Refusal of Recognition and Execution: The Measures of Coercion in Cross-
          Border Cases 18
    3.5   Challenging the Investigation Order 20
4   Conclusion 23
References 24

1   Introductory Remarks. The Long Path Towards a European Transnational Investigative Procedure

The topic of free movement and the admissibility of transnational evidence has been among the most debated issues of EU cross-border cooperation in criminal matters over almost the last two decades.[1] A close look at its development in academic discussions and EU initiatives since the *Corpus iuris* project[2] shows, however, that the issue of obtaining evidence in and from other Member States not only has been of varying importance, with through periods of intensive discussions and phases of relative stasis, but has also shown a extraordinary, chameleon-like adaptability to the evolution in EU legislation in criminal matters.

Thus, the 2001 Green Paper on the establishment of a European Prosecutor established, following the approach of the Tampere Council,[3] the duty of any Member State to admit unconditionally the evidence gathered in other Member States.[4] This rigid approach, which was in line with the vertical perspective of the European Prosecutor initiative, was rapidly abandoned, and therefore in the EEW proposal of 2003—launched by the Commission with the aim of applying the strict mutual recognition logic of the FD EAW to the field of evidence gathering[5]—there was no trace of any duty of admission by national authorities of evidence collected in other Member States. It is, however, well known that this legislative proposal had to face so many hurdles and criticisms that adoption of the new instrument was delayed by over 5 years. The issue of the admissibility of evidence re-emerged in the Green Paper of 2009 on obtaining evidence in criminal matters from one

---

[1] Amongst the many researches and studies conducted in this field, see Vervaele (2005), Gleß (2006), and Illuminati (2009).

[2] For the first version of the project, see Delmas-Marty (1997), *passim*. The project was then revised and published in 2000 in Delmas-Marty and Vervaele (2000), *passim*.

[3] Tampere Conclusions, point 36.

[4] COM (2001) 715 final, point 6.3.4.1. On this topic see Allegrezza, Part II, Sect. 3.1.

[5] Proposal for a Council Framework Decision on the European Evidence Warrant for obtaining objects, documents and data for use in proceedings in criminal matters [COM/2003/0688 final].

Member State to another and securing its admissibility.[6] Moreover, the introduction by the Lisbon Treaty of a new general framework allowing for legal approximation in the field of admissibility of evidence in criminal matters with cross-border dimensions [Art. 82(2)(a) TFEU] led to the immediate launching of new initiatives aimed to replace in the EU area most instruments both of judicial assistance and mutual recognition with a new instrument of evidence gathering based on the principle of mutual recognition and potentially related to *all* types of evidence. These initiatives were also promoted by the Stockholm Programme of 11 December 2009,[7] which underlined the need for a new approach to bring order to the fragmentary system of the existing instruments.

Thus, in its Action Plan Implementing the Stockholm Programme,[8] the European Commission—following the approach expressed in the Green Paper of 2009—announced two (at first sight separate) legislative proposals aimed respectively (a) at introducing a comprehensive system for obtaining evidence in criminal matters based on the principle of mutual recognition and covering all types of evidence and (b) at laying down common standards for gathering evidence in criminal matters in order to ensure its admissibility. At the same time, eight Member States launched a proposal for a Directive with the scope of introducing into the EU area a new means of executing investigative measures aimed at taking evidence in other Member States.[9] Neither of these initiatives has been completed yet. The Commission's proposals did not even lead to any legislative initiative and were dropped after the PD EIO was launched, whilst the PD EIO—after more than 3 years of legislative works—has not yet led to a binding legislative act. Moreover, over the course of more than 1 year, the draft text was intensively discussed in the Council, which established a general approach in December 2011.[10] After the orientation vote of May 2012 by the European Parliament, the Conference of Presidents decided in June 2012 that the European Parliament would suspend its cooperation with the Council, *inter alia*, on the EIO dossier until a satisfactory outcome is achieved on Schengen governance.[11] Meanwhile, in November 2012 the Presidency of the Council drew up a document containing responses to some controversial issues and some suggestions on technical questions.[12]

A brief look at the main steps of this uncompleted path shows, however, a different approach. Once the perspective, expressed in the Green Paper of 2001, of mutually binding Member States to the admissibility of foreign evidence, had

---

[6] COM (2009) 624 final.

[7] The Stockholm Programme—an open and secure Europe serving and protecting citizens (2010/C 115/01).

[8] COM (2010) 171 final.

[9] Interinstitutional File: 2010/0817 (COD), COPEN 115 EJN 12 CODEC 363 EUROJUST 47.

[10] See doc. 18918/11, COPEN 369 EJN 185 CODEC 2509 EUROJUST 217.

[11] See http://www.europarl.europa.eu/news/en/pressroom/content/20120614IPR46824/html/EP-suspends-cooperation-with-Council-on-five-justice-and-home-affairs-dossiers.

[12] Interinstitutional File: 2010/0817 (COD), COPEN 245 EJN 83 CODEC 2643 EUROJUST 100.

been abandoned, the focus of EU legislation shifted to allowing free movement of evidence to *facilitate* its admissibility. The 2008 FD EEW is a clear example of this approach, and its limited scope of application (objects, documents and data) demonstrates that priority attention was then given to those types of evidence to which real movement applies. Despite the ambiguous wording of Article 82(2) (a) TFEU and the strong criticism raised against the legitimacy of a EU legislative intervention on the admissibility of transnational evidence,[13] the PD EIO has launched the even more ambitious proposal of an almost comprehensive tool of evidence gathering. Moreover, the proposed extension of the scope of EU intervention from documental evidence (or evidence already existing) to dynamic evidence has marked a clear change of approach, thus shifting the focus of EU intervention from the movement of evidence amongst Member States to the collection of evidence through investigative activities conducted in a State other than that of the relevant proceedings. Such an approach involves attaching priority importance to the procedures of taking evidence rather than to the limits of admissibility of evidence collected abroad.

Against this background, the EIO proposal raises many questions, which have been addressed in detail in the analysis of my distinguished colleagues and the short statements of my chair assistants, listed below. Both the articles and the short statements have been elaborated in response to a *Questionnaire*, which is published as an Annex of this book. The present paper aims to provide an introductory view of the issues and the unanswered questions regarding the proposed new tool as they emerge from the proposed format. For the sake of clarity I shall deal with the general and the specific issues separately.

2 The European Investigation Order. General Issues

2.1 Subject of the Proposed Directive: A New Legislative Action Aimed at Providing a Single Instrument for Gathering Evidence in Other EU Member States

The Directive proposal has been presented as a new legislative action aimed to provide a single instrument of gathering evidence overseas within the EU. This starting point raises two main questions.

A) The first question concerns the approach of the proposed instrument, i.e., the *replacement of all the existing instruments with an EIO with a global scope*. At first glance, the draft Directive is fully in line with the Commission's proposal of introducing a new comprehensive instrument of obtaining evidence based on the principle of mutual recognition. Furthermore, of the four possible policy options for

---

[13] See, among others, Spencer (2010), p. 604.

the EU—i.e., (1) no new action in the EU, (2) non-legislative action, (3) abrogation of the FD EEA with a return to the system of mutual legal assistance, (4) new legislative action—the PD EIO opts for a new legislative action. This should not, however, constitute an EEW II, i.e., a new instrument aimed at extending the EEW I *with its logic* to all types of evidence. In several passages the Accompanying Document to the PD EIO stresses the inadequacy of the EEW mainly due to the rigidity of this instrument,[14] thus proposing a new approach focused on the measure to be executed rather than on the evidence to be collected.

I shall address this point below, under Sect. 2.2. Now it is noteworthy that the original draft was not entirely in line with the announced goal, since some measures—i.e., the setting up of JITs and the gathering of evidence within a JIT, as well as some forms of interception of communications (interception with immediate transmission and interception of satellite telecommunications)—were excluded from the sphere of application of the EIO [Art. 3(2) of the original proposal]. During the discussions in the Council,[15] however, this area was considerably reduced by including all forms of interceptions of telecommunications within the scope of the Directive proposal. Moreover, despite the announced approach of the proposal, the collection of evidence already in possession of the executing State appeared in the text agreed in December 2011 amongst the main goals of the new instrument [Art. 1(1) PD EIO], which encompassed also the evidence gathered before (and independently from) the order being issued. On the other hand, any form of supranational gathering of evidence has always been left outside the scope of application of the EIO proposal, which in its most recent versions remains concerned with the horizontal level. This regards the collection of evidence through the future EPPO as well as—taking into account the wide scope of application of the EIO proposal, extended to administrative proceedings—through supranational bodies or agencies such as OLAF.

Against this framework, the coherence of the new instrument should be assessed on two levels. On a first level, it should be ascertained whether the proposed model applies properly to *all* the different forms of investigative activities covered by the draft Directive, which at the present encompasses at least three models of obtaining evidence overseas: (a) ordering an investigative activity overseas, (b) obtaining the results of investigative activities already in possession of the executing authority, and (c) conducting extraterritorial investigations. On a second level, the analysis of the legislative initiative should address the relationship between the collection of evidence following the proposed tool and what has been left out of the scope of the draft proposal, i.e., the models of extraterritorial investigations, joint inquiries and supranational investigations.

---

[14] Accompanying Document to the Proposal for a Council Directive regarding an European Investigation Order in criminal matters, Detailed Statement, 9288/10 ADD 2, COPEN 117 EJN 185 CODEC 384 EUROJUST 217, § 3.1.2.

[15] See already doc. 8474/11, COPEN 67 EJN 13 CODEC 550 EUROJUST 49 PARLNAT 13.

B) The second question concerns the need for replacing all the existing instruments with an EIO with a global scope, i.e., the *practical and theoretical justification of the new legal action*. There is no doubt that the co-existence of tools of evidence gathering inspired by different approaches can lead to confusion and difficulties in law enforcement, since the competent authorities—in absence of "one channel" for the obtaining of evidence—will have to avail themselves of different instruments to obtain legal assistance.[16] This does not, however, imply that the introduction of a new instrument—applicable to all types of evidence and based on the principle of mutual recognition or a new method of mutual recognition—is the best way to prevent inefficiency in international cooperation. Indeed, affirming the *need* to replace all existing instruments with a new single one should presuppose the ascertainment of the causes of the current inefficiencies in the MLA system. In the Stockholm Programme the European Council pursued a similar approach, by stressing that the adoption of a comprehensive means of obtaining evidence in criminal cases with a cross-border dimension had to follow an *impact assessment* of the existing instruments in this area.[17]

The rapidity both of the Commission's and the Member States' intervention did not, however, permit such analysis. At the time of the Commission's Green Paper, many Member States had not yet transposed the FD OFPE, and the deadline for incorporating the FD EEW not only had not yet expired, but had been transposed only by one Member State (Denmark).[18] Moreover, at the time of the Commission's and the Member States' intervention (respectively, 2009 and 2010), there were neither sufficient scholarly studies nor, most importantly, empirical research supporting its arguments.[19] Furthermore, some studies conducted on a factual basis[20] have pointed out that, among the various causes of the inefficiency of the system of mutual legal assistance, linguistic barriers and defects in the execution of requests (delays, even disappearance of requests, etc.) are a frequently recurring problem in cross-border cooperation.[21] Taking into account the prime importance attached to language issues in the Roadmap for strengthening procedural rights of suspected and accused persons in criminal proceedings,[22] it would have been wise to wait for EU intervention in this field. And after the Directive 2010/64/EU, the impact of EU harmonization of the right to interpretation and translation in criminal proceedings on the MLA system would have merited careful assessment.

---

[16] Bachmaier Winter (2010), p. 583.

[17] The Stockholm Programme (footnote 7), § 3.1.1.

[18] Gleß (2011b), p. 599.

[19] Allegrezza (2010), p. 570.

[20] Amongst them, cf. the Preliminary Report by Wade (2011) on the Euroneeds-Project, undertaken by the Max Planck Institute for Foreign and International Criminal Law.

[21] Bachmaier Winter (2010), p. 589.

[22] Resolution of the Council of 30th November 2009 (2009/295/01).

2.2 Approach and Goals of the Draft Proposal Instrument: A New Way of Providing Mutual Recognition

It has been noted that the draft Directive aims to provide a new approach in the field of transnational inquiries, an approach consisting, above all, of an unprecedented way of providing mutual recognition. The complex nature of the proposed Directive shows a significant shift from a conception of the MR model *as an alternative of the MLA system* to a view of the MR model *combined with* the MLA system. What is sought in the draft proposal is, in other words, a virtuous combination of the efficiency of the *order model* (MR system) with the flexibility of the request model (MLA system). This was not, however, entirely consistent with the approach of the original proposal. On the one hand, the provision that granted the issuing authority unprecedented power to choose the investigative measure—i.e., the subject of the order—led to the not less innovative move to allow the executing authority (provided for in Article 13 of the Framework Decision 2009/829/JHA) to choose an investigative measure other than that requested (Art. 9 of the original proposal). On the other hand, the grounds for refusal were drastically reduced and no room was even left for grounds reflecting fundamental rights of the defendant, such as the *ne bis in idem* principle [Art. 10(1) of the original proposal]. Moreover, insufficient guarantees were provided in the field of legal remedies, which were granted to the extent provided by domestic law.

In its most recent versions, however, the draft proposal has led to more adequate balances between efficiency and flexibility, as shown by the complex structure of the provision on the grounds for refusal [Art. 10(1) PD EIO]. To be sure, the combination of the MR and the MLA system does not constitute a novelty in itself: on the one hand, many legislative instruments of the intermediate and recent phases of MLA, such as the CISA and the EUCMACM had already anticipated some features of the MR system and, on the other hand, the developments in the MR system show that it has gradually been smoothened by re-incorporating typical elements of the MLA. In the context of this draft proposal, furthermore, such a combination is aimed to achieve further goals. Alongside with the purpose of improving and speeding up the EU cross-border cooperation, the new instrument should ensure the admissibility of evidence, while maintaining a high level of protection of fundamental rights (especially procedural rights), reducing the financial costs, increasing mutual trust and cooperation between the Member States, and preserving the specificities of the national systems and their legal culture.[23] It must be assessed whether the proposed combination of MR and MLA allows for the achievement of such ambitious objectives.

To start with, it is worth observing that amongst these goals, the admissibility of evidence may seem to be out of place, since the PD EIO—unlike the Commission's proposals—does not aim at securing the admissibility of evidence. This does not,

---

[23] Accompanying Document (footnote 14), § 1.

however, lead us to conclude that the admissibility issue has not been addressed at all. Indeed, like the FD EEW, the PD EIO imposes upon the issuing authority the duty of checking the availability of the investigative measure before issuing the order, and allows the issuing authority to require certain procedural formalities of *lex fori* to be complied with in the execution of the order. In light of this, it might be said that the issue of admissibility has been addressed in an indirect way, i.e., by setting up the conditions to facilitate the admissibility of the evidence collected in the proceedings pending in the issuing State—an issue that remains, however, a business of the competent authority of *this* State. The analysis of the draft proposal contained in this study will have to ascertain whether this approach—i.e., targeting international cooperation on facilitating the *national* admissibility of the evidence gathered overseas—is consistent with the provision of Article 82(2)(a) TFUE.[24]

On the other hand, it should, however, be stressed that the principle of mutual recognition, even if combined with the MLA model, still constitutes the basis of the new order [Art. 1(1) PD EIO], although some special measures contained in Chapter IV of the draft Directive reproduce literally the corresponding provisions of the 2000 EUCMACM, which are inspired by the pure assistance model (*e.g.*, covert investigations). There is no doubt that both the eight Member States which have launched this legislative proposal and the EU institutions still trust the potential of the order model and the adequacy of the MR system. Nevertheless, the developments in the European scenario towards a European territoriality principle, as well as the proposals launched, albeit in different ways, in this direction (especially the proposal of the transnational procedural unity[25]), should lead to a re-thinking of the worth of the prevailing approach in the AFSJ, an approach strongly based on the system—typical of the assistance models—of evidence taken by competent authorities in their territory upon the request/order of the authorities responsible for the relevant proceedings.

3 The European Investigation Order. Specific Issues

3.1 Defining the Investigative Activity to Be Conducted

The first specific issue to be addressed should, in my view, be the subject of the investigation order, i.e., the definition of the investigative activity to be carried out in other Member States. It has been observed that the fact that, unlike any previous EU legislative instrument in the field of transnational criminal inquiries, the PD EIO empowers the issuing authority to choose the measure to be executed consti-tutes one of the most innovative mechanisms of the draft Directive. This novelty,

---

[24] This topic has been discussed in detail by Belfiore, Part III, Sect. 4.

[25] Cf. Schünemann, Part IV, Sect. 5.

which implies the shift of the focus from the evidence to be collected to the measure to be executed, is in line with the main goal of the proposal to extend the MR principle to the collection of dynamic evidence—a goal that still maintains priority importance in the context of the draft Directive, even if the developments in the legislative text have led to introducing the gathering of documental evidence into its scope of application. This confirms that the issue of movement of evidence becomes a matter of secondary importance compared with the question concerning the *forms* of conducting investigative activities in other Member States.

It has, moreover, been noted that the provision of a strict duty of execution, concerned not only with the evidential result but also with the specific measure chosen by the issuing authority, has led to introducing an unprecedented compensation mechanism, consisting of the power of the executing authority the enforce another measure aimed at achieving the same investigative goal. This solution was unavoidable to prevent the risk that individuals might be limited in their fundamental rights through investigative means which either are not provided for in the executing State or are subject to specific limits other than those provided for in the issuing State. In such cases the provision of an unconditioned duty of execution would have caused unbearable discriminations in a common area of freedom security and justice, depending on the fact that people are subject to investigative means in the context of a domestic or a transnational criminal procedure.

On the other hand, the compensation mechanism is strictly linked to the possibility of the new instrument being adopted to collect evidence abroad by coercive means, to which those limitations apply. Significantly, pursuant to the FD EEW the executing authority was entitled not only to choose what measure should be carried out in its territory but furthermore to decide whether it is necessary to use measures of coercion [Art. 11(1) and (2) FD EEW]. This guarantee was, however, blurred by the duty of the executing authority to make any measure available (even search and seizure) in the event of any of the offences listed under Article 14 to which the dual criminality requirement does not apply [Art. 11(3)(ii) FD EEW]—a rather questionable exception from a human rights perspective. The link between the possibility to have recourse to another measure and possible use of coercive investigative means was not clearly expressed in the original text of the EIO proposal, which moreover allowed (without obliging) the use of a different measure in cases of non-compliance with the requirement set forth in Article 9. The consequence of this approach was that the executing authority was given considerable leeway to enforce a measure that possibly interfered with the individual rights even of third parties in cases that under domestic law would never allow the adoption of the requested investigative means.

Doubtless, the draft agreed in December 2011 addresses this issue more effectively, in that it obliges, as far as this is possible, the executing authority to adopt another measure where the requested one does not fit the requirements of procedural lawfulness (legal provision and the respect for legal limits) under *lex loci*. However, also the current draft leaves room for human rights concerns. The main concern relates to the fact that, whilst Article 9 aims to ensure the respect for the principle of lawfulness from the perspective of the executing State, no provision prevents the risk of the EIO being misused to obtain the adoption of a measure that does not comply with the requirements of lawfulness under the law of the issuing State. This would expose the defendant to a criminal judgment on the basis of evidence gathered overseas by investigative means not allowed (*e.g.*, online search) or allowed under certain conditions by domestic law (*e.g.*, wiretaps). From an inter-state, bi-dimensional perspective it can, to a certain extent, be accepted that each of the cooperating authorities absolves itself of its responsibility as to the ascertainment of requirements which pertain to the other legal system. But from a tri-dimensional perspective, the focus on the individual[26] makes *both* the cooperating authorities responsible for the respect of human rights.[27] Therefore, mechanisms should be structured to ensure the respect for the principle "*nulla prosecutio transnationalis sine lege*"[28] in relation to the *whole transnational procedure* in order to avoid legal limitations being eluded in either of the cooperating countries.

3.2 Proportionality and Admissibility of the Investigation Abroad

Surprisingly, in the original draft the new approach of the proposed instrument— i.e., the decision to make the issuing authority responsible for the choice of the measure to be executed—had not been accompanied by any provision requiring this authority to check beforehand the necessity and proportionality of the measure and the admissibility of the requested measure from the viewpoint of its own law. To be sure, the original proposal did not completely ignore the importance of a previous test both of the proportionality and the admissibility of the investigative measure. Such assessments were, however, imposed upon the executing authority in line with its aforementioned power to change the measure to be executed. Indeed, the possibility of having recourse to another measure if the requested one did not fit the requirements of lawfulness and especially where the same result could be reached by less intrusive means [Art. 9(1)(c) of the original proposal] clearly pertained to the sphere of proportionality. Outside these cases, no provision gave the executing authority and private parties any opportunity to check the proportionality and admissibility of the measure to be executed under its own law. Nor was there any possibility to challenge under *lex loci* the necessity and admissibility of the procedures requested for the collection of evidence, with the sole exception of Article 8(2), which charged the executing authority with the task of assessing

---

[26] On the cultural shift from a interstate, bi-dimensional to a tri-dimensional, human rights-oriented conception of international cooperation, see Schomburg et al. (2012), pp. 2ff.

[27] On the joint responsibility for the respect of human rights in transnational procedures, cf. Vogel (2012), Vor § 1, pp. 54ff.

[28] Cf., on this topic, Gropp (2012), pp. 41ff.

whether the requirements set by the issuing authority were consistent with the fundamental principles of its own law. In light of a global view of transnational criminal investigations, this approach was clearly inadequate to ensure the *full* proportionality of the requested investigative measure and entailed serious risks for the addressees of the EIO.

In this regard, the text resulting from the amendments in the Council presents an approach that reflects a more adequate balance between the respect for domestic procedural systems and the protection of human rights. Above all, the new Article 5a requires, by reproducing almost literally the wording of Article 7 FD EEW, the issuing authority to carry out a prior check of the investigative measure's necessity, proportionality and availability. The latter control, based on the assessment of a hypothetical national case, is aimed to extend the ordinary requirements of admissibility of domestic evidence under *lex fori* to transnational cases. The validation procedure laid down in paragraph 3 of the same Article 5a falls also within the sphere of proportionality and, compared to the system introduced by the FD EEW, provides a stronger guarantee for the addressee of the investigative measure since validation is *in any case* required.

Also this approach, however, proves unsatisfactory and leaves many questions open from a human rights perspective. The main deficiency derives from the fact that the draft Directive does not specify what is meant by the "necessity," "proportionality" and "availability" of investigative measures in transnational cases— concepts that, in the absence of a harmonized meaning,[29] remain undefined. As noted above, what the draft Directive aims at is requiring the issuing authority to carry out those checks before the EIO has been issued. Nevertheless, the wide scope of application of the proposed instrument makes it extremely difficult to comply with such a difficult task. This is mainly due to the fact that the EIO can be issued in a proceeding other than a criminal procedure. Indeed, even if Article 5a provides for a validation procedure after the EIO being transmitted to the executing State, the possibility of conducting a proper control of these requirements in great part depends, where there is an investigative magistrate or pre-trial judge, on their knowledge of the results and the developments of the investigation, as well as on their independent and impartial position. Moreover, the proportionality and availability of the transnational inquiry should be assessed in relation to the measure that will actually be carried out. In this regard, whereas Article 9(2) requires the executing authority that has decided to use another measure to inform the issuing authority, which may withdraw the request, there is no provision *requiring* a check of availability, necessity and proportionality on the different measure by the issuing authority, nor does it seem to be implied by Article 5a. This considerably weakens the level of individual guarantees in the current text and should lead us to seek a different approach.

Doubtless, the draft agreed in December 2011 has strengthened the availability assessment from the perspective of the executing State by including a further

---

[29] On this topic, see, among others, Bachmaier Winter (2013), pp. 85ff.

ground for changing the subject of the investigative order, i.e., the unavailability of the requested measure in a comparable national case [Art. 9(1)(b)]. This is a very Solomon-like solution which, in the event of diverging assessments concerning the admissibility of the investigative measure, leads to the use of another measure, provided a corresponding admissible measure exists under *lex loci*, otherwise assistance will not be provided [Art. 9(3)]. Neither is this solution, despite its merits, free from defects. The main concern arises, in my view, from the fact that in all these cases the issue of admissibility of evidence is entirely left solely to the executing authority, an approach which is in line with the strictest logic of mutual recognition as a way of enhancing *mutual trust between the cooperating authorities*. Instead, there is no room for any participation of private parties in the decision-making process on the admissibility of the investigative measure. This does not, of course, rule out that these may take part in the decision on the admissibility of the investigative measure in the executing State, whenever *lex loci* allows it. Yet no provision allows for private parties to take part in the decision on availability in the executing State.[30] As a consequence, such difficult assessments—i.e., the capability of another measure to achieve the same result as the requested measure and the admissibility of such a different measure—will be entrusted solely to the executing authority—a conclusion that raises many human rights concerns, taking into account, *inter alia*, that the executing authority may be neither a judicial nor a prosecuting authority [Art. 2(a)(ii)].

3.3 Methods of Obtaining Evidence Abroad and Defence Rights

It has been noted that the fact that the proposed instrument has been launched to cover dynamic evidence poses as the main issue the question of the *methods* of conducting investigations abroad. In this regard the draft Directive follows the approach of the FD EEW and is therefore in line with the consolidated combination, typical of the last phase of MLA,[31] of *lex loci* and the specific procedural formalities of *lex fori* required by the requesting authority. This is a very soft version of a *combined method* that in its strictest form has been enacted in international texts

---

[30] Furthermore, as under Article 29 the PD EIO aims at replacing the *corresponding* provisions laid down in previous judicial assistance instruments, it could be argued that Article 4 ECMACM, which allows for private parties to be present in the execution of the rogatory letters, should analogously be applied to the collection of evidence with the EIO. Along these lines, see Marchetti (2011), pp. 163f. This interpretation cannot, in my view, be shared. It would firstly run counter to the general approach of this draft proposal, which aims to provide a comprehensive new way of conducting investigations abroad. Moreover, this solution would apply only within the scope of application of the 1959 ECMACM, i.e., only in the field of transnational procedures *in criminal matters*.

[31] Cf. Ruggeri (2012), pp. 153ff.

such as the UN MTMACM, which made legal assistance dependent on the demanding conditions of consistency with the law and practice of the host country (Art. 6). A similar approach can be found in some national legislations, such as the Swiss one: Article 65(2) IRSG lays down a very strict condition for applying overseas formalities in the collection of evidence in cross-border cases, i.e., compliance with domestic procedural rules, including the general rules of Swiss StPO on coercive means (Arts. 196 et seq.).[32]

Doubtless, the introduction of combined methods of evidence gathering has marked a revolutionary cultural change in the field of judicial assistance. Under the traditional MLA system, the strict application of *lex loci* allowed both parties to ignore foreign law and it is no surprise that even those countries that continue to use the old MLA system waive their right to verify whether *lex loci* has been respected, thus acknowledging a presumption of compliance with *lex loci*.[33] This could no longer happen with the introduction of combined systems. Indeed, the complete realisation of such combinations presupposes the knowledge of foreign law on the part of both cooperating authorities, which is an obvious precondition for the proper application of foreign criminal law in the field both of substantive and procedural law.[34] In this regard, the possibility for officials and private parties of the relevant proceedings to attend at the execution of letters rogatory, which had already been provided for in the traditional international instruments of MLA, has undoubtedly gained a new role by helping the requested authority to fulfil such a difficult task.[35]

Against this background, the first applications of combined methods in the MLA system in the strict version outlined above did not clearly promote efficient international cooperation, since it allowed the adoption only of those foreign formalities that, albeit not identical, were fully consistent with domestic law. On the other hand, this approach, while preventing the risk of the unbalanced hybridisation of procedural law, facilitated the solution of the practical problems arising from the application of foreign law. It is well-known that the need for efficiency and speediness in transnational cooperation, alongside with the concerns related to the admissibility of transnational evidence, has historically led to smoothing the interaction between domestic and foreign law, by obliging domestic authorities to comply with *all* the procedural formalities requested with the sole exception of those which infringe the fundamental, relevant, etc. principles of domestic law. This approach, inherited by the EIO proposal, raises serious concerns related both to the efficiency of international cooperation and the protection of the rights of the individuals in transnational procedures.

---

[32] Gleß (2011a), p. 89.

[33] See, in Spain, Supreme Tribunal, judgement of 5 May 2003 (ROJ 3023/2003). On this topic, cf. Gascón Inchausti (2013), p. 484.

[34] On the application of foreign law in the field of criminal law, see Cornils (1978), *passim*.

[35] Significantly, outside Europe, the IACMACM strengthened this possibility allowing officials and private parties of the home State not only to be present but furthermore to take part in the execution of letters rogatory (Art. 16).

To start with, the PD EIO does not reproduce those limitation clauses laid down in various judicial assistance texts[36] and aimed to restrict the possibility of setting formalities of *lex fori* to the cases in which they are "necessary" under the law of the requesting state. To be sure, this requirement had been better specified in the first EU legislation, as shown by the FD OFPE, which required the formalities to be necessary to ensure the "validity" and use of overseas evidence [Art. 5(1)]. Similar provisions are laid down at a domestic level. For instance, Article 727(5*bis*) it. CCP, introduced by Act 367/2001, allows for the Italian authorities—whenever provided for in international agreements[37]—to specify, while lodging a request for legal assistance, which domestic formalities must be applied abroad by indicating the "necessary elements to [ensure] the procedural usability of the evidence sought." The failure to specify in the draft Directive which formalities can be requested gives enormous leeway to the issuing authority in the choice of the procedures to be fulfilled in the collection of evidence.[38]

Such a solution proves unsatisfactory for many reasons. In the absence of indications as to the parameters for choosing the procedural forms to be followed overseas, the choice can overcome what is necessary to ensure the admissibility of evidence in the relevant proceedings. Any decision to impose upon procedures of domestic law entails the risk of incoherent hybridisation of heterogeneous procedures, which can rarely be homogenised or cannot be homogenised at all. Many international instruments enacting the soft version of the combined method show awareness of this problem but do not provide any mechanism to solve it: *e.g.*, the SAP ECMACM envisages that the requested authority might be in the position of applying procedures that are "unfamiliar" to its own legal order (Art. 8). This elevates the risk that the requested formalities are not fully consistent with domestic law, which clearly endangers the realisation of a proper combination of procedural laws. Furthermore, this approach can jeopardise the effectiveness of the transnational investigation. As noted above, if the combination is aimed at reducing the risk of inadmissibility of evidence, the success of the combined method clearly requires that foreign law can be applied properly. In this regard, however, not only does the clause of non-infringement of the fundamental principles of *lex loci* achieve at best a minimum and even forced combination, but it can also entail serious practical problems for the requested authority while applying procedures that might be unknown and culturally very distant from domestic law. Last but not least, this approach can also cause additional costs above what is usually provided for by national law.[39]

---

[36] See, *e.g.*, Art. 8 SAP ECMACM.

[37] This is the main limitation of this domestic regulation, which has a very limited scope of application since Italy has no general legislative framework for applying the most advanced instruments of MLA. On this topic, see Caprioli (2013), pp. 449f.

[38] On this issue, see Schünemann, Part IV, Sect. 4.

[39] This would happen, for instance, where Italian authorities request the transcription of telecommunications following the formalities (especially the procedure laid down for expert evidence) provided for by Article 268(5) and (6) it. CCP.

The seriousness of such problems is further aggravated by the characteristics of the MR system. Although the wording of Article 8(2) PD EIO follows almost literally the provision of Article 4(1) EUCMACM, the same rule has obviously a very different function in a mutual recognition context, where as a rule, assistance *must* be afforded. This reduces proportionally the margin of decision of the executing authority, which is called upon to carry out the difficult task of applying foreign procedures properly and the not less difficult task of harmonizing them with its own law and practice. Moreover, this legislative proposal has not reproduced the clause laid down in Article 12 FD EEW, which releases the executing authority from its obligation to comply with foreign formalities requiring the application of coercive measures. The only way out for the executing authority to refuse execution is to invoke the infringement of the fundamental principles of its own law, which is clearly different from the violation of the law of *lex loci*[40] and even more different from being consistent with the law and practice of the country to which the request is made.[41]

Finally, unlike most instruments of MLA, the PD EIO does not provide for any form of participation of private parties in the execution of the EIO [Art. 8(3)]. This is a general lacuna of the MR system and, even if the participation of the defence can be requested as any other procedure of *lex fori*, there is surprisingly no provision that recognises its contribution in similar terms as those used for the involvement of the authorities sent by the issuing State under Article 9(3). This leads to a rather unjustified imbalance between private parties and the authorities of the issuing State. Such conclusions are further aggravated by the fact that under the draft agreed in December 2011 the authorities of the issuing State can exercise law enforcement powers pursuant to *lex loci* upon agreement of the executing and the issuing authorities [Art. 9(3a)]. This system introduces an unprecedented system of extraterritorial enquiries *within the MR model*, which goes beyond the distinctions of models of international assistance drafted so far[42] and raises many human rights concerns due to the rather vague notion and position of these "authorities" sent by the issuing country. In this context the failure to involve private parties clearly impinges, on a first level, on the effectiveness of the defence rights[43] both of the defendant and of third parties in relation not only to the conduction of investigations but also to the collection of the evidence already gathered abroad. In a deeper sense, however, this lacuna means underestimating the importance of the contribution of the defence to ensuring an appropriate application of foreign procedural formalities. Also here, this solution does not reflect at all the need to combine the MR system with the flexibility of the MLA model, but it is in line with the pure logic of mutual recognition: to achieve the goal of an efficient application of the provisions on

---

[40] See, for example, Art. 10(2) IACMACM.

[41] See, for example, Art. 6 UN MTMACM.

[42] Among others, see the four models outlined by Van Hoek and Luchtman (2005), p. 28. For a different approach, cf. Ruggeri (2013), pp. 533ff.

[43] See Marchetti (2011), p. 163.

execution of the EIO, there is room only for a dialogue between the cooperating authorities.

Against this background, it should be analysed whether this approach reflects a proper way of achieving the goals posed by the draft Directive or whether a new approach must be sought to find a more adequate balance between the efficiency of transnational inquiries and the effectiveness of defence rights.

3.4   The Refusal of Recognition and Execution: The Measures of Coercion in Cross-Border Cases

It has been observed that the draft agreed in December 2011 not only has considerably widened the list of grounds for refusal of recognition and execution of the EIO compared to the original text but has also set up a double level of grounds. Even though the distinction between the grounds for refusal has been drawn on the basis of the "coerciveness" of the measures,[44] this approach can lead to confusion and contradictory interpretations of the entire system.[45] Indeed, what is to be meant by "coercive measures" in the context of the proposed EIO and, more generally, of transnational investigative procedures in the EU?

To be sure, one might doubt that this text reveals a coherent notion of "means of coercion" in the field of cross-border evidence gathering. The only provision that explicitly relates to "coercive means" in the context of Article 10 is paragraph 1(f), which states that assistance can be refused where the EIO was issued for obtaining a *coercive measure* in respect of an act allegedly committed outside the home state and wholly or partially in the territory of the host state, but this act does not constitute a criminal offence under *lex loci*. Instead, paragraph 1a contains a generic reference to "any non-coercive investigative measure" (lit. b), whereas paragraph 1b applies to all measures "other than those" referred to in paragraph 1a. This rather complicated approach (even from a linguistic viewpoint) reveals the lack of a clear notion of "coercion" in the context of cross-border inquiries, which can both endanger the efficiency of the transnational procedure and cause serious risks for the individuals involved.

To start with, the case of non-coercive means seems to be restricted only to paragraph 1a(b). But then, how should the other measures mentioned in paragraph 1a be considered? Their autonomous position in the context of paragraph 1a should lead us to conclude that their execution can entail the use of coercion, since otherwise they would fall into the scope of application of paragraph 1a(b), which contains a comprehensive clause relating to *any* non-coercive measure. This conclusion appears to be confirmed by the reference to search and seizure (letter f).

---

[44] See doc. 10749/11 REV 2, COPEN 130 EJN 70 CODEC 914 EUROJUST 85, p. 3.

[45] On this issue, see, in detail, Bachmaier Winter, Part III, Sect. 3.2.

But what is then the nature of the measures covered by paragraph 1b? Would they paradoxically be other than both non-coercive and coercive measures?

An alternative interpretation could be to deem *all* the measures provided for by paragraph 1a as always non-coercive, as the reference to hearings of victims, suspects and third parties (letter a) would suggest. However, this interpretation, apart from the aforementioned incongruence in respect of lit. b), would run counter to the clear nature of search and seizure, which cannot of course change because of the simple fact that in the home state the proceedings were initiated for an offence belonging to the list of 32 offences for which dual criminality is not required. Moreover, given that the measures are subject only to the grounds for refusal laid down in paragraph 1, how could the provision under paragraph 1a(f) apply to non-coercive measures where the territoriality exception presupposes the use of coercive means? Finally, since paragraph 1a rules out the application of the sole Article 9(1) to the measures listed therein, Article 9(1bis) should also apply to these measures. But how can the executive authority use a different measure capable of achieving the same result by less *intrusive* means, if these measures should not be intrusive at all?

This interpretation cannot be shared and therefore it cannot be ruled out than even the measures listed in paragraph 1a may entail the use of coercion. Such a conclusion certainly applies firstly to search and seizure, which gives therefore rise to the same concerns observed in relation to the EEW regulation, but it cannot ruled out in regard with other cases. A particularly worrying case is concerned with evidence already in possession of the executing authority. It is truly surprising that the PD EIO has included this case among the non-coercive measures, since of course even the information already in possession of the executing authority under paragraph 1a(c) could have been obtained by coercive means and therefore in the context of a procedure for an act that necessarily had to constitute an offence in the host State. As a consequence, the position of this reference in the list of paragraph 1a allows for the issuing authority to obtain the documental results of an investigation carried out prior to, or independently from, the issuing of the EIO through measures that would not be conducted abroad on the basis of the same instrument. In this regard a new approach should be adopted taking into account the risks emerging from the analysis of those countries, such as Italy, in which case law shows frequent recourse to informal agreements with foreign authorities to obtain evidence by means of a procedure other than letters rogatory.[46]

In such cases the approach of the draft Directive exposes both the defendant and third parties to risks that they would never have to face in domestic proceedings. This conclusion is not only due to the fact that the execution of "other measures" presupposes the fulfilment of the further requirements of dual criminality and the respect for the limitations relating to specific lists of offences and to certain punishment thresholds as laid down by its own law—requirements that should clearly be required also in relation to some of the measures listed in Article 10

---

[46] In this regard, see Caprioli (2013), pp. 451ff.

(1a). Furthermore, since Article 10(1a) rules out the application of the Article 9 (1) to the measures listed therein, the lawfulness and availability tests under *lex loci* should paradoxically apply to *none* of the measures provided for in paragraph 1a, including those that clearly entail the use of coercion in its most traditional sense.

Moreover, concerns can arise in relation to measures of an apparently non-coercive nature, such as the hearings provided for in paragraph (1a)(f) for many reasons. In some criminal justice systems such hearings may be conducted coercively or through investigative means that are forbidden in some Member States (*e.g.*, lie detection). Furthermore, according to the so-called *Annexkompetenz* doctrine, hearings could imply coercion only for their practical implementation. But again, why should, for example, co-accused persons be exposed to the risk of coercive transfer in case of non-attendance at the requested hearing if this is not allowed under the law of the executing State, with the additional risk of exposing themselves to criminal liability for an act that does not constitute an offence in that State or an act that anyway does not authorize the use of the requested measure?

In light of this, the draft Directive provides a useful opportunity for an in-depth reflection on coercive measures in transnational criminal procedures.[47] A fruitful starting point for such analysis is the German doctrine on measures impinging on fundamental rights (*Grundrechtseingriffe*).[48] This concept, which lies on the assumption that the development of science and technology in particular has led to the emergence of new investigative means that are not perceived by the affected individuals as coercive,[49] shows the outdatedness of the notion of "coercive measures," which no longer constitutes a useful reference point for EU legislation. Starting from such a notion, it should be ascertained whether the theoretical underpinnings of the protection of fundamental rights need to be expanded and especially whether measures neutral to fundamental rights (*grundrechtsneutrale Ermittlungshandlungen*) can be still conceived in the complex scenario of cross-border criminal inquiries.

3.5 Challenging the Investigation Order

The possibility for the individuals affected by the EIO to effectively challenge the investigative measure reflects the capability of the proposed instrument to satisfy both the right to an effective remedy and the right to an effective defence as enshrined in the ECHR.[50] The original text did not pursue any harmonisation at all, since it only related to the availability of remedies provided for at a national level. Moreover, the power to challenge the substantive reasons of the EIO was

---

[47] On this topic, see recently Ruggeri (2012), pp. 147ff.

[48] Cf., among others, Amelung (1976).

[49] Along these lines, see Kühne (2010), p. 248.

[50] In this regard, see Schünemann, Part IV, Sect. 1.2.1.

limited to an action to be brought before a *court* of the issuing State. This distribution of competences, typical of the MR model, reflected the pure logic of division of labours[51] and appeared, at first sight, consistent with the practical need to challenge the substantive conditions of the investigative measure before a court of the State in possession of the information required to carry out such an assessment.

This approach proved unsatisfactory for many reasons. To start with, the effectiveness of the substantive remedy depends on the features of the judicial control in the issuing State. These were, however, in great part unclear. The competence of the court was undefined, since it was not specified whether it had competence in criminal matters. Neither was it clear whether the information required to carry out a control of the substantive reasons had to be made available to this court. Furthermore, the possible change of the contents of the order by the executing authority should lead to granting the affected parties the right to challenge the substantive reasons of the *new measure* before a court of the executing, rather than of the issuing, State. However, there was no provision requiring the necessary information to be forwarded to the executing State to carry out this difficult task.

Certainly the availability of information plays an essential role in judicial controls and there is no doubt that the maintenance of an approach based on the division of labours requires a proper exchange of information to enhance the effectiveness both of the right to a remedy of private parties and of the judicial control of the competent authorities. Significantly the European Parliament, in its position at first reading, has proposed an Amendment to Article 13, according to which both the issuing and the executing authority must, unless confidentiality is to be ensured, provide the interested parties with all the relevant and appropriate information to guarantee the effective exercise of the right to a legal remedy.[52] This duty of information goes beyond the obligation, provided for in the text agreed in December 2011, to inform the parties about the "possibilities for seeking the legal remedies" [Art. 13(4)] and seems to encompass also substantive information on applicable preconditions, grounds for change of the measure, etc.

Even so, distributing the remedies between the two States may be an inadequate solution. The main deficiency of this system is perhaps that it does not allow for the measure to be judicially reviewed as a whole.[53] This leads to reflecting on the inconveniences of a rigid division of labours, which can, moreover, give rise to insurmountable difficulties, also from a linguistic viewpoint, both for defendants and suspicionless parties who wish to challenge the investigative order before a court, using a procedure they are not familiar with. Furthermore, a strict distribution

---

[51] On the international division of labours (*international Arbeitsteilung*), see Schomburg et al. (2012), pp. 28ff.

[52] Draft European Parliament Legislative Resolution on the adoption of a Directive of the European Parliament and of the Council regarding the European Investigation Order in criminal matters [09288/2010—C7-0185/2010—2010/0817(COD)], amended Article 13(4) PD EIO.

[53] See Schünemann, Part IV, Sect. 1.2.1.

of remedies implies the need to regulate the consequences of the action on the investigation sought and the collection of evidence, as well as the need to coordinate the results of two legal remedies or the results of the action brought in one of the two States and the course of the proceedings in the other one. Concerning the first issue, it is clear that the radical solution of suspending the transfer of evidence pending the outcome of the remedy, as proposed by the European Parliament in its position at first reading, would entail the risk of frustrating the transnational enquiry in cases of unfounded remedies.[54] A proper balance amongst conflicting interests could be achieved by empowering the executing authority to suspend the transfer of evidence after a comparative evaluation of the effects of the suspension on the speediness of the investigation and the chances of success of the remedy.[55] Concerning the second issue, what the draft agreed in the Council imposes upon the issuing authority, after evidence has been transferred, is the duty to take into account, according to national law, the decision of the court of the executing State that has ruled in favour of the party who has proposed the legal remedy. This Solomon-like solution does not, however, provide a proper coordination between the action brought in the executing country and the relevant proceedings in the issuing State, thus exposing the individual to risks that he or she would not face in national procedures. For instance, if the action brought in the executing State successfully challenges the lawfulness of the requested measure pursuant to *lex loci* or the failure to respect the limits established thereby, the decision of the issuing authority to use the transferred evidence—due to the fact that, for example, the measure exists and does not infringe any limitation of *lex fori*—would clearly frustrate the individual right of an effective remedy. On the other hand, the draft Directive does not contain any rule on the effects of the action brought in the issuing State on the course of the investigation in the executing State. But how will the executing authority act after the proportionality or availability of the investigative measure pursuant to *lex fori* has been successfully challenged in the issuing country?

Taking into account such problems, we should consider the need for a new approach, which does not, moreover, necessarily consist of unifying the system of legal remedies under a single jurisdiction. The complex character of the system of legal remedies in transnational cases reflects the pluralism of perspectives and

---

[54] Draft European Parliament Legislative Resolution (footnote 44), amended Article 13 (5) PD EIO.

[55] Such a comparative evaluation is required according to a provision originally introduced in May 2011 into a new paragraph 5a of Article 13 (doc. 10749/11 REV 2, COPEN 130 EJN 70 CODEC 914 EUROJUST 85) and then transposed to Article 12, a provision according to which "The executing authority may suspend the transfer of the evidence, pending the decision regarding a legal remedy, unless sufficient reasons are indicated in the EIO that an immediate transfer is essential for the proper conduct of its investigations or the preservation of individual rights." The position of this rule, albeit related to the transfer of evidence, in the context of Article 12, unlike that of the December 2011 text, was to be preferred, since it aimed to regulate the *effects of the remedy* on the transfer of evidence.

balances between conflicting values involved in cross-border inquiries, which cannot often be safeguarded by means of an action of a single court. On the one hand, the individual charged with a criminal offence would have to face huge difficulties in challenging investigative measures carried out in countries to which he or she does not belong substantially. But on the other hand a regulation aimed at a fair transnational procedure could not overlook the interests of those suspicionless individuals affected in their fundamental rights by offloading onto them the burden of challenging the execution of investigative means in foreign countries and through foreign procedures.

4 Conclusion

This introductive analysis of the draft Directive on the EIO has provided a general view of some of the issues raised by the new proposal, which despite its ambitious purposes does not go in the right direction towards the creation of a fair investigative procedure in cross-border cases. This calls for in-depth reflection of the general approach of the proposed instrument as well as of specific issues concerned, *inter alia*, with the choice of the type of investigation to be carried out in other Member States, the proportionality and admissibility of the investigative measure, the methods of obtaining evidence abroad, the individual guarantees especially in cases of interferences with fundamental rights, and the respect for the right to a defence and to an effective remedy.

On the other hand, this still imperfect instrument poses important challenges for future legislation in the AFSJ. Can mutual trust be promoted by means of orders and duties of execution? Does this new, smoothened version of mutual recognition, combined with the flexibility of the MLA model, provide for proper balance between the need for efficiency and the protection of the defence rights of the individuals involved in transnational investigations? May the collection of evidence in other Member States of the *common* area be dealt with in the same terms of obtaining evidence *abroad*? What is to be meant by "*other* Member States" and how will the *forum* be established in transnational matters? Who will have competence to proceed and who will have to support and cooperate? Is it a proper solution that transnational cases, which often reflect the complex nature of an increasingly transcultural criminal law,[56] are dealt with by a *single* jurisdiction especially where organised crimes or complex crimes with more accomplices are at stake? And what *lex* will the competent authority of this *forum* have to apply? What possibilities are there to set up a multicultural, integrated investigative procedure?

---

[56] On the transcultural criminal law, see Vogel (2010), pp. 1ff.

References[57]

Allegrezza S (2010) Critical remarks on the green paper on obtaining evidence from one Member State to another and securing its admissibility. Zeitschrift für die internationale Strafrechtsdogmatik 9:569–579

Amelung K (1976) Rechtsschutz gegen strafprozessuale Grundrechtseingriffe. Duncker & Humblot, Berlin

Bachmaier Winter L (2010) European investigation order for obtaining evidence in the criminal proceedings. Study of the proposal of a European directive. Zeitschrift für die internationale Strafrechtsdogmatik 9:580–589

Bachmaier Winter L (2013) The role of the proportionality principle in cross-border investigations involving fundamental rights. In: Ruggeri S (ed) Transnational inquiries and the protection of fundamental rights in criminal proceedings. Springer, Heidelberg, pp 85–110

Caprioli F (2013) Report on Italy. In: Ruggeri S (ed) Transnational inquiries and the protection of fundamental rights in criminal proceedings, A study in memory of Vittorio Grevi and Giovanni Tranchina. Springer, Heidelberg, pp 439–455

Cornils K (1978) Die Fremdrechtsanwendung im Strafrecht. De Gruyter, Berlin

Delmas-Marty M (ed) (1997) Introducing penal provisions for the purpose of the financial interests of the European Union. Editions Economica, Paris

Delmas-Marty M, Vervaele JAE (eds) (2000) The implementation of the Corpus Juris in the Member States. Intersentia, Antwerp

Gascón Inchausti F (2013) Report on Spain. In: Ruggeri S (ed) Transnational inquiries and the protection of fundamental rights in criminal proceedings. Springer, Heidelburg, pp 475–495

Gleß S (2006) Beweisrechtsgrundsätze einer grenzüberschreitenden Strafverfolgung. Nomos, Baden-Baden

Gleß S (2011a) Internationales Strafrecht – Grundriss für Studium und Praxis. Helbing Lichtenhahn, Basel

Gleß S (2011b) Europäische Beweisanordnung. In: Sieber U, Brüner FH, Satzger H, von Heintschell-Heinegg B (eds) Europäisches Strafrecht. Nomos, Baden-Baden, pp 596–610

Gropp W (2012) Kollision nationaler Strafgewalten – nulla prosecutio transnationalis sine lege. In: Sinn A (ed) Jurisdiktionskonflikte bei grenzüberschreitend organisierter Kriminalität. V&R Unipress, Osnabrück, pp 41–63

Illuminati G (ed) (2009) Prova penale e Unione europea. Bononia University Press, Bologna

Kühne H-H (2010) Strafprozessrecht. Eine Systematische Darstellung des deutschen und europäischen Strafverfahrensrechts. C.F. Müller, Heidelberg

Marchetti MR (2011) Dalla Convenzione di assistenza giudiziaria in materia penale dell'Unione europea al mandato europeo di ricerca delle prove e all'ordine europeo di indagine penale. In: Rafaraci T (ed) La cooperazione di polizia e giudiziaria in material penale nell'Unione europea dopo il Trattato di Lisbona. Giuffrè, Milano, pp 135–167

Ruggeri S (2012) Investigative powers affecting fundamental rights and principles for a fair transnational procedure in criminal matters. A proposal of mutual integration in the multicultural EU area. Crimen 2:147–168

Ruggeri S (2013) Transnational inquiries and the protection of fundamental rights in comparative law. Models of gathering overseas evidence in criminal matters. In: Ruggeri S (ed) Transnational inquiries and the protection of fundamental rights in criminal proceedings, A study in memory of Vittorio Grevi and Giovanni Tranchina. Springer, Heidelberg, pp 533–573

---

[57] The chapter contributions contained in this book have been quoted with the only reference to the Author's surname, the Part in which the contribution is contained and the number of the paragraph concerned.

Schomburg W, Lagodny O, Gleß S, Hackner T (2012) Einleitung. In: Schomburg W, Lagodny O, Gleß S, Hackner T (eds) Internationale Rechtshilfe in Strafsachen, 5th edn. C.H. Beck, München, pp 2–50

Spencer S (2010) The green paper on obtaining evidence from one Member State to another and securing its admissibility: the reaction of one British lawyer. Zeitschrift für die internationale Strafrechtsdogmatik 9:602–606

Van Hoek AAH, Luchtman MJJP (2005) Transnational cooperation in criminal matters and the safeguarding of human rights. Utrecht Law Rev 1:1–39

Vervaele JAE (ed) (2005) European evidence warrant. Transnational judicial inquiries in the EU. Intersentia, Antwerp

Vogel J (2010) Transkulturelles Strafrecht. Goltdammer's Archiv für Strafrecht 157(1):1–13

Vogel J (2012) Vor § 1. In: Grützner G, Pötz P-G, Kreß C (eds) Internationaler Rechtshilfeverkehr in Strafsachen, 4th edn. C.F. Müller, Heidelberg, pp 1–196

Wade M (2011) EuroNEEDs. Evaluating the need for and the needs of a European Criminal Justice System. http://www.mpicc.de/shared/data/pdf/euroneeds_report_jan_2011.pdf

Part II
Critical Analysis of the EIO Proposal: General Issues

The European Investigation Order: A Rush into the Wrong Direction

Bernd Schünemann

Abstract The European Investigation Order (EIO) [Initiative of seven Member States (Belgium, five smaller countries and Spain) for a Directive of the European Parliament and of the Council regarding the European Investigation Order in criminal matters, 20120/0817 (COD)—21/05/2010. My statement takes the text of the draft Directive into consideration as published 21/12/2011 (18918/11, COPEN 369), widely disregarding the proposed amendments by the Committee on Civil Liberties, Justice and Home Affairs of the European Parliament (see Committee draft report, PE 478–493—23/01/2012) which, in my opinion, is little more but consolation money] not only shares the fundamental flaws of existing mutual recognition instruments, but also carries them a step further as it covers almost any investigative measure. It is regrettable that such a step is taken before the judicial systems have had time to experience the existing system under the European Evidence Warrant. Moreover, it contains no sufficient provisions to allow for an effective defence.

Keywords Defence rights • Evidence gathering • Fair trial • Mutual recognition

Contents

1 The Hurried and Uninformed Legislative Process 30
  1.1 Concerns Regarding the FD EEW 30
  1.2 Green Paper 30
2 Fundamental Flaws of Mutual Recognition, in Particular Concerning the Gathering
  of Evidence 31
3 Most Serious Flaws of the EIO in Particular 31
  3.1 Flexibility as a Denial of Legal Certainty 31
  3.2 No Ground for Refusal When a Measure Has Not Been Ordered by a Court 32

B. Schünemann (✉)
Juristische Fakultät, Ludwig-Maximilians-Universität München, Prof.-Huber-Platz Nr. 2,
Munich, Germany
e-mail: bernd.schuenemann@jura.uni-muenchen.de

S. Ruggeri (ed.), *Transnational Evidence and Multicultural Inquiries in Europe*,
DOI 10.1007/978-3-319-02570-4_2, © Springer International Publishing Switzerland 2014

3.3 Defence Rights 33
3.4 Lack of a General Double Criminality Requirement and/or a Sufficient
     Territoriality Requirement 33
4 Conclusion 34
References 34

1 The Hurried and Uninformed Legislative Process

Even before the Framework Decision on the European Evidence Warrant
(FD EEW), which was already controversial, has been transposed in the Member
States, a new initiative was brought forward. What's more, the consultation process
initiated by the Commission's Green Paper on obtaining evidence in criminal
matters from one Member State to another and securing its admissibility (COM
[2009] 624 final) has been plainly ignored.

1.1 Concerns Regarding the FD EEW

The FD EEW already arose serious concerns regarding its compatibility with the
fundamental rights of a fair trial. As I pointed out in my paper on solution models
(Sect. 4, items 3–5), it does not address the specific needs of the defence in a system
where the prosecutorial powers have been unleashed by the mutual recognition
paradigm.

1.2 Green Paper

The Commission's Green paper has been criticised even more, by a vast majority of
scholars[1] and, notably, some legislative bodies of the Member States (including
Germany[2]). It was pointed out that the gathering of evidence is a very delicate part
of criminal proceedings that is closely linked to the establishment of the truth later
on during trial, and can therefore not be considered alone. And while the FD EEW
was limited to the collection of existing items and few coercive measures, the
Commission intended to go further and cover all investigative measures. This has
been criticised too, and especially the German legislative bodies considered that the
EEW should first be implemented and its practical results considered before taking
it a step further.

---

[1] See for example the analysis by Schünemann and Roger (2010), p. 92.

[2] See *Beschluss des Bundesrats*, 866. *Sitzung am* 12. 2. 2010, BR-Dr 906/09; *Beschlussempfehlung und Bericht des Rechtsausschusses des Bundestages* v. 9.2.2010, BT-Dr 17/660.

But instead of taking advantage of the expertise of numerous reputable scholars, practitioners and legislative institutions, a group of seven Member States proposed the EIO, going even further than what the Commission suggested in the green paper. The whole consultation process was plainly ignored, although it raised serious concerns regarding the mutual recognition approach, in particular in the field of evidence gathering.

2 Fundamental Flaws of Mutual Recognition, in Particular Concerning the Gathering of Evidence

The fundamental bias of the mutual recognition principle results from the transposition of this liberal common market principle to the field of criminal justice. Here it turns from liberal to authoritarian effects and leads to the consequence that the most punitive criminal law system of one Member State can be executed in all other Member States, potentially on the lowest common level of defendant's rights. Concerning the gathering of evidence in particular, the mutual recognition approach does not take into account that the rules on evidence vary considerably between Member States. Every national procedural law provides for a comprehensive and coherent set of rules that balances (or at least is reckoned to balance) the interests of effective prosecution and the safeguarding of the defendant's rights. Because they strike this procedural balance in different ways, these national laws cannot be simply combined.

Basically, any gathering of evidence in criminal matters must be regulated with regard to its sole goal and justification that is the use of evidence in the trial—a trial that needs to be fair. In this respect, mutual recognition is deficient as it creates hybrid procedural laws, enhancing the powers of the prosecution without granting the defence sufficient rights to compensate and re-establish the balance of the proceedings. Not only are there practical barriers for a defendant that faces charges from a foreign state, but also his legal remedies are split between different judicial systems, rendering the task of the defence very complex and potentially unfeasible.

3 Most Serious Flaws of the EIO in Particular

3.1 Flexibility as a Denial of Legal Certainty

The flexibility of the EIO would make it easier to handle for the authorities, but at the expense of legal certainty, a requirement that to a certain extent also applies to procedural law—"*nullum judicium sine lege*," as the European Court of Human

Rights has put it.[3] I would like to pick two main points that the hybridised procedure under the EIO fails to regulate stringently:

A) First, the few grounds for refusal according to Article 10 Proposed Directive (PD) EIO are not mandatory, but at the discretion of the executing authority. So even if one acknowledges that they aim to secure some aspects of a fair trial, they do not convert into effective rights for the defence.

B) Second, the execution under the *forum regit actum* principle, which may allow to apply only one single, coherent procedural law and therefore offer a good solution for the admissibility issue, is left to the discretion of the issuing authority that indicates the formalities and procedures [Art. 8 (2)]. So rather than ensuring the stringent application of one single procedural law, the optional forum principle may be chosen or not for tactical reasons, in order to use the most permissive rules available in the concrete case, thereby reducing the rights of the individual concerned.[4]

C) Both aspects are likely to weaken the defence in concrete cases. Also, they jeopardise the general principle of legal certainty, as it becomes impossible to foresee which procedural law will apply, or which limits will be drawn to the execution of an EIO.

3.2 No Ground for Refusal When a Measure Has Not Been Ordered by a Court

In many legal orders, only a judge may order certain coercive measures. This is generally considered a fundamental guarantee of legality, impartiality and proportionality for such invasive measures. The EIO, however, might also be issued by other authorities, even non-judicial ones, and would nevertheless have to be executed in another Member State. As a result, the executing state would have to enforce the lowest standards of judicial protection. Therefore, it is indispensable that the execution should be refused unless a measure has been issued (or at least validated) by a judge in the issuing state, when such a measure would have to be ordered by a court in the executing state. Even the European Parliament Committee on civil liberties, justice and home affairs (LIBE) has proposed to amend the directive in this respect.

---

[3] E.C.J., *Coëme et al. v. Belgium*, 22 June 2000, n. App. 32492/96, (102).

[4] Dissenting Satzger (2012), § 8 para. 36.

3.3 Defence Rights

As I mentioned earlier, mutual recognition threatens the balance of criminal proceedings and puts the defendant into an inferior position, facing a prosecution released from territorial boundaries. This issue is not addressed by the directive proposal, and in particular, no measures are taken to enable an effective defence against an EIO. Neither the "roadmap on procedural rights"[5] nor pursuant directives offering any serious solution to these issues, nothing but an institutional guarantee would put the defence into a situation comparable to the prosecution's under the aspect of "equality of arms." As a crucial test, the Council has just decided to narrow down the proposed directive on the right of access to a lawyer, allowing even non-judicial authorities to limit this right, and substantially weakening the double defence (in both the issuing and the executing state) proposed for European Arrest Warrant cases,[6] thus unmasking the "roadmap" as a pure lip service.

As for legal remedies, Article 13(3) PD EIO holds that "The substantive reasons for issuing the EIO may be challenged only in an action brought in the issuing State." This is a consequence of the mutual recognition principle—being actually its procedural core—and, lacking any complementary strengthening of the defence, establishes a serious impediment to the right to an effective legal remedy according to Article 47 EU FRCh. The defendant confronted with a coercive measure in state A cannot have the legality of this measure thoroughly assessed by the local courts supposed to control the exercise of power; and on the other hand, he is in an extremely weak position to take action before the courts of a remote country, the language of which he might not even speak or understand, apart from additional court and lawyer fees and other obstacles.

3.4 Lack of a General Double Criminality Requirement and/or a Sufficient Territoriality Requirement

A) Like the prior Framework Decisions on the European Arrest Warrant and Evidence Warrant, the EIO Directive widely abolishes double criminality as a requirement for legal assistance (see for details Art. 10). For some measures—presumably considered less invasive—it has been completely suppressed. Even for more invasive measures, a "positive list" is to be applied, covering 32 offences for which no double criminality check shall be made. As it has often been criticised,[7] this list mocks any pretence of legal certainty. As a result,

---

[5] Resolution of the Council of 30 November 2009 on a Roadmap for strengthening procedural rights of suspected or accused persons in criminal proceedings (2009/C 295/01).

[6] Art. 11 (3) COM (2011) 326 final.

[7] Braum (2005), pp. 681–692; Hefendehl (2006), pp. 161–167; Satzger (2012), § 8 para. 26; Schünemann (2003), pp. 531et seqq.; it has even been criticised by authors who consider that the double criminality requirement may be waived: Mavany (2012), pp. 125et seqq.

the executing State may be forced to take coercive measures for the prosecution of behaviours that its own legal order does not deem criminal offences.

B) This is all the more alarming when we consider that it is not guaranteed that the issuing state has legitimate jurisdiction. Article 10(1)(f) of the proposal only allows refusal when

> the EIO relates to a criminal offence which is alleged to have been committed exclusively outside the territory of the issuing State and wholly or partially on the territory of the executing State, the EIO seeks the use of a coercive measure and the conduct in connection with which the EIO is issued is not an offence in the executing State.

Put another way, there is a positive territoriality condition (regarding the executing State) and cumulatively a negative one (regarding the issuing State). So if an offence is said to have been committed in a third State, the executing authority must obey the issuing authority. The same applies when it has been committed almost exclusively in the executing State, but also for a very small part in the issuing State. In both cases, the law of the issuing State prevails if it is more punitive. This is significantly more severe than the territoriality clause in the FD EEW, in which the "positive" and "negative" territorial exceptions were alternative, not cumulative grounds for refusal.

4   Conclusion

To sum up, the directive proposal of a European Investigation Order once more aims to take a hasty step further into the direction of a European criminal prosecution where, on the contrary, a thorough assessment of the existing rules would have been necessary and the strengthening of the defence inevitable. This was done without considering the concerns expressed by both scholars and national legislative bodies with respect to the previous steps and especially to the Commission's Green paper on obtaining evidence in criminal matters. Therefore this "*fait accompli*" proposal should be abandoned completely to allow instead for an informed and careful legislative process.

Acknowledgement   The author wishes to express his sincere gratitude to *Benjamin Roger*, Maître en Droit, for his essential and indispensable cooperation.

References

Braum S (2005) Das Prinzip der gegenseitigen Anerkennung Historische Grundlagen und Perspektiven europäischer Strafrechtsentwicklung. Goltdammer's Archiv für Strafrecht 681–699

Hefendehl R (2006) Europäischer Umweltschutz: Demokratiespritze für Europa oder Brüsseler Putsch? Zeitschrift für internationale Strafrechtsdogmatik 161–167

Mavany M (2012) Die europäische Beweisanordnung und das Prinzip der gegenseitigen Anerkennung. C.F. Müller, Heidelberg
Satzger H (2012) International and European criminal law. Beck–Hart–Nomos, Münich
Schünemann B (2003) Die parlamentarische Gesetzgebung als Lakai von Brüssel? Zum Entwurf des europäischen Haftbefehlsgesetzes. Strafverteidiger 531–534
Schünemann B, Roger B (2010) Die Karawane zur Europäisierung des Strafrechts zieht weiter. Zur demokratischen und rechtsstaatlichen Bresthaftigkeit des EU-Geldsanktionengesetzes. Zeitschrift für internationale Strafrechtsdogmatik 515–523

General Considerations on the European Investigation Order

Tommaso Rafaraci

Abstract This paper deals with the issue concerning movement of evidence between the 27 Member States of the EU in view of the adoption of the Directive on the European Investigation Order. By a critical approach, the paper focuses in particular on mutual recognition and its application in the criminal law sector, legality and proportionality of investigative measures, and defence rights in legal assistance procedures.

Keywords Admissibility • Investigative measures and evidence • Legality and proportionality • Lex mitior • Mutual recognition • Procedural rights

Contents

1 Preliminary Remarks 38
2 On the Basis of Mutual Recognition 38
3 The Check on "Double Procedural Legality" (and the Ground for Refusal in Case
   No Type of Measure Fits the Request) 40
4 The Margin of Appreciation on Proportionality of the Investigative Measure
   in the Specific Case 41
5 Favour for the Admissibility of Evidence and Silence on Defence Rights in
   Transnational Procedures 42
References 43

T. Rafaraci (✉)
Department "Seminario giuridico", University of Catania, Via Gallo no. 24, Catania, Italy
e-mail: trafaraci@lex.unict.it

S. Ruggeri (ed.), *Transnational Evidence and Multicultural Inquiries in Europe*,
DOI 10.1007/978-3-319-02570-4_3, © Springer International Publishing Switzerland 2014

1   Preliminary Remarks

The debate on the Proposal for a Directive on the European Investigation Order (hereinafter PD EIO) deserves a constructive approach even where criticism is expressed.

The objective to overcome the fragmentation of the current framework for the gathering of evidence in the EU and replace it with a single measure allowing the gathering of—almost—any type of evidence in transnational cases justifies the application of mutual recognition, the method now codified under Art. 82.1 TFEU to strengthen judicial cooperation in criminal matters in light of the creation of an Area of Freedom, Security and Justice. In this context we will not stress the limits that in general affect mutual recognition as such, and those that in particular affect mutual recognition applied in the criminal law sector (where this principle risks producing authoritarian effects, rather than libertarian results, as it does in the common market). Otherwise, we may directly come to a conclusion. Given that issues relating to evidence in criminal proceedings are among the thorniest ones, since national legal systems are very different one from each other and have their own features as far as the separation between the investigative stage and the trial is concerned, it should not be possible to eliminate such differences by simply allowing free movement of evidence in the EU. However, such a conclusion would not be of any help. Even though it is not sure whether agreement on the PD EIO will be reached soon, the issue concerning movement of evidence in transnational cases in the EU remains at the center of attention, thanks to the attention paid to mutual recognition. Attention is paid to this issue also in light of the investigative acts of a possible future European Public Prosecutor Office or its national delegates, depending on the structure and functional articulation—not necessarily vertical—that this Office will be given.

Thus, it is better to analyse the currently available PD EIO (December 2011) with no prejudice and by assessing to what extent natural concerns on mutual recognition can be limited. The following considerations are directed to this end, without pretention to completeness, aware that the PD EIO impinges on delicate and complex issues.

2   On the Basis of Mutual Recognition

The new measure, although founded on the principle of mutual recognition, aims also at taking into account flexibility of the traditional system of mutual legal assistance, as expressly stated in recital nr. 6. However, the PD EIO does not realise a mixed system, as one could think. Indeed, all the features that characterise mutual recognition can be found. The grounds for refusal provided for in the PD EIO[1] are

---

[1] On this issue, see Bachmaier Winter, Part III.

not meant to keep together tradition and new policies of judicial cooperation, but rather show that automatism resulting from mutual recognition—in its adaptation to criminal matters and as it is framed at present—is not the real "hot issue." The features of flexibility provided for in the PD EIO do not represent a tribute to tradition, but rather a new form of dialogue between the issuing and the executing authorities following direct contacts, in order to facilitate the assimilation of mutual recognition in this delicate context of legal assistance.

Mutual recognition is applied without significant theoretical differences and material limitations, as it is clear from the following observations:

a) The scope of application of the EIO is very wide, both *ratione materiae* and *ratione personae*. *Ratione materiae*, it applies to any type of evidence and to any criminal proceeding (there is no limitation to specific offences); to a certain extent, it also applies to non-criminal proceedings (see Art. 4). *Ratione personae*, it can be issued by many different authorities (see Art. 2). However, although an EIO shall be validated when it is issued by an authority different from a judge, court, public prosecutor or investigating magistrate [Art. 5a(3)], nothing ensures that the EIO has been validated by a judge, especially where intrusive measures liable to impinge on fundamental rights are at stake. The executing authority will have to execute an EIO even if the requested measure needs to be validated by a judge according to its national legislation and the measure has not been validated in the issuing Member State by this specific judicial authority.

b) The issuing authority has to check the legality as well as the necessity and proportionality of the investigative measure (Art. 5a). Legality is satisfied if the investigative measure could have been ordered under the same condition in a similar national case [Art. 5a(1)(b)]. Necessity and proportionality are satisfied if the piece of evidence to be obtained by an EIO is necessary and proportionate for the purpose of the proceedings [Art. 5a(1)(a)], and if the investigative measure chosen is necessary and proportionate for the gathering of that piece of evidence (recital nr. 10a).

When these conditions are satisfied, the executing authority executes the EIO in the same way and under the same modalities as if the investigative measure in question had been ordered by an authority of the executing Member State, unless the executing authority invokes one of the grounds for non-recognition or non-execution or one of the grounds for postponement, as provided for in the Directive [Art. 8 (1)]. Among the grounds for refusal relevant in this context, there is the one concerning the lack of what may be defined as "double procedural legality" or "double proportionality" (Art. 9), which stems from the margin of appreciation left to the executing authority (see below, Sects. 3 and 4).

In line with this system, Article 13(3) provides that the substantive reasons for issuing the EIO may be challenged only in an action brought in the issuing State.

c) The number of grounds for refusal is very limited. They are few and only optional [Art. 10 (1)], and do not include the absence of double criminality, required only to a restricted extent. Indeed, double criminality must be satisfied only for the investigative measures other than those listed under Article 10(1a) (search and seizure, here listed, cannot be refused because the requirement of double criminality is not fulfilled, even if they are intrusive measures liable to affect fundamental rights) and only if two additional requirements are satisfied: (1) the offence must be different from those listed in the Annex; (2) the offence must be punished in the issuing State by a custodial sentence or a detention order for a maximum period of at least 3 years. The requirement of double criminality is therefore reduced to its minimum terms, this showing that it is being progressively marginalised as far as mutual legal assistance in the EU is concerned.

3   The Check on "Double Procedural Legality" (and the Ground for Refusal in Case No Type of Measure Fits the Request)

The requirement of "double procedural legality"[2] does not always cede in favour of mutual recognition. What we refer to is the provision concerning the cases where the investigative measure provided for in the EIO does not exist under the law of the executing Member State or it would not be available in a similar domestic case (Art. 9): the executing authority *must*, wherever possible, have recourse to an investigative measure other than that provided for in the EIO, when this other measure will have the same result. The executing authority shall inform the issuing authority, which may decide to withdraw the EIO. Where there is no other investigative measure which would have the same result as the measure requested, the executing authority must notify the issuing authority that it has not been possible to provide the assistance requested. In other words, without impinging on the check of legality and proportionality carried out by the issuing authority, the executing authority cannot refuse the execution of the EIO if it has not tried to find an alternative measure with similar effects.[3] However, this possibility does not apply to those measures listed under Article 10(1a), in relation to which existence and availability in a similar national case under the law of the executing Member State are presumed. The check on "double procedural legality" applies to the measures different from those listed under Article 10(1a), which are—perhaps—the most intrusive ones [although search and seizure are listed under Article 10(1a)].

---

[2] Procedural legality is of utmost importance to ensure the guarantee of certainty and predictability of criminal procedural law.

[3] Similar mechanisms directed to overcome the differences between national legal systems have already been foreseen in the Framework Decision 2009/829/JHA on the application of the principle of mutual recognition to decisions on supervision measures as an alternative to provisional detention, and the Framework Decision 2008/909/JHA on the application of the principle of mutual recognition to judgments in criminal matters imposing custodial sentences or measures involving deprivation of liberty for the purpose of their enforcement in the European Union. See Belfiore (2011), pp. 105ff., and Rafaraci (2012), pp. 67ff.

We believe that the abolition of the check for the measures under Article 10(1a) aims to simplification, with the objective of preventing that legal assistance is refused because of variable interpretations on the conditions required under the law of the executing Member State for the availability of an existent measure. In other words, the check on legality should not go beyond a check on legality *stricto sensu*.

4 The Margin of Appreciation on Proportionality of the Investigative Measure in the Specific Case

The provision according to which the executing authority *may* have recourse to an investigative measure other than that provided for in the EIO when this other investigative measure will have the same result by less intrusive means [Art. 9(1bis)], is meant to prevent that the executing authority refuses an EIO where the investigative measure exists under the law of the executing Member State and would be available in a similar case, but the proportionality of the measure is not satisfied. Proportionality is of course something different from legality *stricto sensu*; yet, it is a very important criterion for the assessment of tolerability of limitations to fundamental rights. In light of this consideration, the margin of appreciation left to the executing authority is welcome: where the measure is deemed to be disproportionate in the specific case, the executing authority may ensure legal assistance only by a less intrusive measure, after informing the issuing authority, which may decide to withdraw the EIO [Art. 9(2)].

Unfortunately, this provision does not result in the application of the *lex mitior*. Indeed, the executing authority is granted a mere option, as it may (not must) have recourse to a less intrusive measure, and the issuing authority is not obliged to accept the assessment carried out by the executing authority concerning the equivalence between the measure provided for in the EIO and the less intrusive one, since it can always withdraw the EIO. On the other hand, we believe that the application of the *lex mitior* should be promoted with more incisiveness in the context of judicial cooperation, especially in all those cases concerning pretrial or investigative measures affecting fundamental rights. The principle inspired by the *lex mitior* should be applied to its maximum extent so as to become the principal criterion to assess proportionality of the measure to be executed in the specific case. Currently, this principle is rather a reserve instrument to be applied from time to time and by option for the purpose of mitigating the asperities of mutual recognition.[4]

---

[4] See Rafaraci (2013), pp. 341f., and De Bondt and Vermeulen (2010), p. 166.

5   Favour for the Admissibility of Evidence and Silence on Defence Rights in Transnational Procedures

The executing authority executes the investigative measure provided for in the EIO according to its national law [Art. 8(1)]. However, the application of *lex loci* is liable to be considerably limited by initiative of the issuing authority, which may indicate formalities and procedures to be complied with in the execution of the measure. The executing authority shall comply with these formalities and procedures, unless they are contrary to fundamental principles of law of the executing Member State [Art. 8(2)].

Similarly, the executing authority shall comply with the request that one or several authorities of the issuing State assist in the execution of the EIO in support to the competent authorities of the executing Member State to the extent that the designated authorities would be able to assist in the execution of the investigative measure in a similar national case, provided that such assistance is not contrary to the fundamental principles of law of the executing Member State or does not harm its essential national security interests [Art. 8(3)].

Article 8 is meant to favour admissibility of evidence in the issuing Member State, by preventing the dilemma whether admitting a piece of evidence even if it does not fulfill all the requirements for admissibility, or not admitting the piece of evidence thus frustrating legal assistance. This provision favours judicial cooperation in consideration of the problems that admissibility of evidence gathered abroad according to different standards raises. In fact, the issue of admissibility is so thorny that Article 82 TFEU provides that, to the extent necessary to facilitate mutual recognition of judgments and judicial decisions and judicial cooperation in criminal matters having a cross border dimension, the EU may establish minimum rules concerning mutual admissibility of evidence.

However, Article 8 is not clear in all its departments. The optional nature of the request to comply with specific formalities and procedures—in consideration of both the option on whether to put forward such a request or not, and its optional content—may result in uncertain effects on the actual rule of evidence to be applied. Plus, formalities and procedures may address very different needs. Compliance with formalities and procedures does not always ensure the respect of fundamental rights of the individuals concerned. Not to mention that the issue on admissibility of evidence does not correspond to the issue concerning the respect of adequate standards of guarantee; in fact, the one must not be confused with the other. Nothing ensures that specific formalities and procedures are meant to favour admissibility of evidence in the issuing Member State (the initiative by the issuing Member State does not bind upon the future admissibility of evidence); formalities and procedures may rather favour a wider scope of application of the measure in the investigative stage.

Therefore we believe that, even if the provision at issue is liable to be virtuously used, it remains ambiguous since it does not definitely ensure the respect of standards which are not contrary to fundamental rights, especially defence rights.

In light of this, the deficit in the gathering of evidence abroad in States with low standards of protection of fundamental rights should be addressed irrespective of the needs of the issuing Member State on rules governing the admissibility of evidence.

On the other hand, the EIO is a measure directed to apply mutual recognition; a measure that competes with the thorny issue of admissibility of evidence in the name of a more efficient legal assistance, while ignoring and postponing the issue of fundamental guarantees and defence rights in transnational procedures. One could think that the inconveniences stemming from the implementation of the European Arrest Warrant will not occur, since the unbalance in favour of law enforcement objectives should be prevented by the progressive implementation of the *Roadmap for strengthening procedural rights of suspected or accused persons in criminal proceedings*.[5]

However, that the general approach of the Roadmap is the most appropriate can be debated. What is needed is the elaboration of defence rights and individual guarantees to be adopted specifically in transnational procedures, which, after all, fall within the competence of the EU in criminal matters. Thus, it is questionable that the elaboration of a general measure, meant to rule the issue concerning legal assistance in the EU, does not include the mechanisms of mutual recognition together with guarantees specific to the gathering of evidence in transnational procedures. This does not need to be done by a single legislative act (in order to prevent confusion between the two faces of mutual trust: the virtual one, i.e. mutual recognition, and the real one, i.e. common rules). But, if different measures will be adopted, they should be adopted at the same time. On the other hand, the way forward indicated by the *Roadmap* is slow and—most important—indifferent to specificities of transnational procedures.

References[6]

Belfiore R (2011) Mutuo riconoscimento delle decisioni sulle misure alternative alla detenzione cautelare. In: Rafaraci T (ed) La cooperazione di polizia e giudiziaria in materia penale nell'Unione europea dopo il Trattato di Lisbona. Giuffrè, Milano, pp 105–117

De Bondt W, Vermeulen G (2010) The procedural rights debate. A bridge too far or still not far enough. Eucrim 4:163–167

---

[5] Adopted by Resolution of the Council of 30 November 2009, OJ 2009/C 295/01, and scheduled under the Stockholm Programme (OJ 2010/C 115/01). At present, two measures provided for in the Roadmap have already been adopted: Directive 2010/64/EU on the right to interpretation and translation in criminal proceedings, and Directive 2012/13/EU on the right to information in criminal proceedings (they both apply to the procedures under the European Arrest Warrant).

[6] The chapter contributions contained in this book have been quoted with the only reference to the Author's surname, the Part in which the contribution is contained and the number of the paragraph concerned.

Rafaraci T (2012) The application of the principle of mutual recognition to decisions on supervision measures as an alternative to provisional detention. In: Ruggeri S (ed) Liberty and security in Europe. A comparative analysis of pre-trial precautionary measures in criminal proceedings. V&R Unipress, Göttingen, pp 67–83
Rafaraci T (2013) The right of defence in EU judicial cooperation in criminal matters. In: Ruggeri S (ed) Transnational inquiries and the protection of fundamental rights in criminal proceedings, A study in memory of Vittorio Grevi and Giovanni Tranchina. Springer, Heidelberg, pp 331–343

The European Investigation Order: Fundamental Rights at Risk?

Richard Vogler

Abstract This chapter describes the difficult legislative history of the proposal for a European Investigation Order, noting the reluctance of its sponsors to integrate human rights protections except by formal declaration. It is argued that such protections should be woven deep into the fabric of legislation such as this, if it is to have any chance of promoting mutual recognition and reciprocity between nations in the conduct of investigations.

Keywords European Commission • European Court of Human Rights • European Investigation Order • European Parliament • Human rights • Mutual recognition

The proposal for a "European Investigation Order" (EIO) has been a long time in gestation. It was conceived as an attempt to apply the "mutual recognition" methodology of the European Arrest Warrant to the field of transnational investigations, hitherto governed by a complex array of partial expedients. It began to take definite form in November 2009 when the European Commission produced a Green Paper on the subject[1] and shortly afterwards a meeting of experts was convened in Brussels to consider national responses to the Member States' questionnaire.[2] At this point, however, no public consultation was attempted and before the Commission could take the project further, a group of seven Member States, under the

---

[1] Green Paper on Obtaining Evidence in Criminal Matters from one Member State to Another and Securing its Admissibility, COM(2009) 624 Final (Brussels, 11 November 2009).

[2] Spencer (2010).

R. Vogler (✉)
Sussex Law School, University of Sussex, Falmer BN1 9QQ, UK
e-mail: R.K.Vogler@Sussex.ac.uk

S. Ruggeri (ed.), *Transnational Evidence and Multicultural Inquiries in Europe*,
DOI 10.1007/978-3-319-02570-4_4, © Springer International Publishing Switzerland 2014

leadership of Belgium, intervened to deliver their own Proposed Directive for a European Investigation Order (PD EIO).[3]

What is most striking about both the Commission's Green Paper and the Member States' PD EIO, is their unashamed appeal to values of "efficiency" and "flexibility"[4] to the almost complete exclusion of any sustained discourse relating to human rights, as exemplified by the European Convention on Human Rights (ECHR) and the European Union Charter of Fundamental Rights ("the Charter"). The Green Paper made no mention whatsoever of the human rights impact of the proposal and asked no questions in relation to this topic in its questionnaire to Member States. The PD EIO itself used language which reinforced this impression. References to human rights principles, where they existed at all, were inserted grudgingly and inconspicuously in the text. Instead of headlining the protection of human rights as a primary objective of the PD EIO, paragraph 3 instead introduced a purely negative qualification to the effect that

> (t)his Directive shall not have the effect of modifying the obligation to respect the fundamental rights and fundamental legal principles as enshrined in Article 6 of the Treaty, and any obligations incumbent on judicial authorities in this respect shall remain unaffected.

The unspoken assumption behind this curious formulation is that in other circumstances, such rights and obligations might well be "modified" or "affected", should the more pressing interests of efficiency and flexibility so require!

The European Council's *Explanatory Memorandum* goes on to explain, almost apologetically, that paragraph 3 had been included "as it is the case in all instruments on mutual recognition in criminal proceedings."[5] The *Detailed Statement*, released 20 days later, indicated that the "general objective" of the PD EIO was to "improve the search for truth in criminal proceedings with a transnational aspect."[6] It suggested that this general objective was composed of seven specific subsidiary objectives, of which the fourth (sandwiched between simplifying procedure and saving costs) was described as "maintaining a high level of protection of fundamental rights, especially procedural rights."[7] The *Detailed Statement* then offered a highly unconvincing "Impact Analysis" of the PD EIO, in which, without evidence or sustained discussion, the consequences for fundamental rights were declared to be "neutral."[8]

Such equivocation in European legislation which is likely to present a grave threat to the most vulnerable defendants, is profoundly disappointing and explains in part the slow progress towards implementation of the PD EIO. The original draft

---

[3] Proposal for a Directive of the European Parliament and of the Council regarding the European Investigation Order and other Matters, 9145/10, COPEN115 (Brussels, 29 April 2010).

[4] European Council, *Explanatory Memorandum*, 9288/10 ADD 1 (Brussels, 3 June 2010).

[5] *Ibid.*, p. 3.

[6] European Council, *Detailed Statement*, 9288/10 ADD 2 (Brussels, 23 June 2010), p. 20.

[7] *Ibid.*

[8] *Ibid.*, p. 35.

was at once subjected to a barrage of criticism based on its failure to address rights concerns. Sayer, for example, described it as, in most respects "a tool for interstate police cooperation in the guise of mutual recognition?"[9] Heard and Mansell, on behalf of *Fair Trials International*, concluded that the human rights protections were simply "inadequate" and pointed out that disregard for them was not included in the limited grounds for refusal of an EIO.[10] These concerns had already been forcefully expressed by a number of other human rights agencies such as *Statewatch*,[11] *Justice*[12] and *CEPS, Liberty and Security in Europe*.[13] A Report commissioned by the European Parliament from the *European Union Agency for Fundamental Rights* in February 2011 commented that there were serious problems, not only in respect of defendants' rights[14] but also in respect of victims' rights,[15] data protection and privacy[16] and that grounds available for refusal of an EIO were also inadequate. The Agency called for an "evidence-based assessment of both the needs of and the fundamental rights implications for individuals."[17]

A *Commentary* issued by the European Commission in August 2010[18] took the same view, concluding that there was "neither a proper impact assessment nor an explanatory memorandum that provides enough material to state that the draft Directive respects the Charter and the ECHR."[19] The *Detailed Statement* was also criticised on the grounds that it misunderstood the provisions of the Charter by failing to identify and assess the more important fundamental rights potentially affected by this proposal. The *Commentary* concluded that the proclaimed statement of compliance with the Charter was not acceptable and in order to address this problem, the Commission proposed a list of rights provisions which should be made explicit.[20] The European Justice Commissioner, Viviane Reding, at the same time promised that "we are ready to help Member States ensure that their proposals respect our EU Charter of Fundamental Rights during the negotiations and later in the practical application of this EU instrument."[21]

Despite the weight of criticism directed specifically towards the PD EIO's reluctance to acknowledge the primacy of human rights protections in its text, its

---

[9] Sayers (2011), p. 6.

[10] Heard and Mansell (2010), p. 6.

[11] Peers (2010).

[12] Blackstock (2010, 2011).

[13] Sayers (2011).

[14] European Union Agency for Fundamental Rights (2011), pp. 4–6.

[15] *Ibid.*, p. 6.

[16] *Ibid.*, pp. 7–9.

[17] *Ibid.*, p. 13.

[18] European Commission, *Commentary*, JUST/B/1/AA-et D(2010) 6815 (Brussels, 24 August 2010).

[19] *Ibid.*, p. 7.

[20] *Ibid.*, pp. 7–9.

[21] European Commission *Press Release*, IP/10/1067, 24 August 2010.

promoters were still disinclined to make concessions. A "General Approach" was agreed at the Justice and Home Affairs Council in December 2011 and the European Parliament suggested amendments in May 2012. These included a recital of the specific process rights which should be protected in the course of a transnational investigation[22] and the assertion that:

> mutual recognition is to be applied in legal areas that are not harmonised and that have different legal traditions and criminal procedural systems, and may therefore result in legal anomalies to the detriment of the rights of suspects, as demonstrated by the experience gained with using the European Arrest Warrant. Measures must be established which will allow a national court to substantially intervene in cases where such anomalies may arise.[23]

They insisted that the "challenge in terms of European criminal integration is therefore to ensure respect for and guarantee fundamental rights."[24] During the subsequent "Trilogue" discussions in November,[25] the European Presidency conceded that, notwithstanding that the "general reference" to fundamental rights was, in its view perfectly sufficient, it was "not entirely inappropriate" that the rights of the defence should receive particular attention in the text.[26] Here again, the topic of rights protection, where mentioned at all, was introduced in a negative and seemingly reluctant manner. Despite the obligation under Article 48(2) of the Charter to respect the rights of the Defence, the Presidency was not prepared to concede that they should enjoy equal rights to the Prosecution in obtaining transnational evidence. Instead they proposed a much weaker form of words:

> In this regard, when implementing this Directive, Member States should give due consideration to the rights of the defence, in conformity with the relevant rules under their national law, to request that certain investigative measures be carried out also at the initiative of the defence if this is allowed by a Member State's legal system.[27]

Amendments were nevertheless proposed by the European Parliament in an attempt to strengthen the "double criminality" and territoriality principles and to propose a human rights ground as a full ground for refusal.[28] Given the entrenched positions on both sides, it is not surprising that little progress has been made towards the implementation of the PD EIO.[29] In March 2013, nearly 4 years after their original intervention, the Justice Ministers of the seven sponsoring states

---

[22] European Parliament Committee on Civil Liberties, Justice and Home Affairs, *Orientation Vote Result*, 2010/0817(COD), 8 May 2012, Amendment 20.

[23] *Ibid.*, Compromise Amendment 21.

[24] *Ibid.*, p. 54.

[25] Answer to Parliamentary Question, James Brokenshire, 12 December 2012.

[26] Council, *Note to Delegations*, 16120/12, COPEN 245 (Brussels, 15 November 2012), p. 2.

[27] *Ibid.*, p. 5.

[28] See European Scrutiny Committee of the UK Parliament, 13 March 2013, at http://www.publications.parliament.uk/pa/cm201213/cmselect/cmeuleg/86-xxxv/8617.htm.

[29] Trilogue discussions were interrupted when the European Parliament suspended co-operation due to disagreements regarding the Schengen Evaluation Mechanism.

wrote in exasperated tones to insist that "we believe that the time has come" to finish the work on this "modern instrument."[30]

The unhappy legislative history of the PD EIO demonstrates all too clearly that the widest possible debate is necessary before the enactment of provisions which so clearly impact on the rights of the most vulnerable. Individuals involved in transnational investigations are exponentially more likely to be exposed to the risk of abusive practices than those involved in merely domestic proceedings.[31] The reasoned perspectives of Police and Prosecution experts, whatever their honourable intentions in combatting the scourge of transnational crime, are no substitute for a detailed evaluation of the practical implications of an instrument such as this and its effect on individuals under suspicion. It should be well understood by now that a merely formal recital of compliance with the Charter and the ECHR in a document which offers multiple possibilities for the most egregious breaches, is completely inadequate. This is a legislative strategy shared by the procedure codes of countries, particularly in the Soviet era, which systematically abused the rights of arrestees and it should have no place in the legal culture of contemporary Europe. Human rights protections must be woven deep into the fabric of legislation such as this, at every point at which rights are likely to be threatened. Only in this way can the mutual trust between nations, on which the whole system of transnational investigation depends, enjoy some chance of successful development.

References

Blackstock J (2010) Briefing on the European Investigation Order for Council and Parliament. Justice, London

Blackstock J (2011) Briefing on the European Investigation Order for Council and Parliament. Partial general approach. Justice, London

European Union Agency for Fundamental Rights (2011) FRA opinion on the draft directive regarding the European Investigation Order (EIO). European Union Agency for Fundamental Rights, Vienna

Heard C, Mansell D (2010) Fair Trials International's response to a European member states' legislative initiative for a directive on a European Investigation Order. Fair Trials International, London

Peers S (2010) The proposed European Investigation Order: assault on human rights and national sovereignty. Statewatch, London

Sayers D (2011) The European Investigation Order – travelling without a 'roadmap'. Centre for European Policy Studies, Brussels

Spencer J (2010) The Green Paper on obtaining evidence from one member state to another and securing its admissibility: the reaction of one British lawyer. Zeitschrift für Internationale Strafrechtsdogmatik 9:602–606

Vogler RK (2013) Transnational inquiries and the protection of human rights in the case-law of the European court of human rights. In: Ruggeri S (ed) Transnational inquiries and the protection of fundamental rights in criminal proceedings. Springer, Heidelberg, pp 27–40

---

[30] Council, *Note to Delegations* 6532/13 COPEN 18 (Brussels, 5 March 2013), pp. 2–3.

[31] Vogler (2013).

Collecting Criminal Evidence Across the European Union: The European Investigation Order Between Flexibility and Proportionality

Silvia Allegrezza

Abstract As always, the aim of theoretical analysis is to bring to light the many obstacles piled on the road of the European criminal law enforcement. One's confidence in European criminal law turns on how well it is perceived. And this is largely a fact of whether and how it can improve the effectiveness and the quality of criminal justice. This kind of task confronts critical theory with concrete needs for both law enforcement and individual rights.

This paper discusses the pros and cons of the proposal for a directive on the European investigation order. First, it will focus on definitions, stressing the difference between collecting evidence abroad—that means nothing more than a request and an answer between different States—and the so-called "free movement of evidence," that concerns only evidence already existing or already gathered or used in trial by the requested member State. Second, the role and the real meaning of mutual recognition will be discussed. Those who advocate against the mutual recognition principle seem to forget how difficult the position of the defence is in transnational cases governed by the traditional mutual legal assistance. This paper stresses the neutral nature of the method itself: its dangerousness for the defence will depend on the concrete applications in criminal matters. Having in mind the need to implement the effectiveness of judicial cooperation in criminal matters, this paper will deal with the proportionality requirement in the draft directive. Many elements justify a moderate optimism.

Keywords European criminal law • Evidence • Mutual recognition

Contents

1 Introduction 52
2 One-Size Fits All Approach: Flexibility as a Value 53

S. Allegrezza (✉)
Department of Law, University of Bologna, Via Zamboni 27/29, Bologna, Italy
e-mail: Silvia.allegrezza2@unibo.it

S. Ruggeri (ed.), *Transnational Evidence and Multicultural Inquiries in Europe*,
DOI 10.1007/978-3-319-02570-4_5, © Springer International Publishing Switzerland 2014

3 Mutual Recognition, Free Movement of Evidence and Transnational Investigation 55
   3.1 Mutual Recognition 55
   3.2 Free Movement of Evidence 57
   3.3 Admissibility of Evidence in Trial Is Still Out of the EU Mandate 58
4 Building a EU Proportionality Requirement 59
   4.1 A Key Topic for Mutual Distrust? 59
   4.2 Taking the EAW Experience as a Model 60
   4.3 Proportionality and Evidence 61
   4.4 Proportionality and Evidence in the Draft Proposal on the EIO 62
   4.5 The "Less Intrusive Measure" Rule 63
References 65

1 Introduction

The proposal for the European investigation order introduces a new tool for cross-border investigations and for trans-national gathering of evidence. The mechanism is quite simple: no specific formality is required for the issuing authority that needs to investigate in another Member State. The proposal includes a form to be filled up and sent directly to the judicial authority of the executing State. The requested authority shall execute the measure required "in the same way and under the same modalities if the investigative measure in question had been ordered by an authority of the executing State" (Article 8). Grounds for non recognition or non execution are limited (Article 10).

The draft directive intends to solve the fragmentary legal framework actually in force for police and judicial cooperation during the investigation. As it is stated in Recital Nr. 5,

> with the adoption of Framework Decisions 2003/577/JHA and 2008/978/JHA it has become clear that the existing framework for the gathering of evidence is too fragmented and too complicated. A new approach is therefore necessary.

The first point to note is that the primary scope of the proposal is not only a speedier and more effective judicial cooperation, but also to solve the current fragmented picture. The legislative European patchwork in this field is actually inefficient and needs to be updated and completed. A substantial number of new EU criminal justice or policing measures have already been adopted since the Lisbon Treaty came into force in December 2009. Most of those measures have not yet been implemented by the Member States. A fragmentary approach is a common character: some of them only apply to certain evidence[1] or imply a two-step procedure.[2]

---

[1] Framework decision 2008/978/JHA only applies to already existing evidence.

[2] See the Council Framework decision 2003/577/JHA that only applies to the freezing phase and needs a separate order for the transfer of evidence.

To this aim, after the adoption, the Directive would replace Framework Decision 2003/577/JHA, which covers orders for freezing property or evidence, and Framework Decision 2008/978/JHA, which is the European Evidence Warrant provision. The last one has been implemented only by a few Member States. The reasons are many: on one hand, national authorities already know the existence of the proposal for a general and more comprehensive instrument such as the EIO. On the other hand, as it happened 10 years ago with the European Arrest Warrant, many Member States show no enthusiastic approach towards innovative instruments that limit or abolish any political control on judicial cooperation in criminal matters.

Nevertheless, the great importance of the proposal is shown by the choice of the UK and Ireland to "opt-in" to the directive at stake, notwithstanding the growing "Eurosceptical approach" towards the former third pillar legal framework. In the meanwhile indeed the UK government announced the possibility for that country to opt-out to the whole third pillar *acquis*.[3]

Even if one of the areas where 'more work' is to be expected in the coming years relates to the enforcement side of criminal justice cooperation,[4] re-nationalisation seems to be the key-word of the new trends.[5] As a consequence, the political debate on the EIO has suffered of the conflicts between the European Parliament and the Council. The file on the EIO was frozen after the Council unilaterally changed the legal basis of a proposal on the reintroduction of internal border checks in the Schengen zone. Recently negotiations restarted and on the 15th November 2012 the Council presented a few amendments to the text agreed as a general approach at the end of 2011.[6]

2 One-Size Fits All Approach: Flexibility as a Value

A positive aspect of the draft directive is the wide range of measures that could be targeted with the EIO: judicial authorities may use the new tool in order to collect almost any kind of information.[7]

The draft directive will in practice significantly contribute to facilitate the gathering of evidence in cross-border criminal cases, since yet frustrated by bureaucracy and insufficient cooperation. It has abandoned the choice of the EEW that, adopting the "piecemeal approach," did not help to simplify the judicial cooperation between Member States, stressing further a system already fragmented. As the EEW is applicable exclusively to pre-existing elements of evidence, whereas

---

[3] Hinajeros et al. (2012), pp. 1ff.

[4] Allegrezza (2009b), p. 167.

[5] Carrera and Guild (2012), p. 12.

[6] Eucrim 2/2012, 50.

[7] Bachmaier Winter (2010), p. 586; De Amicis (2010), p. 1ff.

for all other evidentiary materials that might be also needed, practitioners will still have to use the letters rogatory of the mutual legal assistance system.[8]

The future European investigation order adopts the so-called "one size fits all" approach[9] as it was followed in the Stockholm Programme, in which the EU underlined that for cross-gathering of criminal evidence "A new approach is needed, based on the principle of mutual recognition but also taking into account the flexibility of the traditional system of mutual legal assistance." Flexibility means one tool for all the data and activities required. Even in the Communication to the European Parliament and the Council on "An area of freedom, security and justice serving the citizen"[10] the Commission supported a comprehensive approach instead of a piecemeal approach. Flexibility is also sponsored by the LIBE Committee. The Rapporteur suggests the adoption of "an effective and flexible instrument, thereby ensuring swifter action."[11]

Only a few restrictions are still provided by the last version of the proposal: Article 3(2) states that the EIO cannot be used to set up a Joint Investigation Team and the gathering of evidence within such a team.

Some scholars stressed how inappropriate the "one size fits all approach" might be in the absence of harmonized, coherent rules on admissibility, data protection and investigative procedures in an EU where the principle of equality of arms is not a feature of many legal systems.[12]

Despite a comprehensible scepticism for the "one size fits all approach," it seems preferable to combine mutual recognition with the flexibility of traditional MLA tools. As recent studies have highlighted, prosecutors and courts do not want to multiply the requests. That is why many member States have not yet implemented the EEW framework decision.

Other objections seem frankly exaggerated: according to Fair Trial International the EIO would "like the EAW overwhelm busy police forces with orders from other countries to investigate offences as minor as bike thefts."[13] It is up to national courts, as it happened for the EAW, to find out concrete solutions to those cases and to promote, with a bottom-up approach, a wider check on proportionality in the executing State.

---

[8] Klimek (2012), p. 277; Spencer (2010), p. 604; Allegrezza (2010), p. 573; Belfiore (2009), p. 2 ff.; Mavany (2012), p. 77 ff.; Mitsilegas (2009a), p. 116; De Amicis (2011), p. ff.; Stefanopoulou (2013), p. 54 ff.

[9] Heard and Mansell (2011), p. 353.

[10] COM(2009) 262.

[11] See the Draft Report on the adoption of a Directive of the European Parliament and of the Council regarding the European Investigation Order in criminal matters [09288/2010—C7-0185/ 2010—2010/0817(COD)]—Committee on Civil Liberties, Justice and Home Affairs Rapporteur: Nuno Melo.

[12] Heard and Mansell (2011), p. 353.

[13] Heard and Mansell (2011), p. 356.

3 Mutual Recognition, Free Movement of Evidence and Transnational Investigation

3.1 Mutual Recognition

As a consequence of the legislative choice to simplify formal procedures, suggesting the direct contact between judicial authorities of different Member States and reducing the grounds for refusal of investigative measures requested by another Member State, the European authorities have increased the effectiveness of the mutual recognition, transforming traditional legal assistance tools in a system adopting mutual recognition as a cornerstone.

Scepticism towards the mutual recognition in this field has been widely highlighted. In the frame of the first pillar, mutual recognition is used to support freedom, in the sense that it allows the individual to

> take with him advantageous standards of his home country into the host country and is freed from the double burden of having to comply fully with the standards of both home and host county.[14]

In the criminal law field mutual recognition threatens freedom because the individual is followed by judicial decisions (mostly arrest warrants, convictions or freezing orders) that are free to circulate in the EU area.[15]

Furthermore, in criminal matters, the primary aim of building a single "area" has not been achieved "by attempting to create common rules and standards underpinning free movement."[16] There has been no attempt to rethink the territoriality clause, to harmonise basic principles of criminal law or to create a common understanding between different national systems as far as evidence law is concerned. As Mitsilegas underlines:

> Rather, the emphasis has been placed at the national level: equating people with court decisions, the logic of this system dictates that it is national judicial decisions, and consequently national legal and constitutional systems, that must move freely with the minimum of formality and be respected by other national jurisdictions in the EU.[17]

Nevertheless, after Lisbon mutual recognition is enshrined in the Treaties as the real cornerstone of the criminal justice area and it is time to admit that principle has worked as an "effective method of the European integration in criminal matters."[18] Mutual recognition is not a dogma and it is not an enemy itself of fundamental rights in criminal justice: it is a neutral method to be applied. Results and concerns

---

[14] Möstl (2010), p. 409; Mazza (2009), p. 393 ff.; Maduro (2007), p. 814 ff.; Murphy (2011) p. 224 ff.; Peers (2004) p. 5 ff.; Vermeulen et al. (2010), p. 1 ff.; Ouwerkerk J (2011), p. 1 ff.

[15] *Ibid.*, p. 409.

[16] Mitsilegas (2006), p. 1309.

[17] *Ibid.*, p. 1309.

[18] Mitsilegas (2009b), p. 560.

depend on how it is applied. As the experience in courts of the EAW shows, conflicts arise due to the lack of harmonization of criminal law and procedures. It is time to propose concrete solutions—even compromises—and amendments in order to guarantee a better framework in which mutual recognition might work without prejudice for fundamental rights of the individual. Recent directives on procedural rights represent a first important step, but a lot of work still needs to be done.

National courts play a key role in such a process, introducing a kind of step-by-step harmonisation in criminal law and suggesting concrete amendments to the EU stakeholders. Pressures coming from the EAW case law suggested to the Commission to introduce explicitly a proportionality check to be carried out by the issuing authorities in order to ban warrants for petty crimes, even in a context not sufficiently harmonised.[19]

Given the scepticism and fear towards any new instrument accepting mutual recognition as a theoretical basis, first it must be clear what the real goals of the EIO are.

The proposal is not focusing on cross-border evidence sharing. The new EIO gives to national authorities the power to obtain investigative activities in another Member State in full respect of the rules in force in the issuing State. In other words, it introduces a new mechanism for the EU member States to seek the collection of evidence in criminal matters in a cross-border context.[20]

The proposal does not imply a kind of "free movement" of evidence within the EU, that is no more that "something of a provocation itself"[21] and it is never mentioned in the EU official documents.[22] Only the Green Paper on a European Public Prosecutor of 2001 introduced the concept of "mutual admissibility of evidence" as a principle under which

> any national Court trying a criminal case in which the Community's financial interests were at stake would have to admit any evidence lawfully obtained in accordance with the law of another Member State.

As that Green Paper was dealing exclusively with crimes affecting the EU financial interests, it is obvious that the Commission was supporting a kind of

---

[19] See the Final report of the Council on the fourth round of mutual evaluations—The practical application of the European Arrest Warrant and corresponding surrender procedures between, 28 May 2009, 8302/4/09. This report was adopted by the Council in June 2010. The amended handbook now sets out the factors to be assessed when issuing an EAW and possible alternatives to be considered before issuing an EAW. If the amended handbook is followed by Member States, it will provide a basis for some consistency in the manner in which a proportionality check is applied; see the report from the commission to the European Parliament and the Council on the implementation since 2007 of the Council Framework Decision of 13 June 2002 on the European arrest warrant and the surrender procedures between Member States [SEC(2011) 430 final]. See Vervaele (2005), p. 131 ff.; Williams (2005), p. 69 ff.

[20] Klimek (2012), p. 251.

[21] Gless (2005), p. 122.

[22] Klimek (2012), p. 251.

"forced admissibility of evidence" limited to those cases in which a common interest (EU founds) are at stake. It cannot be intended as a broad principle applicable to the whole FSJ area.

It is meaningful that only for EU financial crimes Article 86 of the TFEU provides for the introduction of a common European Public Prosecutor Office by means of regulations. These regulations

> shall determine the general rules applicable to the European Public Prosecutor's Office, the conditions governing the performance of its functions, the rules of procedure applicable to its activities, as well as those governing the admissibility of evidence, and the rules applicable to the judicial review of procedural measures taken by it in the performance [Article 86(3) TFEU].

Both the *Corpus Juris* project[23] and the Model Rules, recently published[24], proposed a unified common regulation for criminal investigations of the EPPO because in that field mutual recognition is estimated to be insufficient. But crimes affecting EU financial interests are a specific, peculiar and limited area within the AFSJ.

3.2 Free Movement of Evidence

Furthermore, the proposal on the EIO will not introduce any "free movement of evidence." At least one might identify a kind of "free movement of clues gathered during investigation." It exists already in the everyday life of file exchange between prosecutorial authorities. Italian scholars call this practice "spontaneous transmission" in order to underline the absence of any duty of the requested authority to comply with the request coming from abroad.[25] This spontaneous transmission is mostly secret because it occurs during the investigations, it implies no judicial authorisation and it does not conceive any role for the defence.[26]

Once these elements have been transmitted, there is no obstacle to use them for every decision concerning pre-trial decisions (arrest warrant, search warrant, wire-tapping authorization or decisions concerning the pre-trial detention). Barriers arise mainly during the trial stage.

The risk of establishing a real "free movement of evidence" was stronger in the European Evidence Warrant: the Framework decision explicitly stated that

> The EEW may be used to obtain any objects, documents and data for use in proceedings in criminal matters for which it may be issued. This may include for example objects, documents or data from a third party, from a search of premises including the private

---

[23] Delmas-Marty (1997), 1ff.; Delmas-Marty and Vervaele (2000), 1ff.

[24] Ligeti (2012).

[25] Allegrezza (2009a), p. 1347; Simonato (2011), p. 220; De Bondt et al. (2010), p. ff.; Vermeulen (2011), p. ff.

[26] Caprioli (2013), pp. 451ff.

premises of the suspect, historical data on the use of any services including financial transactions, historical records of statements, interviews and hearings, and other records, including the results of special investigative techniques. (Recital Nr. 7 of the FD EEW)

The last version of the proposal introduces a similar provision in Article 10(1a) (c). It states that limits established by Article 9 do not apply for

The obtaining of information or evidence which is already in the possession of the executing authority and, this information could have been obtained, in accordance with the law of the executing State in the framework of criminal proceedings or for the purposes of the EIO.

Nevertheless, in these cases ordinary grounds for refusal listed in Article 10 apply, leaving room to the judicial authority of the issuing State to assess the legality of the information or evidence gathered abroad. The difference with the previous framework decision on the EEW is huge: no automatism is conceived but in those cases the executing State is not allowed to recourse to a different type of investigative measures.

3.3 Admissibility of Evidence in Trial Is Still Out of the EU Mandate

In the proposal for the EIO there is no automatism between the request and the validity of such evidence in trial across Europe: mutual recognition in regard to the "transfer of evidence" cannot be intended as a "mutual admissibility concept."[27] Mutual recognition for evidence in cross-border cases "is about acknowledging differences between the judicial systems of the Member States and accepting them."[28]

In this light, mutual recognition has to be read narrowly: it only implies that

no objection could be taken to evidence obtained in another Member State on grounds of failure to comply with a formality required by the requesting state, provided the formalities of the executing state had been complied with.[29]

As we already stated previously, mutual recognition and free movement of evidence avoid national authorities from raising barriers to evidence gathered abroad. In other words, mutual recognition fights against the "foreignity argument." No exclusionary rule can be justified in force of the alien origin.[30] The same provision is adopted by the Model Rules for the EPPO, in which Article 19 imposes the primacy of the Model Rules providing that "National courts may not treat as illegally or improperly obtained evidence that has been gathered in accordance with

---

[27] Gless (2006b), p. 124; Gless (2006a), *passim.*

[28] De Hert et al. (2009), p. 62.

[29] Spencer (2006–2007), p. 474; *contra* Vervaele (2009), p. 160.

[30] Allegrezza (2010), p. 572; Mangiaracina (2010), p. 428 ff.; Menna (2011), p. 169 ff.

these Rules." This rule bans the exclusion based on different formalities but it does not imply any compulsory admission of that evidence.

Any wider reading, according to which "any piece of evidence that is gathered lawfully in one Member State becomes automatically admissible in criminal proceedings in another Member State, irrespective of any rule of evidence that would otherwise exclude it" has to be rejected because it would "potentially upset the internal balance of a number of national legal systems."[31] And no reference is made by the proposal in this direction.[32]

No concern for admissibility is provided by the proposal: in line with the Framework Decision on the EEW and, unlike the Green paper of 2009, in which it was a clear asset the harmonization of rules governing admissibility of evidence in criminal trial, the Directive on the EIO does not deal with this critical point. This lack can be read in two different ways. On one side, it shows how difficult it is for the EU to deal with the very heart of any criminal justice system and how it is opportune to respect different legal traditions as provided by Article 82 TFEU, especially as far as the criminal trial is concerned. I do believe that it is not of "any business of the EU to lay down rules requiring certain forms of evidence to be admissible in criminal trials in Member States,"[33] especially outside the specific fields of Article 86 of the TFUE.

On the other hand, this lack leaves room for a possible "double step application" of the proportionality principle in the issuing State, first during the investigation and later on during the trial. That implies several differences in appreciating the evidence gathered abroad in the national legal systems. In Italy legal barriers usually ban the use in trial of pre-trial statements made during the investigations by witnesses; in France,

> une preuve recueillie à l'étranger à sa demande, la probabilité est forte qu'elle se retrouve à exploiter cette preuve quelles que soient les conditions dans lesquelles elle a été prélevée.[34]

It is in the hands of national courts to ascertain whether a piece of evidence has been legally obtained and what should be its probative value.

4   Building a EU Proportionality Requirement

4.1   A Key Topic for Mutual Distrust?

Proportionality principle has always been a key topic in the AFSJ since the discussion on the FD EAW.[35] As the Committee on Civil Liberties, Justice and

---

[31] *Ibid.*, p. 474; Ambos (2010), 557.

[32] Spencer (2010), p. 602; Ruggeri (2013), pp. 565ff.

[33] Spencer (2010), p. 604.

[34] Lelieur (2010), p. 597.

[35] Bachmaier Winter (2013), pp. 88ff.

Home Affairs stressed in its report, an appropriate assessment of the proportionality in criminal matters is a constitutional requirement in several Member States and also a requirement pursuant to Article 8 ECHR. As a result, a clear and obvious lack of proportionality may represent an infringement of human rights and/or an infringement of fundamental national constitutional principles.[36] Furthermore, proportionality is provided by Article 49(3) of the Charter and it is binding on the Member States only "when they are implementing Union law." No doubt that every EIO issued by a Member State will represent an implementation of Union law, as it has been already stated for the EAW[37] or the *ne bis in idem*.[38]

In this light, pivotal importance has to be given to the real meaning of the proportionality requirement. What exactly is the object of the proportionality test? Which are the relevant aspects to be considered in assessing the proportionality of an investigative measure requested by another member State? Who is entitled to carry out such scrutiny?

One might start observing what happened in the field of the EAW since its adoption and its implementation in national systems.

4.2 Taking the EAW Experience as a Model

The experience of the EAW might be useful. In the discussion on the European Arrest Warrant, the majority of the Member States seem to reject the introduction of a ground for refusal based explicitly on proportionality. Such a scrutiny

> would run counter to the idea of mutual recognition, because it would significantly delay the execution of warrants by obliging executing authorities to seek additional information in order to examine the issue of proportionality, resulting also in an assessment of the merits [of the European Evidence Warrant] in the executing State.[39]

As a result, in the text of the Framework Decision there was no explicit reference to the proportionality requirement but, according to some national decisions and many scholars, constitutional rules of the Member States and now the European Charter of fundamental rights could represent a strong legal basis for supporting a proportionality check in the executing State, especially with reference to the adoption of an EAW for petty offences.[40]

---

[36] Draft Report on the adoption of a Directive of the European Parliament and of the Council regarding the European Investigation Order in criminal matters [09288/2010—C7-0185/2010—2010/0817(COD)]—Committee on Civil Liberties, Justice and Home Affairs Rapporteur: Nuno Melo; 12a.

[37] Vogel and Spencer (2010), p. 476.

[38] Amalfitano (2012), p. 3889.

[39] De Hert et al. (2009), p. 65.

[40] Vogel and Spencer (2010), p. 473.

In this light, the execution of an EAW should be refused when the warrant is not necessary and proportionate in the light of the rules of the executing State, having regard to the maximum penalty applicable to the offence in question or, better, to the penalty that is actually likely to be imposed.[41] As it was already mentioned, doubts and concerns coming from national courts have suggested the Commission to amend the "European Handbook on how to issue a EAW" in favour of proportionality. The amended handbook now sets out the factors to be assessed when issuing an EAW and the possible alternatives to be considered before issuing an EAW. In particular,

> the EAW should not be chosen where the coercive measure that seems proportionate, adequate and applicable to the case in hand is not preventive detention. The warrant should not be issued, for instance, where, although preventive detention is admissible, another non-custodial coercive measure may be chosen or one which would imply the immediate release of the person after the first judicial hearing. Furthermore, EAW practitioners may wish to consider and seek advice on the use of alternatives to an EAW.
>
> Taking account of the overall efficiency of criminal proceedings these alternatives could include[42]:
>
> * Using less coercive instruments of mutual legal assistance where possible
> * Using videoconferencing for suspects
> * By means of a summons
> * Using the Schengen Information System to establish the place of residence of a suspect
> * Use of the Framework Decision on the mutual recognition of financial penalties
>
> Although national courts indicated the need to confer such a scrutiny to the executing authorities, the Commission clearly states that "Such assessment should be made by the issuing authority."[43]

4.3 Proportionality and Evidence

Taking into account the commission amendments and suggestions coming from national decisions in the EAW, it appears that the idea of appropriateness in issuing a EAW encompasses different aspects, mainly:

* The seriousness of the offence (considering both the possible penalty and the penalty concretely applied);
* The consequences of the execution of the EAW on the fundamental rights of the individual;
* The possibility of achieving the objective sought by other less troublesome means for both the person and the executing authority;
* A more general cost/benefit analysis of the execution of the EAW, i.e. the cost and effort of a formal extradition proceeding including extradition arrest.

---

[41] Ibid., p. 480.

[42] Council conclusions, 28 May 2010, 8436/2/10.

[43] Ibid.

Not surprisingly, it appears clearly that those who advocate for a proportionality requirement in the EAW procedure had in mind not only the protection of fundamental rights but also the efficiency of the machine. A frequent and unnecessary use of the EAW might lead to a loss of efficiency in the executing State.

Adapting these conclusions to the evidentiary field, things are slightly different. Theoretically, proportionality could be read in the following way:

- The requested measure shall be proportioned to the crime under investigation, but due to the early stage in which usually investigative measures are required that reference has to be made only to the penalty provided by national criminal law of the issuing State, not to the penalty concretely applied;
- The consequences of the execution of the EIO for the individual has to be assessed including all the persons involved, not only the defendant;
- The requested measure shall be proportioned to the evidence to be collected;
- The requested measure shall be proportioned to the purpose of the proceedings as a whole.

A European proportionality test, conferred to every judicial authority who is called to take a decision in the concrete case, would help to overcome scepticism. As stated in a report of a few years ago,

> Experience with the EAW has demonstrated that there is already a legitimate and widely held perception that the "principle of mutual recognition does not benefit the defence and that there is no real balancing of interests between prosecution and defence.[44]

Not without good reasons the critical theorists suspected that without a chance to challenge the proportionality of the measure by the executing authority, there is the risk to exacerbate this feeling of imbalance and encroachment on individual rights.[45]

4.4 Proportionality and Evidence in the Draft Proposal on the EIO

The main concern still under discussion, in a nutshell, is: who should assess the proportionality and according to which law?

One might observe that the proposal is not silent on these issues. There are several provisions which make reference to the proportionality test in the issuing State: first, Article 5a(1)(a) provides that authorities shall adopt an EIO only when it appears "necessary and proportionate for the purpose of the proceedings" to the issuing authorities. Furthermore, Article 5a(1)(b) states that "the investigative measure(s) mentioned in the EIO could have been ordered under the same

---

[44] Vernimmen-Van Tiggelen and Surano (2008), p. 20.

[45] Sayers (2011), p. 20; Peers (2010).

conditions in a similar national case." It is clear that "a similar national case" has to be read in relation to the issuing State legal order; the draft proposal indeed provides for different rules governing the existence or the legitimacy of the measure in the executing State as a refusal ground (see Art. 10).

All these provisions are referred to the issuing State and its law; they do not solve the main problem of "distrust" basically due to the discrepancy between different national laws. The experience with the EAW has taught that the pivotal issue is the control on proportionality carried out by the judicial authority of the executing State, often in the light of its law. In the draft proposal there are at least three interesting provisions. Article 8(2) reproduces the mechanism already introduced by Article 4 of the MLA Convention of 2000 and confirmed in Article 12 of the FD EEW, according to which the issuing State may indicate in the request specific formalities and procedures for the gathering of evidence abroad. In principle, the executing State "shall comply" with these formalities unless they are "contrary to the fundamental principles of law of the executing State." Fundamental principles of law represent an obstacle to the application of foreign rules. Judicial authorities of the executing State will analyse the request and appreciate the risk of breaching "national" fundamental rights in applying different rules governing the collection of evidence.

The second and the third relevant provisions are provided by Article 9: they both extend the powers of the executing State in controlling the proportionality of the requested measure.

4.5 The "Less Intrusive Measure" Rule

Article 9(1)(a) explicitly states the duty for the executing State to have recourse to "an investigative measure other than that provided for in the EIO when the measure does not exist under the law of the executing State."

Preference is given, in this case, to the legal order of the executing State and in particular to its constitutional *acquis*, banning a specific measure. In particular, analysing surveillance measures and in general measures involving advanced technological devices. For those measures EU Member States are already harmonised in the sense that to a certain extent there is no rule governing this investigations. What will happen with such an EIO? Several examples: visual surveillance in domestic premises in Italy or in Germany, on-line searches in Germany or blood samples in Italy before Law No. 85 of 2009. It is not clear what will happen in national systems providing for an open rule such as Article 191 of the Italian Code of criminal procedure dealing with the so-called "*preuve atipique*," authorising the admissibility of procedures not expressly ruled. One might expect interesting developments in the interaction between national systems due to the application of this provision.

Furthermore, Article 9(1b) obliges the adoption of a less intrusive measure when the one indicated in the EIO "would not be available in a similar domestic case".

This rule implies a direct reference to requirements and thresholds required by the executing State law as far as evidentiary law is concerned. It means that beyond the formal proclaim concerning mutual recognition, the draft directive recognises a critical role to national rules of the executing State because they may ban the recognition of the EIO for the reason that national requirements are not fulfilled or national thresholds are not satisfied. In other terms, it clearly states the existence of a proportionality test in the executing State in the light of the seriousness of the crime to be investigated or the level of suspicion according to the law of that country.

Moreover, the "less intrusive measure" rule receives even a wider application in the draft proposal. According to Article 9(1bis), the executing State may have recourse to a less intrusive investigative measure if it will produce the same result of the measure required by the issuing State. There is no doubt that this choice would imply a proportionality check made by the executing authorities[46] according to its national rules. The solution is to be welcomed and it seems to be adequate to confirm the *extrema ratio* principle in the adoption of intrusive or coercive measures. Furthermore, this mechanism may create a kind of spontaneous harmonization between different legal systems with a sort of *métissage* of national evidentiary rules.

However, it seems that the "less intrusive measure" rule confers to proportionality test the power to impede the admissibility of evidence: there is no certitude that the different measure adopted by the executing State could be admissible as evidence in trial in the issuing State.[47]

In case of failure of the less intrusive measure test, Article 9(3) states that the executing authority must notify to the issuing authority that it has not been possible to provide the assistance requested.

Finally, one might say that the latest draft of the EIO proposal improves somewhat on the original, by including a proportionality test by the issuing State and several checks on proportionality conferred to the executing State according to its law. It is a satisfactory compromise, even in the light of fundamental rights of the individual.

The proportionality requirement will be increased with the adoption of the amendment to recital 10a suggested by the Council in its conclusions of 15 November 2012, which intends to strengthen the validation procedure in all those cases in which investigative measures for administrative procedures require a validation by the judicial authority.[48]

Several aspects of the draft directive have to be improved. In particular, specific attention has to be given to the great lacunas concerning the weak position of the defence. Two main issues should be considered: the chance for the defence to collect evidence abroad, actually absent in the proposal, and a different assessment of legal remedies.

---

[46] Ruggeri (2013), pp. 557ff.

[47] Marchetti (2011), p. 164.

[48] See Conclusions of the presidency of the EU Council, 15 November 2012, doc. 16120.

References

Allegrezza S (2009a) L'acquisizione della prova all'estero e profili transnazioxxnali. In: Cerqua LD (ed) Diritto penale delle società. Profili sostanziali e processuali, vol II. Cedam, Padova, pp 1323–1363

Allegrezza S (2009b) L'armonizzazione della prova penale alla luce del Trattato di Lisbona. In: Illuminati G (ed) Prova penale e Unione europea. Bononia University Press, Bologna, pp 161–174

Allegrezza S (2010) Critical remarks on the Green Paper on obtaining evidence in criminal matters from one member state to another and securing its admissibility. Zeitschrift für die internationale Strafrechtsdogmatik 9:569–579

Amalfitano C (2012) Cassazione penale 11:3889–3900

Ambos K (2010) Transnationale Beweiserlangung – 10 Thesen zum Grünbuch der EU-Kommission. Erlangung verwertbarer Beweise in Strafsachen aus einem anderen Mitgliedstaat. Zeitschrift für die internationale Strafrechtsdogmatik 9:557–566

Bachmaier Winter L (2010) European Investigation Order for obtaining evidence in the criminal proceedings. Study of the proposal for a European directive. Zeitschrift für die internationale Strafrechtsdogmatik 9:580–589

Bachmaier Winter L (2013) The role of the proportionality principle in cross-border investigations involving fundamental rights. In: Ruggeri S (ed) Transnational inquiries and the protection of fundamental rights in criminal proceedings, A study in memory of Vittorio Grevi and Giovanni Tranchina. Springer, Heidelberg, pp 88–110

Belfiore R (2009) Movement of evidence in the EU: the present scenario and possible future developments. Eur J Crime Crim Law Crim Justice 17:1–22

Caprioli F (2013) Report on Italy. In: Ruggeri S (ed) Transnational inquiries and the protection of fundamental rights in criminal proceedings, A study in memory of Vittorio Grevi and Giovanni Tranchina. Springer, Heidelberg, pp 439–455

Carrera S, Guild E (2012) Does the Stockholm Programme matter? The struggles over ownership of AFSJ Multiannual Programming. CEPS Paper on Liberty and Security in Europe 51

De Amicis G (2010) L'ordine europeo di indagine penale. www.europeanrights.eu

De Amicis G (2011) Limiti e prospettive del mandato europeo di ricerca della prova. In: Grasso G, Picotti L, Sicurella R (eds) L'evoluzione del diritto penale nei settori di interesse europeo alla luce del Trattato di Lisbona. Giuffrè, Milano, pp 475–514

De Bondt W, Vermeulen G, Van Damme Y (2010) EU cross-border gathering and use of evidence in criminal matters: towards mutual recognition of investigative measures and free movement of evidence? Maklu, Antwerpen

De Hert P, Weis K, Cloosen N (2009) The framework decision of 18 December 2008 on the European evidence warrant for the purpose of obtaining objects, documents and data for use in proceedings in criminal matters – a critical assessment. New J Eur Crim Law 55–78

Delmas-Marty M (1997) Corpus Juris, introducing penal provisions for the purpose of the financial interests of the European Union. Editions Economica, Paris

Delmas-Marty M, Vervaele JAE (2000) The implementation of the Corpus Juris in the member states. Intersentia, Antwerp

Gless S (2005) Mutual recognition, judicial inquiries, due process and fundamental rights. In: Vervaele JAE (ed) European evidence warrant. Transnational judicial inquiries in the EU. Intersentia, Antwerpen, pp 121–129

Gless S (2006a) Beweisrechtsgrundsätze einer grenzüberschreitenden Strafverfolgung. Nomos, Baden-Baden

Gless S (2006b) Free movement of evidence in Europe. In: Armenta Deu T, Gascón Inchausti F, Cedeño Hernán M (eds) El Derecho Procesal Penal en la Unión Europea. Tendencias actuales y perspectivas de futuro. Ed. Colex, Madrid, pp 121–130

Heard C, Mansell D (2011) The European Investigation Order: changing the face of evidence-gathering in EU cross-border cases. New J Eur Crim Law 4:353–367

Hinajeros A, Peers S, Spencer JR (2012) Opting out of EU criminal law: what is actually involved? http://www.cels.law.cam.ac.uk/

Klimek L (2012) Free movement of evidence in criminal matters in the EU. Lawyer Q 4:250–290

Lelieur J (2010) L'application de la reconnaissance mutuelle à l'obtention transnationale de preuves pénales dans l'Union européenne: une chance pour un droit probatoire français en crise? Zeitschrift für die internationale Strafrechtsdogmatik 9:590–601

Ligeti K (2012) Model rules for the EPPO. http://www.eppo-project.eu/

Maduro MP (2007) So close and yet so far: the paradoxes of mutual recognition. J Eur Public Policy 14(5):814–825

Mangiaracina A (2010) La circolazione della prova dichiarativa in ambito nazionale ed europeo. La giustizia penale 115:428–448

Marchetti MR (2011) Dalla convenzione di assistenza giudiziaria in materia penale dell'Unione europea al mandato europeo di ricerca delle prove e all'ordine europeo di indagine penale. In: Rafaraci T (ed) La cooperazione di polizia e giudiziaria in materia penale nell'Unione europea dopo il Trattato di Lisbona. Giuffrè, Milano, pp 135–167

Mavany M (2012) Die Europäische Beweisanordnung und das Prinzip der gegenseitigen Anerkennung. C.F. Müller Wissenschaft, Hamburg

Mazza O (2009) Il principio del mutuo riconoscimento nella giustizia penale, la mancata armonizzazione e il mito taumaturgico della giurisprudenza europea. Rivista di diritto processuale 64:393–402

Menna M (2011) Mandato di ricerca della prova e sistemi probatori. In: Rafaraci T (ed) La cooperazione di polizia e giudiziaria in materia penale nell'Unione europea dopo il Trattato di Lisbona. Giuffrè, Milano, pp 169–183

Mitsilegas V (2006) The constitutional implications of mutual recognition in criminal matters in the EU. Common Mark Law Rev 43:1277–1311

Mitsilegas V (2009a) EU criminal law. Hart, Oxford

Mitsilegas V (2009b) The third wave of third pillar law: which direction for EU criminal justice? Eur Law Rev 34:523–560

Möstl M (2010) Preconditions and limits of mutual recognition. Common Mark Law Rev 47 (2):405–436

Murphy C (2011) The European evidence warrant: mutual recognition and mutual (dis)trust? In: Eckes C, Konstadinides T (eds) Crime within the area of freedom, security and justice: a European public order. Cambridge University Press, Cambridge, pp 224–248

Ouwerkerk J (2011) Mutual trust in the area of criminal law. In: Meijers committee (ed) The principle of mutual trust in European asylum, migration, and criminal law. Reconciling trust and fundamental rights. http://www.commissie-meijers.nl/assets/commissiemeijers/Co_opmaakOmslag06.pdf

Peers S (2004) Mutual recognition and criminal law: has the council got it wrong? Common Mark Law Rev 41(5):5–36

Peers S (2010) The proposed European Investigation Order. Assault on human rights and national sovereignty. www.statewatch.org

Ruggeri S (2013) Transnational inquiries and the protection of fundamental rights in comparative law. Models of gathering overseas evidence in criminal matters. In: Ruggeri S (ed) Transnational inquiries and the protection of fundamental rights in criminal proceedings, A study in memory of Vittorio Grevi and Giovanni Tranchina. Springer, Heidelberg, pp 533–573

Sayers D (2011) The European Investigation Order travelling without a 'roadmap'. CEPS, Brussels, pp 1–27

Simonato M (2011) The spontaneous exchange of information between European judicial authorities from the Italian perspective. New J Eur Crim Law 2:222–229

Spencer JR (2006–2007) The problems of trans-border evidence and European initiatives to resolve them, vol 9, Cambridge yearbook of European legal studies. Hart, Oxford, pp 465–480

Spencer JR (2010) The Green Paper on obtaining evidence from one Member State to another and securing its admissibility: the reaction of one British Lawyer. Zeitschrift für die internationale Strafrechtsdogmatik 602–606

Stefanopoulou G (2013) Der Rahmenbeschluss über die Europäische Beweisanordnung. Juristische Rundschau 2:54–58

Vermeulen G (2011) Free gathering and movement of evidence in criminal matters in the EU. Thinking beyond borders, striving for balance, in search of coherence. Maklu, Antwerp

Vermeulen G, De Bondt W, Van Damme Y (2010) EU cross-border gathering and use of evidence in criminal matters. Maklu, Antwerpen

Vernimmen-Van Tiggelen G, Surano L (2008) Analysis of the future of mutual recognition in criminal matters in the European Union. Institute for European Studies. Université Libre de Bruxelles, Brussels

Vervaele JAE (2005) European criminal law and general principles of union law. In: Vervaele JAE (ed) European evidence warrant. Transnational judicial inquiries in the EU. Intersentia, Antwerpen, pp 131–155

Vervaele JAE (2009) Il progetto di decisione quadro sul mandato di ricerca della prova. In: Illuminati G (ed) Prova penale e Unione europea. Bononia University Press, Bologna, pp 153–160

Vogel JR, Spencer JR (2010) Proportionality and the European arrest warrant. Crim Law Rev 6:474–482

Williams C (2005) Overview of the commission proposal for a framework decision on the European evidence warrant. In: Vervaele JAE (ed) European evidence warrant. Transnational judicial inquiries in the EU. Intersentia, Antwerpen, pp 69–76

Part III
Critical Analysis of the EIO Proposal:
Specific Issues

The Proposal for a Directive on the European Investigation Order and the Grounds for Refusal: A Critical Assessment

Lorena Bachmaier Winter

Abstract Since the first draft of a Proposal of a Directive for a European Investigation Order was presented in 2010, there have been numerous meetings, reports, consultations and opinions, with the aim of reaching an agreement on a single instrument for the gathering of evidence in European cross-border criminal investigations. The purpose of this study is to point out those issues that should be recast in order to improve the regulation of the grounds of refusal of recognition and execution of a European Investigation Order: for example, the possible refusal to cooperate in carrying out investigative measures based on the lack of double incrimination, the principle of proportionality, the existence of an immunity or the principle of ne bis in idem. The need to clarify the regulation and avoid unnecessary complexity is essential for a swift and efficient judicial cooperation as well as for fostering the principle of mutual trust.

Keywords Criminal investigation • European area of justice • European criminal procedure • European Investigation Order • European public prosecutor • Judicial cooperation • Mutual legal assistance • Principle of mutual recognition • Transnational criminal prosecution

This paper has been written within the context of the research project "Lucha contra el terrorismo en Europa y restricción de derechos fundamentales en el proceso penal" (DER 2009-11243), financed by the Spanish Ministry of Science and Innovation and sent for publication in December 2012. A previous version of this article was published in Spanish under the title "*La propuesta de directiva europea sobre la orden de investigación penal*: *valoración crítica de los motivos de denegación*," Rev. La Ley 28 diciembre 2012.

L. Bachmaier Winter (✉)
Facultad de Derecho, Departamento de Derecho Procesal, University Complutense of Madrid, Avda. Complutense s/n, Madrid, Spain
e-mail: l.bachmaier@der.ucm.es

S. Ruggeri (ed.), *Transnational Evidence and Multicultural Inquiries in Europe*,   71
DOI 10.1007/978-3-319-02570-4_6, © Springer International Publishing Switzerland 2014

Contents

1 Introduction 72
2 The European Investigation Order and the Principle of Mutual Recognition 73
3 The Grounds for Non-recognition and Non-execution
   of the European Investigation Order 75
   3.1 Grounds for Non-execution Under Article 9(3) PD EIO 75
   3.2 Grounds for Non-recognition or Non-execution Under Article 10(1) PD EIO 77
   3.3 The Meaning of Article 10(1a) PD EIO 85
   3.4 The Lack of Double Incrimination as a Possible Ground of Refusal
       [Art. 10(1b)(a) PD EIO] 86
   3.5 The Measure Is Not Permitted in the Executing State with Regard to the Offence
       Indicated in the EIO [Art. 10(1b)(b) PD EIO] 87
4 Conclusions 87
References 88

1 Introduction

Since the first draft of the Proposal of a Directive for a European Investigation Order (hereinafter PD EIO) was presented in 2010,[1] there have been numerous meetings, reports, consultations and opinions,[2] with the aim to reach an agreement on a single instrument for the gathering of evidence in cross-border criminal investigations within the European Union.

It is not our aim to recall here all the discussions the PD EIO has given rise to[3] nor to comment on all the changes the initial text of the initiative for an EIO has experienced during the past two and a half years. It will be enough to state that after numerous working sessions and consultations on the first draft, a new text of a PD EIO was issued in June 2011,[4] and a new draft was presented on the 21 December

---

[1] The initiative for a PD EIO was first published on the 29 April 2010 (COPEN 15, CODEC 363, EUROJUST 47, EJN 12).

[2] Among others see the reports of CEPS (Centre for European Policy Studies of June 2011 written by D. Sayers (http://www.ceps.eu/book/european-investigation-order-travelling-without-'roadmap'); the JUSTICE Briefing on the European Investigation Order of July 2011 (http://www.statewatch.org/news/2010/aug/eu-justice-briefing-eio.pdf); STATEWATCH, whose reports of May and November 2010 are signed by S. Peers (http://www.statewatch.org/analyses/no-96-european-investigation-order.pdf and http://www.statewatch.org/analyses/no-112-eu-eio-update.pdf) the report of the German Bar Association (*Deutscher Anwaltsverein*) of May 2011 (http://anwaltverein.de/downloads/Stellungnahmen-11/SN-29.pdf); of the *Bundesrechtsanwaltskammer* of January 2011 (http://www.brak.de/zur-rechtspolitik/stellungnahmen-pdf/stellungnahmen-europa/2011/januar/stellungnahme-der-brak-2011-10.pdf).

[3] See, for example Bachmaier Winter (2013), pp. 85–110 and the literature cited there. See also, Ruggeri (2013), pp. 283ff.; Vermeulen et al. (2010), pp. 7ff.; Jiménez-Villarejo Fernández (2011), pp. 175–203; Zimmermann et al. (2011), pp. 56–80; and Aguilera Morales (2012), pp. 1–25.

[4] Made in Brussels 17 June 2011, COPEN 158, EUROJUST 99, EJN 80.

2011.[5] Since that date the working group for the cooperation in criminal matters has introduced minor amendments that mainly affect the Preamble, the forms and the Annex in relation to Article 29(1) PD EIO.[6] These last amendments are not significant and thus this paper will refer to the version done the 21st December 2011.

The purpose of this work is to point out those issues that should be recast with regard to the grounds to refuse the recognition and execution of an EIO. However, before focusing on specific provisions of the PD EIO, it might be appropriate to briefly remind the context in which the PD EIO as a whole is being discussed.

2   The European Investigation Order and the Principle of Mutual Recognition

Since the Council of Tampere, the principle of mutual recognition has become the key concept for the judicial cooperation in Europe, as the way to overcome the difficulties of cooperation between different national legal systems. This has been confirmed in the Treaty of Lisbon and in the Stockholm Programme and, despite the numerous detractors and critics, it may be the only way—or better way—to advance towards a single space of freedom, justice and security in Europe. However, admitting and accepting the mutual recognition as the principle for building a common judicial area, does not impede the questioning of the need, justification and actual wording of the PD EIO.[7]

Accepting the principle of mutual recognition as the guiding principle does not mean that legislative proposals have to be assumed uncritically: the principle of mutual recognition cannot act as the overarching element that legitimizes every legal proposal coming from Europe. And on the contrary, the critics against specific provisions of a European legal proposal cannot be interpreted as an attack against the principle of mutual recognition. It goes without saying that the implementation of an EIO would, in general terms, facilitate the judicial cooperation in criminal matters, making it easier, quicker and thus contribute to a more efficient fight

---

[5] Text agreed as general approach, made in Brussels the 21.12.2011, 18918/11, COPEN 369, EUROJUST 217, EJN 185.

[6] The document made in Brussels in 29 February 2012, COPEN 44, EUROJUST 16, EJN 16, includes amendments of the Preamble and in the Annex, according to the observations made by the delegations after the meeting of the Council the 13 and 14 December 2011, where the new text of the EIO published the 21 December 2011 was approved. Those amendments appear also in the subsequent text of the working group made on 29 May 2012, COPEN 104, EUROJUST 42, EJN 34. The changes affect the recitals 10d, 11, 12, 14, 14b, 14d, 14j, 15, and 15a of the Preamble as well as the Annex related to Article 29 PD EIO. These amendments in the wording and systematic of the Preamble do not represent significant changes.

[7] It would be impossible to cite here the huge number of publications and scientific literature regarding the mutual recognition principle in the judicial cooperation in Europe.

against cross-border criminality. At the same time it goes without saying that the EIO shall be essential for the functioning of a future European Public Prosecutor with competences to carry out criminal investigations over the whole European territory.[8]

In other words, I only want to draw attention to the idea that acceptance of the principle of mutual recognition does not automatically justify any legal instrument for the judicial cooperation, and does not mean that such instruments are absolutely indispensable.

According to the Preamble of the PD EIO the deficiencies of the mutual legal assistance instruments and the need to overcome the fragmentary legal framework of the judicial cooperation in criminal matters justify the implementation of a European Investigation Order. I do not want to insist on the issue whether the EIO is necessary or not, or if there are clear arguments to state that the inefficiency of the current mutual legal assistance instruments can be overcome by implementing the EIO—I still think there are no such arguments—or if this instrument is premature in a context where the premise of mutual confidence between Member States is not enough developed. These issues have already been pointed out by different professional associations and human rights organizations, as well as by scholars in prior studies,[9] and there is no point in explaining them here again. It might be enough to stress that our opinion has been confirmed by the report prepared by the *European Union Agency for Fundamental Rights* (FRA), where it is expressly stated that there is not enough empirical evidence on how the mutual legal assistance mechanisms are functioning in practice.[10] Even if there are already some good studies on the practice of judicial cooperation in the European Union,[11] they do not point out that the solution for the present deficiencies in transnational criminal investigations require the approval of an EIO.

---

[8] Since the text of this article was written, the Commission has published a Proposal for a Regulation, Brussels, 17.7.2013, COM(2013) 534 final.

[9] I already questioned the justification of the need for a PD EIO, as it is explained in the Preamble in our previous study, in Bachmaier Winter (2013), pp. 96ff. In the same sense, see also Ferries (2010), p. 432; the report of the *Deutsches Anwaltsverein* of May 2011 or point 4 of the Report of the *Bundestag* of 6 October 2010, mentioned above, under footnote 2.

[10] The FRA, in the conclusions of its Opinion on the draft Directive regarding the European Investigation Order of 14 February 2013 states: "Thus, the draft legislation might not sufficiently draw on factual, comparative analysis of the shortcomings in the daily functioning of the existing systems across the European Union. Against this background, it seems even more important to build in evidence-based mechanisms both in the observation of how this new instrument is operating in practice as well as in future revisions." See http://fra.europa.eu/en/opinion/2011/fra-opinion-draft-directive-regarding-european-investigation-order-eio.

[11] A good example of a research Project focused on collecting empirical data on the judicial cooperation in criminal matters in the EU is the "Euroneeds Project", directed by the Max Planck Institute for Foreign and International Criminal Law, and coordinated by Prof. M. Wade. The main conclusions of this research Project can be read in Wade (2011), accessible under http://www.mpicc.de/shared/data/pdf/euroneeds_report_jan_2011.pdf.

Notwithstanding these considerations, there is no doubt that for the future European Public Prosecutor, the EIO is essential and therefore, from now on it might be more sensible to strive on the improvement of the PD EIO, rather than continue with the discussion on the shortcomings of the principle of mutual recognition.

3 The Grounds for Non-recognition and Non-execution of the European Investigation Order

It is essential to have a close look on the rules regarding the conditions for issuing, refusing and executing an EIO as well as the rules on remedies to be able to assess if this instrument will facilitate the judicial cooperation in the gathering of evidence.[12] Moreover focusing on these rules will allow to verify if the EIO is consistent with the principles applicable in the state of execution, while providing at the same time enough protection of the fundamental rights of the defendant and the other parties affected during the criminal investigation. An EIO with limited grounds for refusal represents a further step towards the principle of mutual recognition, and conversely, if the grounds for refusal are drafted extensively, the principle of mutual recognition tends to vanish. The text of the PD EIO as of December 2011 has broadened the grounds to refuse the execution of a EIO to an extent that the current preamble recognizes that the PD EIO combines the principle of mutual recognition with the system of mutual legal assistance. This combination provides flexibility to this instrument, while diminishing the automatic execution of the request, something that entails advantages as well as drawbacks.

The grounds for refusal are mainly regulated in Article 10, but other grounds of refusal of the execution are also found in Article 9, and in Article 21(1a)(a) PD EIO. The regulation is so complex, that prior to making any critical assessment, I will try to clarify the meaning of the rules on the grounds of refusal. This paper will focus only on Articles 9 and 10 PD EIO.

3.1 Grounds for Non-execution Under Article 9(3) PD EIO

Article 9 PD EIO is titled "Recourse to a different type of investigative measure" and allows the executing authority to substitute the requested measure in following cases: (1) if the requested measure does not exist under the law of the executing State [Art. 9(1)(a)]. For example, if the issuing authority should request the Spanish authority to bug a domicile and record the conversations held in that private space,

---

[12] Generally on the grounds of refusal see Bachmaier Winter (2013), pp. 100ff.; Jiménez-Villarejo Fernández (2011), pp. 194ff.; Aguilera Morales (2012), pp. 11ff.

the Spanish authority, instead of refusing directly the EIO because the measure is not provided under Spanish law it should try to substitute it by another legal measure that could achieve equal or similar results. In this example, the executing authority could substitute the bugging by the telephone tapping: (1) if such a measure is possible and could in the relevant case lead to analogous results; (2) when the indicated measure, although existing in the execution State, would not be available in a similar domestic case; and (3) when the same results to be obtained by the measure requested in the EIO could be achieved by less intrusive means.[13] By allowing the substitution of the requested measure by an equivalent one, the PD EIO intends to limit the scope of the refusals and thus promote a pragmatic approach to the cooperation in the criminal investigation, following the simple scheme that "if someone request apples, and we do not have apples or cannot provide them, we can give pears." It is not exactly the same, but should be equivalent and thus serve for the same aim. But this reasoning is not always applicable in cases of criminal investigation and the substitution of the requested measure by another one, without asking the requested authority first, may not only frustrate the obtaining of evidence, but also endanger the whole investigation. For example, if the measure requested is to obtain some computer file by way of an electronic surveillance of the computer or the server, and the requested authority substitutes this secret investigative measure, by ordering the search and entry of the home to seize the computer, the evidence obtained might be the same, but the consequences for the success of the whole investigation can be clearly different.

While I agree that the non-existence of the same investigative measure should not lead straight away to a refusal of the request, it should be noted that the requesting authority should be consulted before the requested measure is substituted by another measure that would achieve equivalent results. Such consultation should be done quickly and without any special formalities, and except in cases of urgency, it should be mandatory.

Article 9(1) PD EIO—apart from regulating the cases where the requested measure could or should be substituted—also includes a ground for refusal: in those cases where the requested measure is not available and its substitution is not possible or would not have the same results "the executing authority must notify the issuing authority that it has not been possible to provide the assistance requested," and thus refuse its execution.

This case of non-execution of the indicated measure would not pose any further problems save for the expression: "the investigative measure indicated in the EIO would not be available in a similar domestic case" [Art. 9(1)(b) PD EIO]. How should this provision be interpreted? It can mean that the measure is expressly excluded for the offence indicated in the EIO, but it can also be interpreted in the sense that, even if there is no specific provision excluding the measure, according to

---

[13] In case there should be a less intrusive measure for achieving the same results, the substitution should be mandatory, as it is pointed out in the report of JUSTICE under point 9. The same critical remark is expressed more recently also by Aguilera Morales (2012), p. 17.

the assessment of the principle of proportionality in the executing State the measure should be refused. As it has been stated earlier, it seems that Article 9(1)(b) allows the refusal of an EIO that does not fulfil the proportionality requirement according to the test applicable in the executing State.[14] In this sense, and due to the ambiguous wording of Article 9(1)(b) PD EIO, there is an overlapping with the grounds of refusal foreseen under Article 10 PD EIO.

3.2 Grounds for Non-recognition or Non-execution Under Article 10(1) PD EIO

The list of grounds of refusal included in this article is extremely complex. It is not only that one must read several times this provision to grasp the meaning, or that it requires making a scheme to differentiate between grounds of refusal in cases of coercive measures and grounds of refusal for the rest of measures or evidence requested. The problem is that the lack of clarity not only adds difficulty in understanding, but also causes legal uncertainty.

I will try to explain here the content of Article 10 PD EIO and point out those parts that should be reviewed and redrafted.

The first recital of Article 10 PDEIO lists the grounds that can be invoked to refuse the recognition or the execution of the requested EIO.[15]

3.2.1 Immunity or Privilege According to the Law of the Executing State [Art. 10(1)(a) PD EIO]

The mere existence of an immunity should not automatically hinder the execution of the request of evidence under the EIO.[16] Paragraph 3 of the same Article 10 states that if the executing State has the power to waive the immunity "the executing authority shall request it to exercise that power forthwith." But, if the power to waive the immunity lies not within the executing State, it is the issuing authority the one competent to request the waiver. It should be further analysed what are the practical implications of the existence of immunities in the international judicial cooperation and more precisely within the ambit of the European Union. Even if international law immunities and state immunities are not the most adduced reasons

---

[14] See Bachmaier Winter (2013), pp. 100–101.

[15] Most of these grounds for refusal are found already in Article 13 of the Council Framework Decision 2008/979/JHA on the EEW for the purpose of obtaining objects, documents and data for use in criminal proceedings, of 18 December 2008.

[16] On immunity of jurisdiction and execution of states, its scope, content and alternatives in Spain see the comprehensive analysis made by Gascón Inchausti (2008), pp. 97–106 and pp. 415ff.; Kloth (2010), pp. 88ff.

for refusing the judicial cooperation in cross-border gathering of evidence—in fact they are very exceptional—as such cases may be closely linked to the State sovereignty, they have to be properly regulated. For example, in a case where a judicial authority of a European Member State issues an EIO to gather bank information of a representative of a Member State or the Head of State. According to Article 10(1)(a) PD EIO, before refusing the execution of the EIO on the basis of an immunity, it should seek to request the waiver of the immunity, which may be legally difficult, but also raise diplomatic concerns.

The application of this provision can become even more complex if, following the opinion of German scholars the notion of "privilege" refers also to the right of the witness not to declare against relatives and other persons, or the privilege of the counsel-defendant relationship.[17] Here again the question that arises is which law applies to the right not to testify? Who is competent to "request the waiver" of such a privilege? I only want to point out here the difficulties arising from the interpretation of this paragraph to state that more clarification will perhaps help in answering some of these questions, and thus promote confidence through certainty.

Before refusing the recognition and execution of the EIO under this ground, the requested authority shall consult the issuing authority [Art. 10(2) PD EIO].

3.2.2 Protection of Freedom of the Press and Freedom of Expression [Art. 10(1)(a) PD EIO]

After mentioning the existence of an immunity or privilege, the same recital Art. 10.1 a) makes reference to another ground of refusal, that does not seem to be linked to the previous one. The EIO might be refused when *"there are rules on determination and limitation of criminal liability relating to freedom of the press and freedom of expression in other media."* This ground of refusal, which was to be found already in the first draft of the PD EIO, clearly seeks to protect the freedom of expression and the freedom of press, but its meaning is still confusing. It is not clear if it refers to the protection of the sources of information or if it is a specific double incrimination requirement that has to be checked when the EIO deals with an offence related to the freedom of press or freedom of expression. Unless I am mistaken, the Preamble of the PD EIO does not shed light on how this ground for non-recognition and non-execution shall be interpreted. Finally, as with regard to the previous ground for refusal, before deciding on the non-execution of the EIO, the issuing authority shall be consulted [Art. 10(2) PD EIO].

---

[17] For example, Gless (2011), p. 605; Mavany (2012), pp. 130–131, although with regard to the European evidence warrant regulated in the Council Framework Decision 2008/979/JHA; Gstöhl (2008), pp. 188ff.

3.2.3   National Security Interests, Protection of the Source of the Information and Classified Information [Art. 10(1)(b) PD EIO]

The grounds of refusal set out under Article 10(1)(b) PD EIO are that its execution "would harm essential national security interests, jeopardise the source of the information or involve the use of classified information relating to specifics intelligence activities." This possible grounds of refusal are very similar to the one stated in the Framework Decision 2008/978/JHA on the EEW [Art. 13(1)(g)], and are also to be found in Article 2(b) of the ECMACM of 20 April 1959, applicable also to the EUCMACM of 29 May 2000, although in the conventional rules the clause of *ordre public* and the exception of sovereignty are further mentioned.

At this point the PD EIO does not introduce any relevant innovation, but just adopts the causes already provided traditionally in the conventional rules. Nevertheless the inclusion of these same non-execution grounds in an instrument based upon the principle of mutual recognition should make us pause to consider whether this implies any change to the treatment of these grounds of refusal. The principle of mutual recognition should make that the executing authority deals with the request made through the EIO, if as it were a domestic judicial assistance request. From this point of view, the mere allegation that the evidence requested affects national security interests or classified information, should not alone justify the non-execution of the requested EIO and thus impede the access to evidence that could be essential for the criminal proceedings. The right of the State to keep certain information secrete and refrain from disclosing classified information should also be subject to control in order to avoid that the excuse of national security interests or the need to protect intelligence activities, could contribute to the impunity of serious crimes.[18]

No doubt that this is a sore point and that the States are especially sensitive when it comes to protecting their national security interests and their intelligence activities. However, according to the principle of mutual recognition, the executing authority should proceed in the same way as if it were handling with a domestic case and such information were necessary for his/her own investigation. In other words, if the laws of the requested State would allow the judge to control the secret character of the information requested or, if he/she would be authorised to require and obtain the declassification of classified documents, this should also be the proceeding to be followed in the execution of an EIO issued by the judicial authority of another Member State.

Of course it is obvious that the strict implementation of the principle of mutual recognition with regard to State secrecy and classified information is not a priority for the Member States or the European legislator. Nevertheless the interpretation

---

[18] On the problems related to the use of state secrets and the access to classified information in judicial proceedings, albeit with regard to the US criminal justice system, see the interesting study of Vervaele (2012), pp. 229–261.

here proposed would still be the most consistent with the principle of mutual recognition as established under Article 1(2) and Article 8(1) PD EIO where it says:

> The executing authority shall recognise an EIO (...) and ensure its execution in the same way and under the same modalities as if the investigative measure in question had been ordered by an authority of the executing State, unless that authority decides to invoke one of the grounds for non-recognition or non-execution or one of the grounds for postponement provided for in this Directive.

As with regard to the previous grounds of refusal, here applies also Article 10(2) PD EIO: before deciding on the non-recognition or non-execution of the EIO, the requested authority shall consult the issuing authority.

3.2.4 The Requested Measure Would Not Be Authorised for a Similar Case in a Non-criminal Procedure in the Executing State [Art. 10(1)(d) PD EIO]

Pursuant to Article 4(b) and (c) PD EIO, a European Investigation Order can also be issued with the aim of an administrative procedure that can end up in a criminal case.

For example, the German legal system provides for some offences to be considered as administrative offences or *Ordnungswidrigkeiten*. The sanctioning of such offences does not fall within the criminal jurisdiction, but the decision taken by the administrative body can lead to a criminal procedure before the criminal courts. Similarly in other legal systems, certain behaviours are considered *administrative offences* and only by way of review the criminal jurisdiction can make a final decision.[19] This explains why the PD EIO is also foreseen for the obtaining of evidence with regard to proceedings that initially are not criminal proceedings. In this context, Article 10(1)(d) PD EIO provides for a specific ground of refusal: that under the law of the executing State the requested measure would not be authorised in a similar domestic case. In this case, before refusing the execution of the EIO the requested authority does not need to consult with the issuing authority [Art. 10(2) PD EIO].

Article 10(1)(d) coincides partially with the content of Article 9(1)(b) PD EIO (possible substitution of the requested measure). Does this mean that in case of Article 10(1)(d) the EIO can be refused without prior looking for a substitute measure that would make the same result? Or on the contrary, a requested measure can only be refused under Article 10(1)(d) PD EIO if there is no possible substitute measure, as stated under Article 9(3) PD EIO?

---

[19] At present a proposal for decriminalizing petty offences now regulated in the Criminal Code is discussed in Spain. It is early to make any assessment of this intended future reform, but for those future administrative offences Article 4(b) and (c) PD EIO could be applicable, obviously only if the proportionality test is met.

If this last interpretation is accepted it would mean that Article 10(1)(d) would only repeat what is provided in Article 9(1)(b) PD EIO, as this last provision is applicable to criminal proceedings as well as to administrative proceedings that can lead to a criminal procedure. But if Article 10(1)(d) just wanted to say that EIOs issued within administrative procedures can be refused straight away without resorting to a substitute measure, this cannot be clearly inferred from the wording of this provision.

In sum, these issues might not be of great importance neither for the approval of the PD EIO nor for its future practical implementation, but the overlapping of provisions, apart from showing a poor legal technic, does not contribute to the clarity a legal cooperation instrument should provide.

3.2.5   Ne Bis in Idem [Art. 10(1)(e) PD EIO]

Article 10(1)(e) PD EIO states that the execution of an EIO may be refused if it contravenes the principle of *ne bis in idem*. This ground of refusal may not be alleged when the requesting authority provides

> an assurance that the evidence transferred as a result of an execution of an EIO shall not be used to prosecute a person whose case has been finally disposed of in another Member State for the same facts (...).

The infringement of the principle of *ne bis in idem*, although it was already set out in Article 13(1)(a) FD EEW, it was not included in the first draft of the PD EIO, something which was widely criticised.[20]

Much has been discussed and written about the principle of *ne bis in idem* and its transnational horizontal effect in Europe. There is broad consensus on the idea that the development of a common justice area requires adequate mechanisms to avoid that a person is tried twice for the same criminal facts.[21] The principle of *ne bis in idem* has been recognized at the supranational level in the European Union, since it is expressed in Article 50 EUFRCh. This rule applies not only within the domestic legal orders of the Member States, but imposes also the duty to respect the *ne bis in idem* between the Member States. Differently from Article 4 of VII Additional Protocol ECHR,[22] Art. 50 of the EU Charter is also applicable in a European

---

[20] See generally Bachmaier Winter (2010), pp. 584–585. Later, in the same sense the report of the *Bundestag* of 6 October 2010, cit., point 12; and the report of STATEWATCH, cit., p. 6.

[21] Among others, see following monographic studies: Mansdörfer (2004), pp. 135ff.; Kniebühler (2005), in particular on the Convention implementing the Schengen Agreement, see pp. 169ff.; Jagla (2007), pp. 45ff.; Costa Ramos (2009), pp. 115ff. See also, Vervaele (2005), pp. 100–118. In Spain see, for example, De la Oliva (2008), pp. 167–185. In the same volume see Cedeño Hernán and Aguilera Morales (2008), pp. 187–241.

[22] Article 4 of Protocol 7 of the ECHR: Right not to be tried or punished twice: "No one shall be liable to be tried or punished again in criminal proceedings under the jurisdiction of the same State for an offence for which he has already been finally acquitted or convicted in accordance with the law and penal procedure of that State." For the case law of the ECtHR on Article 4 of Protocol VII, see Van Boeckel (2010), pp. 173–203.

transnational setting.[23] The concept and the scope of the *ne bis in idem* principle differs greatly in the domestic legal rules of the Member States.[24] At the same time, the protection at the national level is not equivalent to that provided at the supranational level by the European rules. Very briefly and without entering into the numerous debates regarding the principle of *ne bis in idem* in the European Union, Article 54 CISA—incorporated to the *acquis communitaire*—states:

> A person whose trial has been finally disposed of in one Contracting Party may not be prosecuted in another Contracting Party for the same acts provided that, if a penalty has been imposed, it has been enforced, is actually in the process of being enforced or can no longer be enforced under the laws of the sentencing Contracting Party.

And Article 50 of the European Charter reads:

> *Right not to be tried or punished twice in criminal proceedings for the same criminal offence.* – No one shall be liable to be tried or punished again in criminal proceedings for an offence for which he or she has already been finally acquitted or convicted within the Union in accordance with the law.

The principle of *ne bis in idem* is not only recognized as a European constitutional principle, but it also extends its material and territorial scope of application: it applies horizontally between the Member States and also vertically, between resolutions of the European bodies and tribunals of the Member States.[25] As it is defined in Article 50 of the EU Charter, *ne bis in idem* prevents not only a double punishment, but also grants protection against a second indictment: it is applicable to the case where the defendant has been acquitted through a final decision of the courts of another Member State, for the same facts. However, this provision does not respond to the question of what happens if the first proceedings ended up with a deal or an agreement without a formal judgement.

The PD EIO solves any possible doubts regarding the issue of which rule shall be applied within the ambit of an EIO, because Article 10(1)(e) PD EIO refers expressly to the conditions set out under Article 54 CISA.[26] Hence, as a general rule the requested authority may refuse the execution of the indicated measure if it has notice that the defendant has been previously tried for the same facts, has been convicted by a final decision and the conviction has been enforced, is being enforced or is impossible to enforce. The PD EIO opts for a limited scope of application of the *ne bis in idem* principle. The Preamble does not explain this

---

[23] See Mansdörfer (2004), pp. 238ff.

[24] For an interesting comparative law study of the principle of *ne bis in idem* in Europe and beyond, see Mansdörfer (2004), pp. 57ff. (Germany, Austria, Switzerland, France, Benelux, *common law* legal systems, Scandinavian legal systems, and Spain and Italy); Kniebühler (2005), pp. 17ff. (Germany and Belgium); Jagla (2007), pp. 156ff. (Germany, United Kingdom and France).

[25] Eser (2011), pp. 571–576.

[26] Article 54 CISA has not been superseded by Article 50 EU FRCh and, as both provisions tend to overlap, it can be concluded that Article 54 CISA has to be interpreted according to Article 50 of the European Charter. On the other hand, Article 54 CISA could be considered as a concretion of the broader constitutional provision. On this issue see Buchard and Brodowski (2010), pp. 310ff.

choice. If the PD EIO provides for a facultative ground of refusal based on the protection of the ne bis in idem, it does not appear to be logical not to follow the principle of *ne bis in idem* set out in the Charter, and thus also allow the requested authority to refuse the execution if the same defendant has been already acquitted in that State for the same facts.

The aforesaid notwithstanding, the execution of the EIO may not be refused on the basis of the *ne bis in idem* principle when the requesting authority gives assurance that the transferred evidence will not be used if it infringes the *ne bis in idem* principle as defined in the CISA.

From a formal point of view, it appears that the PD EIO gives adequate protection against the double punishment for the same facts and the refusal to cooperate in the evidence gathering in such cases seems to be logic. However, from the point of view of its practical implementation, some questions arise.

First, in practice to control if the investigative measure requested in the EIO is aimed to investigate a case that has been previously tried in another Member State is anything but easy. Unless the case has got international relevance in the media, usually the requested authority will not know if the execution of the EIO is contrary to the principle of *ne bis in idem*. If the ECRIS system providing information on the criminal records at the European level is already implemented in the requested Member State,[27] the judicial authority might check trough this system if the defendant named in the EIO has already been convicted for the same facts. But even then, the identification of the *idem*, will not be easy, because the description of the facts contained in the form for the EIO are quite brief. Checking if there is a prior conviction against the same person—if the system is functioning and it is comprehensive, updated and user-friendly—will require additional effort and time for the executing authority. This raises doubts whether the principle of *ne bis in idem* will in practice be adequately protected *ex officio*.

There is no doubt that the protection will be best afforded, if it is the defendant who alleges and proves the existence of a prior conviction relating the same facts. However this will only be feasible if two conditions are met: (1) if the defendant has appeared before the criminal proceedings in the issuing state; (2) if the defendant is informed on the issuing of the EIO.

I do not pretend to say that the wording of Article 10(1)(e) PD EIO is not adequate, I only want to point out that if there are not other measures and instruments in place to guarantee the respect of the *ne bis in idem* principle, in practice it will be difficult and burdensome for the executing authority to check if the EIO complies with this principle.

On the other hand, if the issuing authority assures that the evidence transferred will not be used in violation of the *ne bis in idem* principle, the executing authority will not be able to refuse the execution of the EIO on this ground. It appears that the mere allegation of the issuing authority in this regard should suffice, as no other

---

[27] See Council Framework Decision 2009/315/JHA of 26 February 2009 on the organisation and content of the exchange of information extracted from the criminal record between Member States.

kind of "assurance" can come into consideration. From the point of view of facilitating and speeding up the judicial cooperation, as well as from the point of view of implementing the principle of mutual recognition, this provision is to be seen as adequate and positive. But at the end, the whole system of protection of the principle of *ne bis in idem*, will rely on the express declaration of the issuing authority that it complies with the fundamental rights recognized at the European level and precisely, with Article 50 of the European Charter. By way of this general statement—that could even be included as a general statement in the forms—the requested authority avoids the work of checking the respect of the *ne bis in idem* principle and relies on the "assurance" given by the issuing authority. This mechanism clearly reflects the principle of mutual trust that shall govern the judicial cooperation in criminal matters in Europe. Nevertheless, it does not help to strengthen the protection of fundamental rights and does not contribute to the confidence of the defendants in the judicial cooperation instruments.

3.2.6   The Territoriality Clause [Art. 10(1)(f) PD EIO]

Article 10(1)(f) PD EIO regulates as a possible ground for refusal the so-called territoriality clause or exception of jurisdiction, as it was already provided for in Article 13(1)(f) of the Framework decision 2008/978/JHA. Four conditions have to be met to apply this ground of non-execution of the EIO: (1) the EIO relates to a criminal offence which is alleged to have been committed exclusively outside the territory of the issuing State; (2) the offence has been committed wholly or partially in the territory of the executing State; (3) the EIO requests a coercive measure; and (4) the conduct the EIO refers to is not an offence in the executing State. Pursuant to Article 10(2) PD EIO, before refusing the EIO under this ground, the issuing authority shall be consulted. The primary justification of this ground for refusal of an EIO is the avoidance of abusive extraterritorial exercise of jurisdiction, which does not make much sense in the context of free movement of evidence.[28] However, the answer to the problems deriving from the extraterritorial extension of the criminal jurisdiction and the solution of the conflicts of jurisdiction caused thereof is not to be found in the refusal to cooperate in the evidence gathering requested through an EIO. Although it is admissible that each Member State may refuse the cooperation in order to protect its own criminal jurisdiction—mainly linked to the territoriality principle—from the viewpoint of the efficient prosecution of transnational crimes this ground for refusal is not the best solution.

---

[28] Jiménez-Villarejo Fernández (2011), p. 189.

3.3 The Meaning of Article 10(1a) PD EIO

Article 10(1a) PD EIO states that Article 9(1) PD EIO does not apply to the measures—mostly non-coercive measures, but not only[29]—listed in this provision. It should be recalled that Article 9(1) PD EIO sets out the substitution of the requested investigative measure when it does not exist under the law of the executing State or would not be available in a similar domestic case. Having this in mind, what is the objective of the provision of Article 10(1a) PD EIO? Is it aimed to prevent that the measures listed here are substituted by a different one or rather to prohibit the refusal of the EIO on the ground that the measure does not exist or is not available in the executing State? Or rather, does this rule pursue both objectives?

As a rule, the measures listed under this recital—hearing of a witness, a victim, a suspect, the identification of the holder of a phone number, etc.—are ordinary measures foreseen in the criminal procedure of any of the Member States. This fact already would make it impossible to deny the execution of the EIO on the basis that such a measure does not exist or is not admissible. Moreover, departing from the premise that all measures listed under Article 10(1a) PD EIO exist in all domestic legal systems of the Member States and are generally accessible in the criminal investigation, it would be useless to provide for the express prohibition to apply Article 9(1) PD EIO.

Nevertheless, let us suppose that there is a non-coercive measure [Art. 10(1a) (b) PD EIO] that does not exist in the executing State. In this event, according to the wording of Article 10(1a), measures listed under this recital shall be neither substituted nor refused on the basis that they do not exist or are not admissible, even if they should not exist in the executing State. With regard to the measures of search and seizure this means that, despite being coercive, if they relate to an offence listed in the Annex and punished with more than 3 years imprisonment, the grounds for refusal under Article 9 PD EIO would not be applicable. Thus, even if the search and seizure were not admissible for the offence described in the EIO, the executing authority would not be able to invoke Article 9(3) PD EIO. The ground of refusal included under Article 10(1b)(b)—the measure is restricted under the law of the executing State to a list or category of offences or to offences punishable by a certain threshold—is not applicable either, because Article 10(1b) is not applicable to the measures of Article 10(1a) PD EIO, where the search and seizure is included.

---

[29] Article 10(1a) PD EIO lists: (a) the hearing of a witness, victim, suspect or third party; (b) any non-coercive investigative measure; (c) the obtaining of information or evidence which is already in the possession of the executing authority and this information or evidence could have been obtained through the execution of an EIO; (d) the obtaining of information contained in databases held by police or judicial authorities and directly accessible by the executing authority in the framework of criminal proceedings; (e) the identification of persons holding a subscription of a specified phone number or IP address; (f) search and seizure in relation to one of the 32 offences listed in the annex if they are punishable in the issuing State by a custodial sentence or detention order for a maximum period of at least 3 years.

In sum, the EIO requesting any non-coercive measure or a search and seizure to investigate an offence listed in the Annex and punished with more than 3 years imprisonment in the issuing State, cannot be refused. The conclusion is clear, but the way to come to this conclusion due to the complex draft of this legal instrument, is quite cumbersome.

3.4   The Lack of Double Incrimination as a Possible Ground of Refusal [Art. 10(1b)(a) PD EIO]

The lack of double incrimination has been introduced as a possible ground for refusal under Article 10(1b) PD EIO albeit with certain limitations.[30] First, this ground of refusal is not applicable to those cases where the requested measure is listed under Article 10(1a) PD EIO; and second, it cannot be invoked with regard to the EIO issued in relation of an offence listed in the Annex and such an offence is punishable with more than 3 years custodial penalty in the issuing State.

It seems appropriate that the lack of double incrimination might not be used to refuse the cooperation when it relates to an offence included in the Annex and it is considered a serious offence in the issuing State (penalty of more than 3 years), although with regard to the offences listed in the Annex there hardly will appear any problems of lack of double incrimination. In practice the Annex will facilitate the cooperation: if the issuing authority refers in the requesting form that the offence is one of the 32 offences listed in the Annex, the requested authority will not need to check any double incrimination requirement and will not have to check if there would be a possible ground for refusal.

With regard to the requirement that the offence is punished with at least 3 years custodial penalty, it must be noted that this threshold might not be strictly necessary. In practice this case will not be frequent, as most of the 32 offences listed in the Annex are serious offences and are generally punished with more than 3 years. Moreover, in order to facilitate the cooperation, it should be enough that the offence is punishable in both States. Thus, if it is listed in the Annex, this should, as a rule be enough and the fact that the offence is punished with less than 3 years imprisonment

---

[30] Art. 10.1b PD EIO reads: "Without prejudice to paragraph (1), where the investigative measure indicated by the issuing authority in the EIO concerns a measure other than those referred to in paragraph (1a), the recognition or execution of the measure may also be refused:

(a) if the conduct for which the EIO has been issued does not constitute an offence under the law of the executing State, unless it concerns an offence listed within the categories of offences set out in the Annex X, as indicated by the issuing authority in the EIO, if it is punishable in the issuing State by a custodial sentence or detention order for a maximum period of at least three years; or

(b) if the use of the measure is restricted under the law of the executing State to a list or category of offences or to offences punishable by a certain threshold, which does not include the offence covered by the EIO."

in the executing State should not as a rule be a problem for executing an EIO as the principle of proportionality already appears protected under Article 9(1)(b) and 10(1b)(b) PD EIO: if the measure were not available for a similar domestic case or is restricted to offences of a minimum penalty.

The PD EIO mentions expressly the offences connected to taxes or duties, stating that a EIO related to them shall not be refused on the basis that the executing State does not impose the same kind of tax or duty [Art. 10(1c) PD EIO]. This provision is a further clarification on the limits of the ground of refusal based on the absence of double incrimination.

3.5 The Measure Is Not Permitted in the Executing State with Regard to the Offence Indicated in the EIO [Art. 10(1b)(b) PD EIO]

This paragraph of Article 10 PD EIO allows the refusal of the execution when, in accordance with the law of the executing State, the measure is restricted "to a list or category of offences or to offences punishable by a certain threshold, which does not include the offence covered by the EIO." This provision overlaps with the ground for refusal provided for in Article 9(1)(b) in connection with Article 9(3) PD EIO. Unless I am mistaken, this ground for refusal is covered by Article 9(1)(b). If this is the case, the reiteration only adds confusion.

4 Conclusions

The text of a PD EIO is currently under discussion and until now there is not a common agreement either on the need or on the scope of a future European Investigation Order. This lack of agreement might be due to the lack of mutual trust between the Member States, especially visible when it comes to criminal justice; or the cause might be found in the unwillingness to yield powers traditionally linked to the sovereign power of the State; or because there is always initial resistance towards something unknown and new; or perhaps because the advantages and guarantees provided by the PD EIO have not been adequately explained[31]; or, finally, the opposition of some Member States and organizations to this proposal may be found in a combination of all the reasons that have been just mentioned. Whatever the reasons might be the fact is that some Member States do not support

---

[31] This may explain the publication of the document "Frequently asked questions" with regard to the PD EIO, with the aim of making the citizens and other stakeholders aware of the content, and scope of the future European Investigation Order The document "Frequently asked questions" was made in Brussels on 4 April 2012, COPEN 71, EUROJUST 25, EJN 20.

the PD EIO—for example Germany or the United Kingdom—and claim this judicial cooperation instrument might be premature.

The complexity and confusing wording of some of the provisions of this initiative do not help to overcome such resistance. Moreover, if legal uncertainty and complexity are to be avoided in any legislative instrument, in the case of an instrument which is aimed at fostering and simplifying cooperation on the basis of mutual trust, the complexity can have clear damaging effects, as it impedes the instrument to achieve its objective. Legal uncertainty strikes deeply the confidence, and this counteracts the element that underpins the implementation of an instrument based on the mutual recognition.

On the one hand, if the regulation is complex and is difficult to understand— which has been seen with regard to the rules on the grounds for non-execution— instead of contributing to the swiftness of the cooperation, it adds difficulties in the recognition and execution of the requested EIO. On the other hand, the fact that the grounds for refusal are optional, which is very positive to promote the mutual recognition principle and the cooperation, at the same time it also produces some degree of legal uncertainty: it will not be easy to know in advance if the requested authority will make use of the possibility to deny the cooperation or not. This may also cause that the same EIO directed to the same State, sometimes will be executed and sometimes refused, depending on the assessment made by the executing authority of the grounds of refusal: the absence of uniform interpretation criteria may be another undesired factor of uncertainty.

In previous studies I already pointed out the convenience to amend certain provisions of the draft PD EIO, as for example the possibility to refuse certain EIOs in absence of double incrimination. I also stressed the need to further clarify the role the principle of proportionality should play in the judicial cooperation in criminal matters.[32] One can be satisfied to see that the critics expressed have been taken into account in the following texts of the PD EIO. Notwithstanding these improvements, I still consider that the wording and systematic of the PD EIO can be further improved, especially with regard to the possible grounds of non-recognition and non-execution of the European Investigation Order.

References

Aguilera Morales M (2012) El exhorto europeo de investigación: a la búsqueda de la eficacia y la protección de los derechos fundamentales en las investigaciones penales transfronterizas. BIMJ 2145:1–25

Bachmaier Winter L (2010) European investigation order for obtaining evidence in the criminal proceedings. Study of the proposal of a European directive. Zeitschrift für die internationale Strafrechtsdogmatik 9:580–589

---

[32] Bachmaier Winter (2010), p. 584 and Bachmaier Winter (2013), pp. 98ff.

Bachmaier Winter L (2013) The role of the proportionality principle in cross-border investigations involving fundamental rights. In: Ruggeri S (ed) Transnational inquiries and the protection of fundamental rights in criminal proceedings, A study in memory of Vittorio Grevi and Giovanni Tranchina. Springer, Heidelberg, pp 85–110

Buchard B, Brodowski D (2010) The post-Lisbon principle on transnational ne bis in idem: On the relationship between article 50 charter of fundamental rights and article 54 convention implementing the Schengen agreement. Case note on District Court Aachen, Germany, Decision of 8 December 2010. New J Eur Crim Law 1(3):310ff.

Cedeño Hernán M, Aguilera Morales M (2008) El principio *non bis in idem* a la luz de la jurisprudencia del Tribunal de Justicia. In: De la Oliva A (ed) La Justicia y la Carta de derechos Fundamentales de la Unión Europea. Colex, Madrid, pp 187–241

Costa Ramos V (2009) *Ne bis in idem* e Uniao Europeia. Coimbra Editora, Coimbra

De la Oliva A (2008) La regla *non bis in idem* en el derecho procesal penal de la Unión Europea; algunas cuestiones y respuestas. In: De la Oliva A (ed) La Justicia y la Carta de derechos Fundamentales de la Unión Europea. Colex, Madrid, pp 167–185

Eser A (2011) Justizielle Zusammenarbeit auf der Grundlage der gegenseitigen Anerkennung. In: Sieber U, Brüner FH, Satzger H, von Heintschell-Heinegg B (eds) Europäisches Strafrecht. Nomos, Baden-Baden, pp 557–580

Ferries A (2010) The European Investigation Order: stepping forward with care. New J Eur Crim Law 1(04):425–432

Gascón Inchausti F (2008) Inmunidades procesales y tutela judicial frente a Estados extranjeros. Thomson-Aranzadi, Cizur Menor

Gless S (2011) Europäische Beweisanordnung. In: Sieber U, Brüner FH, Satzger H, von Heintschell-Heinegg B (eds) Europäisches Strafrecht. Nomos, Baden-Baden, pp 596ff.

Gstöhl C (2008) Geheimnisschutz im Verfahren der internationalen Rechtshilfe in Strafsachen. Stämpfli, Bern

Jagla SF (2007) Auf dem Weg zu einem zwischenstaatlichen ne bis in idem im Rahmen der Europäischen Union. Lang, Frankfurt

Jiménez-Villarejo Fernández F (2011) Orden europea de investigación: ¿Adiós a las comisiones rogatorias? In: Arangüena C (ed) Cooperación judicial civil y penal en el nuevo escenario de Lisboa. Comares, Granada, pp 175–203

Kloth M (2010) Immunities and the right of access to court under article 6 of the European convention on human rights. Martinus Nijhoff Publishers, Leiden

Kniebühler R (2005) Transnationales 'ne bis in idem'. Zum Verbot der Mehrfachverfolgung in horizontaler und vertikaler Dimension. Duncker & Humblot, Freiburg i. Br

Mansdörfer M (2004) Das Prinzip des ne bis in idem im europäischen Strafrecht. Duncker & Humblot, Berlin

Mavany M (2012) Die Europäische Beweisanordnung und das Prinzip der gegenseitigen Anerkennung. Verlag F.C. Müller, Heidelberg

Ruggeri S (2013) Horizontal cooperation, obtaining evidence overseas and the respect for fundamental rights in the EU. From the European Commission's proposal to the proposal for a directive on a European Investigation Order: towards a single tool of evidence gathering in the EU? In: Ruggeri S (ed) Transnational inquiries and the protection of fundamental rights in criminal proceedings, A study in memory of Vittorio Grevi and Giovanni Tranchina. Springer, Heidelberg, pp 279–310

Van Boeckel B (2010) The ne bis in idem principle in EU Law. Kluwer Law, The Hague

Vermeulen G, De Bondt W, Van Damme Y (2010) EU cross-border gathering and use of evidence in criminal matters. Towards mutual recognition of investigative measures and free movement of evidence? Maklu, Antwerpen

Vervaele JAE (2005) The transnational *ne bis in idem* principle in the EU. Mutual recognition and equivalent protection of human rights. Utrecht Law Rev 1(2):100–118

Vervaele JAE (2012) Secreto de estado y "privilegios probatorios" en los procesos de terrorismo en los estados Unidos. ¿Control judicial de los arcana imperii? In: Bachmaier Winter L (ed) Terrorismo, proceso penal y derechos fundamentales. Marcial Pons, Madrid, pp 229–261

Wade M (2011) EuroNEEDs: evaluating the need for and the needs of a European Criminal Justice System. http://www.mpicc.de/shared/data/pdf/euroneeds_report_jan_2011.pdf

Zimmermann F, Glaser S, Motz A (2011) Mutual recognition and its implications for the gathering of evidence in criminal proceedings: a critical analysis of the initiative for a European Investigation Order. Eur Crim Law Rev 1:56–80

Critical Remarks on the Proposal for a European Investigation Order and Some Considerations on the Issue of Mutual Admissibility of Evidence

Rosanna Belfiore

Abstract This paper focuses on pros and cons of the draft Directive on the European Investigation Order with the purpose of identifying what would have a positive impact on current legal assistance and what would affect it negatively. This paper also puts forward some considerations on mutual admissibility of evidence in the area of freedom, security and justice. Although admissibility is not specifically addressed by the draft Directive, it is a topical issue anyway, since Art. 82(2)(a) of the Treaty on the functioning of the EU provides that Member States may establish minimum rules on mutual admissibility of evidence, to the extent necessary to facilitate mutual recognition of judicial decisions and police and judicial cooperation in criminal matters having a cross-border dimension.

Keywords European Investigation Order • Movement of evidence in the EU • Mutual admissibility of evidence • Mutual recognition

Contents

1 Introduction to the Proposed Directive on the EIO 92
2 Pros of the Proposed EIO 93
    2.1 A Single Regime 93
    2.2 The Investigative Measures 94
    2.3 Deadlines 96
    2.4 Proactive Cooperation 97
3 Cons of the Proposed EIO 97
    3.1 Proportionality 97
    3.2 Prognosis on Admissibility of Evidence 98
    3.3 Blurring Distinction Between Coercive and Non-coercive Measures 99
    3.4 Defence Rights 101
4 Some Considerations on the Issue of Mutual Admissibility of Evidence in the AFSJ ... 103
References 104

R. Belfiore (✉)
Department "Seminario giuridico", University of Catania, Via Gallo n. 24, Catania, Italy
e-mail: rbelfiore@lex.unict.it

S. Ruggeri (ed.), *Transnational Evidence and Multicultural Inquiries in Europe*,
DOI 10.1007/978-3-319-02570-4_7, © Springer International Publishing Switzerland 2014

1   Introduction to the Proposed Directive on the EIO

The initiative for a Directive on the EIO in criminal matters, put forward by Belgium, Bulgaria, Estonia, Spain, Austria, Slovenia and Sweden, has been presented to the Council in April 2010. The Council reached general approach on the draft in December 2011, although some national delegations have maintained parliamentary scrutiny reservations on it.

The proposed text is the result of a long-lasting debate on the thorny issue concerning movement of evidence in the EU.

The first move towards this objective proved to be unsuccessful. FD 2008/978/ JHA on the EEW, formally adopted in 2009, has not become a living instrument— and will never do—since Member States decided to stop the necessary implementation procedure,[1] awaiting for a more comprehensive measure to be adopted at supranational level. Indeed, right after the adoption of the EEW, its limited scope of application and the consequent fragmentation of the framework for the gathering of evidence, suggested the necessity to adopt a more comprehensive measure, in order to allow that any type of evidence and any request of assistance for the gathering of evidence may fall under the umbrella of the well-known principle of mutual recognition, now expressly codified under Article 82(1) TFEU.

Following the Lisbon Treaty, the debate on a new system for obtaining evidence in cases with a cross-border dimension was launched in 2009 by the publication of the *Green Paper on obtaining evidence in criminal matters from one Member State to another and securing its admissibility*,[2] with the aim of pinpointing the main problems with current legal assistance and suggesting possible solutions. The Stockholm Programme[3] scheduled the setting up of a new regime for the gathering of evidence across the EU, which resulted in the draft Directive on the EIO.

This paper focuses on pros and cons of the draft Directive on the EIO with the purpose of identifying what would have a positive impact on current legal assistance and what would affect it negatively. This paper also puts forward some considerations on mutual admissibility of evidence in the AFSJ. Although admissibility is not specifically addressed by the draft Directive, it is a topical issue anyway, since Article 82(2)(a) TFEU provides that Member States may establish minimum rules on mutual admissibility of evidence, to the extent necessary to facilitate mutual recognition of judicial decisions and police and judicial cooperation in criminal matters having a cross-border dimension.

---

[1] The only Member State that implemented the FD on the EEW is Denmark. See Rackow and Birrp (2010), p. 1108.

[2] Brussels, 11 November 2009, COM(2009) 624 final.

[3] OJ C 115, 4 May 2010, p. 1.

2 Pros of the Proposed EIO

2.1 A Single Regime

The first and indubitable positive feature of the proposed EIO towards a coherent system of movement of evidence across the EU lies in the replacement with a single measure of all the previous instruments applicable to judicial assistance in criminal matters.[4]

The EIO will replace the corresponding provisions of: the Council of Europe Convention on mutual legal assistance in criminal matters of 1959 and its two additional protocols; the Convention of 1990 implementing the Schengen Agreement of 1985; and the EU Convention on legal assistance in criminal matters of 2000 and its protocol [Art. 29(1)]. It will also replace: FD 2003/577/JHA on the execution of orders freezing property and evidence (as far as the freezing of items of evidence is concerned); and the already mentioned FD 2008/978/JHA on the EEW. This multiplicity of instruments—potentially applicable to the same criminal proceedings and to a single item of evidence—results in a fragmented system, which practitioners may hardly be familiar with, and which undermines the very objective of simplified and swifter cooperation across the EU.[5]

In the light of the creation of a new comprehensive and coherent regime, we should welcome the provision allowing the issuing of an EIO for the gathering of *any* investigative measure to be carried out in another Member State, with the only exception of the setting up of JITs (Art. 3).[6] No restriction whatsoever is provided for, as far as the scope of application of the EIO is concerned, this removing one of the main concerns affecting the FD EEW.[7]

In the light of the same objective, another provision proves to be of utmost relevance: Article 27e(1) allows the issuing of an EIO for the taking of measures with a view to provisionally preventing the destruction, transformation, moving, transfer or disposal of item that may be used as evidence. The issuing authority may indicate whether the evidence shall be transferred to the issuing Member State or shall remain in the executing Member State [Art. 27e(3)]. The requests on provisional measures currently fall under the scope of application of FD on orders freezing property and evidence, which however does not cover the request for the

---

[4] On the positive effects of a single legal instrument, see, *inter alia*, Spencer (2007), p. 479, and Allegrezza (2010), pp. 569f.

[5] In critical terms see Spencer (2007), p. 477, who affirmed that the existing *acquis* on evidence and evidence-gathering does not amount to a coherent system. As the list of legal instruments concerning mutual legal assistance lengthens, so the fragmentation becomes ever worse.

[6] Article 13 of the EU Convention on mutual legal assistance and FD 2002/465/JHA on JITs continue to apply. As clarified in the Explanatory Memorandum [2010/0817 (COD) Brussels, 3 June 2010, p. 5] of the draft Directive, the added value of the JIT is precisely that evidence freely circulates within the team, which means that there is no need for an EIO among its members.

[7] For some critical remarks on the FD EEW see: Belfiore (2009), pp. 4ff.

transfer of what has been subjected to freezing. This framework results in a two-step procedure, where a freezing order needs to be accompanied by a separate request for the transfer of the evidence (see recital nr. 3). Such a procedure certainly does not help to making cooperation swift and efficient. The EIO, on the other hand, will no longer allow possible multiplication of requests for the same piece of evidence.

2.2   The Investigative Measures

Other positive features of the draft Directive that are worth to be mentioned have to do with the measures that can be ordered via an EIO.

First of all, it is for the issuing authority to choose the investigative measure to be carried out in the executing Member State [Art. 1(1)], after assessing the legality of the measure according to the law of the issuing Member State, i.e. whether the measure ordered in the EIO could have been ordered under the same conditions in a similar national case [Art. 5(1)(a)]. The issuing authority seems to be in the best position to identify the measure needed for the gathering of a certain piece of evidence. The executing authority must recognise an EIO and ensure its execution in the same way and under the same modalities as if the investigative measure in question had been ordered by an authority of the executing Member State [Art. 8(1)]. However, the executing authority is given a certain margin of maneuver. Indeed, it may have recourse to an investigative measure other than that provided for in the EIO when this different investigative measure has the same result as the ordered measure by less intrusive means [Art. 9(1bis)]. This flexibility, aiming at securing efficiency of cooperation while safeguarding individual rights and freedoms, is definitely opportune, especially in consideration of the existing differences between national legal systems. It allows to pursue the objective of gathering evidence at its maximum extent—save when the investigative measure indicated in the EIO does not exist under the law of the executing Member State or would not be available in a similar domestic case, i.e. legality is not satisfied according to the law of the executing Member State [Art. 9(1)(a) and (b)]—while preventing intrusive measures.

Secondly, the ordered measure shall be executed according to the formalities and procedures expressly indicated by the issuing authority, provided that such formalities and procedures are not contrary to the fundamental principles of law of the executing Member State [Art. 8(2)].[8] The issuing authority may even request to assist in the execution of the EIO in support of the competent authorities of the executing Member State, unless such assistance is contrary to fundamental

---

[8] The only exception applies to covert investigations. Article 27a(4) provides that covert investigations shall take place in accordance with the national law and procedures of the Member State on the territory of which the covert investigation takes place.

principles of law of the executing Member State or harms its national security interests [Art. 8(3)].[9] It is clear that these provisions concerning modalities of execution, which are in line with provisions already foreseen under the EU Convention on legal assistance and the FD EEW, are meant to increase the probability that evidence gathered in the executing Member State will be admissible in the proceedings in the issuing Member State, since evidence will be consistent with national procedural requirements. Execution of requests of legal assistance according to the traditional *locus regit actum* principle is being gradually overturned by execution according to the *forum regit actum* principle. Besides the increase of probability of admissibility, execution according to the *lex fori* may lead to further positive results: the concurrent application of different laws may spontaneously foster mutual understanding of national criminal procedures across the EU, this promoting integration, even if in the absence of harmonizing measures.

Thirdly, specific provisions are foreseen for certain investigative measures.[10] Of particular significance, because likely to favour admissibility of what is ordered via an EIO, are the hearing by videoconference or other audio-visual transmission [Art. 21],[11] and the hearing by telephone conference [Art. 22]. These investigative measures are meant to be carried out directly by the issuing authority, of course with the indispensable collaboration of the executing authority. They can be therefore assimilated to measures carried out by the issuing authority in the territory of its own Member State, since no interference by the executing authority occurs. If one considers that in certain legal systems the direct relationship between the judge and oral evidence is a fundamental principle of criminal procedure, it is clear to what extent these specific investigative measures may have a positive impact on the respect of the right to a fair trial—a right expressly granted at EU level by Article 47 EU FRCh. Not to mention that the issuing authority that carries out one of these measures will certainly comply with the formalities and procedures required under its national law: admissibility of evidence will be highly probable.

Finally, the draft Directive envisages detailed provisions on interception of telecommunications [Art. 27(b) and (d)]. This constitutes a positive move in an area where, for a long time, national authorities have applied their own rules, which

---

[9] However, the authorities of the issuing Member States shall be bound by the law of the executing Member State during the execution of the EIO. They shall not have any law enforcement powers in the territory of the executing Member State, unless the execution of such powers is in accordance with the law of the executing Member State and to the extent agreed between issuing and executing authorities [Art. 8(3)(a)]. The authorities of the issuing Member States present in the executing Member State may address an EIO which supplements the earlier EIO directly to the executing authority, while present in that State [Art. 7(2)], without the necessity to transmit it via central authorities, where they exist in accordance to Art. 6(2).

[10] Some derogations to the general regime are provided in terms of additional grounds for refusal.

[11] Hearing by videoconference may also represent an effective alternative to surrender, so as to contribute to the moderate use of EAWs. On other positive effects of videoconferences, see Marchetti (2011), pp. 139ff., and Piattoli (2007), pp. 151ff. For some critical remarks, see Blackstock (2010), p. 496.

markedly differ one from another. Even if the EU Convention on legal assistance already foresees detailed provisions on this issue, this Convention has not been ratified by all the 28 Member States and does not apply the principle of mutual recognition. A single and coherent regime, binding all, is definitely welcome.

2.3 Deadlines

The draft Directive on the EIO, in line with all the other measures applying the principle of mutual recognition in criminal matters, sets specific deadlines for the decision on the recognition of an EIO and for the execution of the order, once recognised. It is provided that: the decision on the recognition or execution shall be taken as soon as possible and no later than 30 days after the receipt of the EIO [Art. 11(3)]; the investigative measure shall be carried out by the executing authority without delay and no later than 90 days after the decision on the recognition or execution of the EIO [Art. 11(4)].[12] The executing authority shall transfer the evidence gathered or already in its possession to the issuing authority without undue delay [Art. 12(1)].

Deadlines represent a novelty in legal assistance procedures, where prompt responses to requests—if any—are traditionally left to the good will of the requested authorities.[13] The relevance of deadlines and their impact on efficiency of cooperation procedures are evident in the implementation of the FD on the EAW: as pointed out in the last report from the Commission,[14] between 2005 and 2009 surrender of persons under the EAW regime took place within 14–17 days if the concerned person gave his consent,[15] and 48 days if such consent was not given. This is definitely a success, if one considers that before the EAW, extradition of requested persons used to take 1-year average.

In addition to these generally applicable deadlines, the draft Directive provides for *ad hoc* deadlines when due to procedural requirements, the seriousness of the offence or other particularly urgent circumstances, a shorter deadline than those generally applicable is necessary. Once the issuing authority states in the EIO that the investigative measure must be carried out on a specific date, the executing authority shall take as full account as possible of this requirement [Art. 11(2)].

---

[12] As clarified in the Explanatory Memorandum (fn. 6), p. 14, the scope of the EIO being much wider (the EEW covered only pre-existing evidence), the 60 days period provided in the FD EEW is extended to 90 days in this proposal. See also Marchetti (2011), p. 164.

[13] As pointed out by Lach (2009), p. 107, it happens that the execution of requests takes several months, or that a request "disappears" without any answer from the requested State.

[14] Report from the Commission to the European Parliament and the Council on the implementation since 2007 of the Council Framework Decision of 13 June 2002 on the European arrest warrant and the surrender procedures between Member States, Brussels, 11 April 2011, COM(2011) 175 final.

[15] During the period taken into consideration, between 51 and 62 % of requested persons consented to their surrender.

This provision introduces a certain level of flexibility that contributes, together with the provision on the indication of specific formalities and procedures for the execution of an order, to increase the probability that evidence gathered in the executing Member State will be admissible in the proceedings in the issuing Member State. Indeed, both these provisions allow taking into consideration specific requirements that stem from national criminal procedures and may be indispensable for the admission of evidence in the proceedings. Thus, they concur to guarantee effectiveness of cooperation. This provision may prove to be useful also when several investigative measures need to be carried out simultaneously in different locations.[16]

2.4 Proactive Cooperation

The draft Directive provides that the executing authority shall inform the issuing authority if the executing authority, in the course of the execution of the EIO, considers without further enquiries that it may be appropriate to undertake investigative measures not initially foreseen or which could not be specified when the EIO was issued, in order to enable the issuing authority to take further action in the specific case [Art. 15(2)(a)(ii)].

This provision on the "obligation to inform"—as it is entitled—seems to imply an obligation to proactive cooperation between national authorities; an obligation which in turn may ensure full efficiency in legal assistance procedures. Indeed, the provision aims at the gathering of any item that may be used as evidence in the proceedings in the issuing Member State, in cases in which the issuing authority may not be aware of the existence of certain items in the territory of the executing Member State, or may have overlooked the necessity to gather further items at the moment of the issuing of the EIO. After all, it is likely that the necessity of further measures arises from the execution of the measure initially ordered: in this case, the executing authority is the only one in the position to identify such necessity and to inform the issuing authority.

3 Cons of the Proposed EIO

3.1 Proportionality

Under Article 5a(1)(a), the draft Directive provides that an EIO may be issued only when it is necessary and proportionate for the purpose of the proceedings at stake. Thus, a proportionality test needs to be carried out by the issuing authority. In this

---

[16] See the Explanatory Memorandum (fn. 6), p. 13.

provision it is possible to read an attempt to limit the issuing of EIOs to proceedings for the most serious crimes, so as to prevent the abuse of the application of this instrument to petty crimes.

This problem has been encountered in the implementation of the FD on the EAW, where nothing on proportionality is provided.[17] Indeed, there are countries where EAWs are issued for any crime, regardless its seriousness, whereas there are countries that apply a rigid proportionality test and limit the issuing of EAWs to the gravest offences. To this regard, the European Handbook on how to issue an EAW has been emended so as to take into full account considerations on proportionality.[18]

However, as rightly pointed out elsewhere,[19] requiring the check on proportionality is not a decisive test: the issuing authority will check it anyway, according to its national legislation. Since this check is a matter of domestic law, the fact that the draft Directive mentions it explicitly does not make any tangible difference.[20] Plus, the proportionality test may implicitly fall under the legality test required by Article 5a(1)(b), according to which the issuing authority must be satisfied that the investigative measure ordered with the EIO could have been ordered under the same conditions in a similar national case.[21] The problems already occurring under the EAW regime will occur under the EIO system as well.

3.2 Prognosis on Admissibility of Evidence

The 2003 proposal for a FD EEW expressly provided that an EEW had to be issued only when the issuing authority was satisfied that the objects, documents and data were likely to be admissible in the proceedings for which they were sought. As clarified in the explanatory memorandum, this could have prevented the EEW from

---

[17] On proportionality and the EAW see Vogel and Spencer (2010), pp. 474ff.

[18] The Council has recommended that "[...] the competent authorities should, before deciding to issue a warrant, consider proportionality by assessing a number of important factors. In particular these will include an assessment of the seriousness of the offence, (...) the possibility of the suspect being detained, and the likely penalty imposed if the person sought is found guilty of the alleged offence. Other factors also include ensuring the effective protection of the public and taking into account the interests of the victims of the offence." See Council conclusions on follow-up to the recommendations in the final report on the fourth round of mutual evaluations, concerning the European arrest warrant, Brussels, 28 May 2010, 8436/2/10, REV 2, p. 3.

[19] Bachmaier Winter (2010), p. 584. For further considerations on this issue, see Bachmaier Winter (2013), pp. 98ff.

[20] We do not share the view of Heard and Mansell (2011), p. 357, who affirm that the proportionality assessment is to be welcomed as it prevents 'forum shopping', understood as the unfair advantage that prosecutors may take from differences between countries' procedural systems. Proportionality is assessed according to national law and can be hardly circumvented by the issuing authority.

[21] For further comments on proportionality, see Belfiore (2014).

being used to circumvent protections in the national law of the issuing Member State on admissibility of evidence, particularly in light of further action on mutual admissibility of evidence obtained pursuant to the EEW.

This provision has not been reproduced in the final text of the FD EEW and has not been incorporated in the draft Directive. No prognosis on admissibility of evidence sought by an EIO must be assessed by the issuing authority. However, such a prognosis is of relevance if one considers that the gathering of evidence that will not be admissible in the proceedings in the issuing Member State is a waste of time and resources, which makes judicial cooperation procedures pointless. In the light of considerations of economic nature, which stem from the final objective of effectiveness of judicial cooperation, it could be useful to expressly require the issuing authority to assess the probability that evidence gathered in the executing Member State will be then admissible in the proceedings for which they are needed.[22]

The prognosis on admissibility may also contribute to prevent the abuse of EIOs: they would be issued only in those cases in which it is possible to predict that the evidence gathered abroad will be admissible in the proceedings at issue. We believe, on the other hand, that this prognosis has nothing to do with prevention from circumventing protections on admissibility of evidence: admissibility is ruled by national legislation of the issuing Member State, which cannot be circumvented, not even if evidence is gathered abroad. What can partially concur to prevent the authority of the issuing Member State from circumventing protections on admissibility of evidence is the legality test provided for under Article 5a(1)(b)—illegal evidence are certainly inadmissible.

3.3   Blurring Distinction Between Coercive and Non-coercive Measures

The draft Directive provides for a minimum number of grounds for refusal, listed under Article 10(1). They apply where: (1) there is an immunity, a privilege, or rules on determination and limitation of criminal liability relating to freedom of press and freedom of expression in other media, which make it impossible to execute the EIO under the law of the executing Member State; (2) the execution of an EIO would harm national security interests, jeopardise the source of the information, or involve the use of classified information relating to specific intelligence activities; (3) the measure ordered would not be authorised under the law of

---

[22] See, however, Bachmaier Winter (2010) pp. 583f., who says that, like for the check on proportionality, requiring the check on admissibility by the issuing authority does not make any difference, since this condition will be assessed anyway (see above nt. 21). We believe that the prognosis on admissibility of evidence should not be given for granted, since this may not be required under national law.

the executing Member State in a similar domestic case and the EIO has been issued for non-criminal proceedings; (4) the execution of the EIO would be contrary to the principle of *ne bis in idem*; (5) the EIO relates to a criminal offence which is alleged to have been committed exclusively outside the territory of the issuing Member State and wholly or partially on the territory of the executing Member State, the EIO seeks the use of a coercive measure, and the conduct in connection with which the EIO is issued is not an offence in the executing Member State.

Article 10(1)(a) then lists a number of investigative measures in relation to which only these grounds for refusal apply. These measures are: the hearing of a witness, victim, suspect or third party in the territory of the executing State; any non-coercive investigative measure; the obtaining of information or evidence which is already in possession of the executing authority; the obtaining of information contained in databases that are directly accessible by the executing authority; the identification of persons; search and seizure in relation to offences falling under the list of 32 crimes for which the check on double criminality is no longer required, if they are punishable in the issuing State by a custodial sentence or a detention order for a maximum period of at least 3 years. Article 10(1)(a) further provides that in relation to these investigative measures is not possible for the executing authority to make recourse to a less intrusive measure other than that provided for in the EIO under Article 9(1).

This provision is obscure for at least two reasons. First of all, it is not clear what all these measures have in common. At first sight it may seem that the provision refers to non-coercive measures[23]; however, search and seizure are included in the list. Secondly, it is not clear why the possibility to make recourse to a less intrusive measure other than that provided for in the EIO is precluded for these specific measures,[24] especially when search and seizure are at issue.

This provision is even more obscure if put into connection with the subsequent provision under Article 10(1)(b), according to which, where the investigative measure in the EIO concerns a measure other than those listed under Article 10 (1)(a), additional grounds for refusal are provided for. These apply where: (1) the conduct for which the EIO has been issued does not constitute an offence under the law of the executing Member State (i.e. double criminality is not satisfied), unless it falls under the list of 32 offences annexed to the Directive, if the offence is punishable in the issuing Member State by a custodial sentence or a detention order for a maximum period of at least 3 years; (2) the use of the measure ordered by the issuing Member State is restricted under the law of the executing Member State to a list, or category of offences, or to offences punishable by a certain threshold, which does not include the offence covered by the EIO.

The nature of additional grounds for refusal may let one think that the measures other than those listed under Article 10(1)(a) are coercive measures, for which stricter legality tests are required. However, search and seizure—which are

---

[23] This is the interpretation given by Heard and Mansell (2011), p. 361.

[24] The same doubt is raised by Heard and Mansell (2011), p. 361.

certainly coercive measures—do not fall under this provision. Thus, it should be excluded that Article 10(1)(b) refers to the general category of coercive measures.

The wording of Article 10 is absolutely reproachful: not only does this provision represent one of the worst example of EU legislation, especially in a delicate subject-matter such as the law of evidence, but it also raises serious doubts on its ratio and concrete application.

Perhaps, in order to both apply a sound ratio aimed at safeguarding national prerogatives together with individual rights, and help legal practitioners in the application of this EU instrument, it could be better to draw a clear-cut distinction between coercive and non-coercive measures (so as to agree on what must be considered coercive and what must not). Additional grounds for refusal may apply only when coercive measures are ordered with the EIO. After all, the additional grounds for refusal have to do with stricter legality tests, which seem to be appropriate when coercive measures are at stake.[25] Also the possibility to make recourse to less intrusive measures is likely to be of relevance when a coercive measure, i.e. a particularly intrusive measure, is ordered.

3.4 Defence Rights

As far as defence rights are concerned, the draft Directive raises all the worries already arising from the FD EEW and the traditional regime of legal assistance: the defence is not granted any right whatsoever with the purpose of both asking for the gathering of evidence to a foreign judicial authority and taking part to the gathering of evidence abroad.

This framework undermines all together the principle of equality of arms between the defence and the public prosecution, the objective of efficiency of legal assistance, and the right to an effective legal remedy.

The principle of equality of arms, which stems directly from the principle of fair trial, is jeopardised by the imbalance between the position of the defence lawyers and that of judicial authorities as far as requesting the gathering of evidence in a territory different from the one of the proceedings is concerned.[26] The defence has no power to directly send a request to a foreign authority when exculpatory evidence is located abroad. The only chance for the defence is to ask the competent judicial authority to forward such a request. However, this may not always be a good move for the defence that would be forced to disclose its defensive strategy to the counter-party before official discovery takes place. Not to mention that judicial

---

[25] Bachmaier Winter (2013), p. 103 points out that the check on double criminality may not be necessary if non-coercive measures are to be adopted in the executing Member State. Of the same opinion, Rackow and Birrp (2010), p. 1117.

[26] Among those concerned about the violation of the principle of equality of arms, see: Bachmaier Winter (2010), p. 587; Heard and Mansell (2011), p. 366; Rackow and Birrp (2010), p. 1121.

authorities may refuse to forward a request as formulated by the defence, and national legal systems may not provide for a remedy against such refusal (as it is in Italy).

The objective of efficiency of legal assistance is undermined by the absence of the defence during the execution of an EIO, where participation of the defence is a requirement necessary for the admissibility of evidence under the law of the Member State of the proceedings. The only possibility to fill this gap may be to request participation of the defence as a modality falling under "formalities and procedures" that can be expressly indicated by the issuing authority. Though, this possibility makes participation of the defence dependent on the arbitrary decision of the issuing authority. What could be decisive in order to induce the issuing authority to request participation of the defence in the execution of the EIO is the prognosis on admissibility of evidence: if participation of the defence is necessary for the admissibility of evidence, the issuing authority will request it as a *condicio sine qua non* (one more reason to expressly provide for such a prognosis, as suggested above).

The exclusion of the defence from the activity of evidence gathering in the executing Member State may also jeopardise the right to an effective legal remedy—which is expressly provided for under Article 13 of the draft Directive[27] and granted by Article 47 EU FRCh. The defence, absent at the moment of the execution of an EIO, does not have the possibility to concretely verify the manner in which evidence has been gathered by the executing authority. This may affect the right to exercise legal remedies in the executing Member State. While the substantive reasons for issuing EIOs may be challenged only in actions brought in the issuing Member State [Art. 13(3)], reasons grounded on the material execution of EIOs may be challenged before the authority of the executing Member State [this seems to be implicit under Article 13(1), that provides that Member States shall ensure that any interested party shall be entitled to legal remedies, which are equivalent to those that would be available in a similar domestic case]. Should the defence be given the chance to take part to the gathering of evidence in the executing Member State,[28] it would be much easier to exercise the right to an effective legal remedy, where needed.

---

[27] For some critical remarks on the system of legal remedies as framed under the draft Directive, see Blackstock (2010), pp. 494f.

[28] In favour of a similar scenario, see Allegrezza (2010), p. 576.

4 Some Considerations on the Issue of Mutual Admissibility of Evidence in the AFSJ

The issue on mutual admissibility of evidence in the AFSJ is not addressed by the draft Directive. However, since the European Council of Tampere of 1999,[29] this issue has been intensely debated. Following the Lisbon Treaty, the possibility to adopt minimum rules on mutual admissibility of evidence has been formally recognized under Article 82(2)(a) TFEU; though, such rules may be adopted only insofar as they facilitate mutual recognition of judicial decisions and police and judicial cooperation in criminal matters.

Mutual admissibility of evidence is often described as the direct consequence of mutual recognition. This statement is questionable.

Mutual recognition is a means through which promoting simpler and swifter cooperation across the EU. It deals with the procedures through which requests of legal assistance are sent and executed, and is characterized by three main features: (a) procedures are judicial only, and the involvement of the executive power is no longer foreseen; (b) grounds for refusal are reduced to a minimum and closed number; (c) responses to requests of legal assistance are fast, since deadlines are provided.[30] Mutual recognition requires Member States to overlook differences in the name of mutual trust they allegedly nurture in each other.

On the contrary, admissibility deals with the formal introduction in the proceedings of a certain item of evidence. In this respect, admissibility does not relate to judicial cooperation. In fact, it is a matter of national laws,[31] the result of delicate checks and balances under domestic legal systems in consideration of specific procedural requirements, which are envisaged to guarantee the fairness of the proceedings and therefore the rights of the accused, while ensuring effective prosecutions and investigations.[32] Evidence is a legal construct: its value cannot be granted but according to the law of the Member State of the proceedings.[33] Interfering with rules on admissibility of evidence would imply upsetting the internal balance of national legal systems,[34] of which those rules are the corollary. Moreover, specific rules on mutual admissibility of evidence gathered in another Member State would

---

[29] The Tampere Conclusions state that evidence lawfully gathered by one Member State's authorities should be admissible before the courts of other Member States, taking into account the standards that apply there. European Council of 15–16 October 1999, Conclusions of the Presidency—SN 200/1/99 REV 1.

[30] See also Belfiore (2009), pp. 6ff.

[31] Spencer (2010), pp. 604f. Also the Court of Strasbourg has constantly stated that the issue of admissibility of evidence lies in the responsibility of the contracting Parties. Indeed, the ECHR does not contain any explicit imperative on the law of evidence. See Gless (2006), p. 128.

[32] Bachmaier Winter (2010), p. 588; Gless (2009a), p. 161; Gless (2005), p. 124.

[33] Gless (2009b), p. 151. See also Allegrezza (2010), p. 573, who points out that the probative value of a piece of evidence always depends on the method followed to produce it or to collect it. The method employed affects the result.

[34] Spencer (2007), pp. 474f.

result in the introduction of a double standard of admissibility, according to which evidence gathered abroad follow a different track than evidence gathered in the Member State of the proceedings. This double-track system is to be avoided: it may undermine the principle of equality, which may in turn jeopardize the principle of fair trial.

Not surprisingly, the European "Model Rules" for the procedure of the future EPPO,[35] which have been drafted by distinguished scholars within a research project carried out at the University of Luxembourg, expressly leave outside their scope of application details relating to the admissibility of information gathered by the EPPO, as it is considered to be the task of national courts—and national criminal procedural laws—to define the evidentiary standards in the trial phase.[36]

What should be questioned in order to assess the opportunity to address the issue of mutual admissibility of evidence across the EU is whether admissibility must be directed to favour judicial cooperation or judicial cooperation must be directed to favour admissibility. Although not in line with Article 82(2)(a) TFEU, we believe that the second statement is the right answer. The possibility of the issuing authority to indicate specific procedures and to assist in the execution of an EIO, and hearings by video and telephone conferences, are all good examples on how provisions on judicial cooperation may really favour admissibility. More in general, judicial cooperation may favour admissibility if procedural rights and guarantees are firmly granted to the accused in all the 28 Member States. The EU seems to have finally set off on this path.

Judicial cooperation should never allow admission of evidence beyond what is provided for under national legislations. It is not admissibility that must cede before judicial cooperation. In fact, rules on admissibility are the ultimate guarantee in order to prevent abuses from both the issuing and the executing authorities.

References

Allegrezza S (2010) Critical remarks on the Green Paper on obtaining evidence in criminal matters from one member state to another and securing its admissibility. Zeitschrift für die internationale Strafrechtsdogmatik 9:569–579

Bachmaier Winter L (2010) European investigation order for obtaining evidence in the criminal proceedings. Study of the proposal for a European directive. Zeitschrift für die internationale Strafrechtsdogmatik 9:580–589

Bachmaier Winter L (2013) The role of the proportionality principle in cross-border investigations involving fundamental rights. In: Ruggeri S (ed) Transnational inquiries and the protection of fundamental rights in criminal proceedings. Springer, Heidelberg, pp 85–110

Belfiore R (2009) Movement of evidence in the EU: the present scenario and possible future developments. Eur J Crime Crim Law Crim Justice 17:1–22

---

[35] The Model Rules are available at: http://www.eppo-project.eu/index.php/EU-model-rules/english.

[36] See the Introduction to the Model Rules, available at the same IP address.

Belfiore R (2014) Exchange of DNA data across the EU: issues and perspectives in light of the principle of proportionality. In: Ruggieri F (ed) Criminal proceedings, language and the European Union, Linguistic and legal issues. Springer, Heidelberg

Blackstock J (2010) The European Investigation Order. New J Eur Crim Law 4:481–498

Gless S (2005) Mutual recognition, judicial inquiries, due process and fundamental rights. In: Vervaele JAE (ed) European evidence warrant, Transnational judicial inquiries in the EU. Intersentia, Antwerpen, pp 121–129

Gless S (2006) Free movement of evidence in Europe. In: Armenta Deu T, Gascón Inchausti F, Cedeño Hernán M (eds) El Derecho Procesal Penal en la Unión Europea, Tendencias actuales y perspectivas de futuro. Ed. Colex, Madrid, pp 121–130

Gless S (2009a) Les perspectives de l'espace judiciaire européen en matière de recherche et d'utilisation des preuves situées à l'étranger. In: Jault Seseke F, Lelieur J, Pigache C (eds) L'Espace Judiciaire Européen Civil et Pénal. Dalloz, Paris, pp 155–165

Gless S (2009b) Strategie e tecniche per l'armonizzazione della prova. In: Illuminati G (ed) Prova Penale e Unione Europea. Bononia University Press, Bologna, pp 141–152

Heard C, Mansell D (2011) The European Investigation Order: changing the face of evidence-gathering in the EU cross-border cases. New J Eur Crim Law 4:353–367

Lach A (2009) Transnational gathering of evidence in criminal cases in the EU *de lege lata* and *de lege ferenda*. Eucrim 3:107–110

Marchetti MR (2011) Dalla Convenzione di assistenza giudiziaria in materia penale dell'Unione europea al mandato europeo di ricerca delle prove e all'ordine europeo di indagine penale. In: Rafaraci T (ed) La cooperazione di polizia e giudiziaria in materia penale nell'Unione europea dopo il Trattato di Lisbona. Giuffrè, Milano, pp 135–167

Piattoli B (2007) Nuove tecnologie e nuove garanzie: l'assunzione della prova tramite videoconferenza. In: Rafaraci T (ed) L'area di libertà, sicurezza e giustizia: alla ricerca di un equilibrio fra priorità repressive ed esigenze di garanzia. Giuffrè, Milano, pp 143–162

Rackow P, Birrp C (2010) Recent developments in legal assistance in criminal matters. Goettingen J Int Law 3:1087–1128

Spencer JR (2007) The problems of trans-border evidence and European initiatives to resolve them. Camb Yearb Eur Legal Stud 9:465–480

Spencer JR (2010) The Green Paper on obtaining evidence from one member state to another and securing its admissibility: the reaction of one British Lawyer. Zeitschrift für die internationale Strafrechtsdogmatik 9:602–606

Vogel JR, Spencer JR (2010) Proportionality and the European arrest warrant. Crim Law Rev 6:474–482

European Investigation Order: The Defence Rights Perspective

Laura Autru Ryolo

Abstract Mutual recognition or judicial cooperation should be viewed as an opportunity to grant justice trough a fair trial.

Despite this reasonable statement, the apparent scope of the EIO seems to permit the gathering of evidence (only for the purpose of Prosecutors and Police investigators) avoiding even the minimum common standard of fairness within the EU. The different approaches by Member States, in a national perspective, and the most controversial issues are pointed out in this paper, reaching the conclusion that the EIO could be detrimental to defence right and be defined as another lost chance.

Keywords Defence rights • European Investigation Order • Fair trial • Fundamental rights • Procedural safeguards • Stockholm roadmap

Contents

1 Is There a Need for the EIO? 107
2 Critical Issues 108

1 Is There a Need for the EIO?

The most frequent asked question is whether there is a need for a single procedural instrument to gather evidence throughout Europe.

L. Autru Ryolo (✉)
Criminal Law Committee of Council of Bars and Law Societies in Europe, Advisory Board of European Criminal Bar Association, Bar Council of Messina, Via C.Battsti, 155, 98123 Messina, Italy
e-mail: autru@hotmail.com

S. Ruggeri (ed.), *Transnational Evidence and Multicultural Inquiries in Europe*, DOI 10.1007/978-3-319-02570-4_8, © Springer International Publishing Switzerland 2014

There are different positions in favour of the proposal and others against it.

Broadly speaking, all the positions have good points on their sides.

The differences and the controversial issues arise when experts and stakeholders face the scope, the rules and the impact of such a measure.

Therefore, the right question should be: what do you expect to find in that directive, what will be the improvement and the added value?

Speed and logistic problems in criminal investigations can be solved in many different ways.

The core point is in the background: what is the idea of the European Union about fundamental rights freedom, security and justice.

The different approaches to the proposal reflect the most relevant diversity of attitude toward fundamental rights.

The measure, as it has been conceived till now, seems to have not any consistency with the overall approach of the Commission and the Parliament to procedural rights, while, on the other hand, reflects the national need for the priority given to speediness and efficiency of investigations, even without a reference to the seriousness of the accuse or public order compelling reasons.

In the opinion of practising lawyers and the most representative association of them (ECBA, CCBE), the legislative process should follow the steps pointed out in the Stockholm Programme, instead of going back, forward and around the already agreed route, in order to grant to the E.U. legislation consistency and improvement in terms of fairness and compliance with the fundamental rights.

2 Critical Issues

So far, attention should be paid to the following essential issues and topics:

A) Relevant diversity of judicial system and procedural safeguards within the Member States: An alternative to the judicial cooperation have to face, first of all, the diversity of the procedural rules about the gathering of evidence during the investigations and admissibility at the trial stage. The second point cannot be solved by the EIO. With regard to the first point, only the introduction of common rules implying high standard in terms of effectiveness of the defence and the reliability of the methods and outcome of investigations are able to overturn the procedural objections in each single Member State.

B) New legislation as a challenge to improve domestic laws: The EIO could be the key to modify domestic legislation and this consequence is not positive or negative. It depends on the content of the Directive.

We cannot think to introduce a sort of double track in the criminal proceedings, applying different rules according to the place where the evidence is gathered.

C) Compliance with the fundamental rights and defence rights: If a Directive points out few rules for gathering evidence throughout EU, assuming that the instrument respect the fundamental rights enshrined in the HCHR, even the constitutional and procedural rules in the single Member States could be at stake.

Neither, it is acceptable that evidence gathered in execution of an EIO could be admissible, regardless of the compliance with the national law, especially on procedural safeguards, where procedural rights are safeguards for the citizens and not obstacle to the judicial cooperation.

D) Domestic criminal policy and individuals' rights: The point of the dual criminality, especially for intrusive measures and the right to not self-incriminate, is not solved at all.

E) Judicial control and remedies: The absence of a judicial evaluation on the pertinence and proportionality of the requested measure in relation to the object of the proceeding and the accuse could lead to abuse in particular in Member States with adversarial system.

There must be provided remedies in case of breach of fundamental rights and the rules of the EIO.

F) Fair trial and equality of arms: The last, but not the least, issue is related to the equality of arms.

Mutual recognition or judicial cooperation should be viewed as an opportunity to grant justice trough a fair trial.

It is questionable that the procedural instrument does not provide any rules about evidence gathered by the defence lawyers or on request of the defence.

In conclusion, it is advisable that the proposal should be withdrawn in order to introduce new procedural instruments within a more ambitious project, consistent with a new model of criminal justice.

The Rules on Legal Remedies: Legal Lacunas and Risks for Individual Rights

Alessandro Arena

Abstract The present paper deals with the rules on legal remedies laid down in the draft directive on the European Investigation Order. The main purpose of this paper is to demonstrate the deficiencies of such regulation, which may lead to unfair treatment, particularly for suspects and defendants. Since Article 13 PD EIO does not define the time limits within which legal remedies can be applied for, two fundamental issues need to be addressed by EU Institutions, i.e., the question of the suspension of the execution or transfer of the measure requested through the EIO and the effects of the remedies. More generally, this contribution also questions the appropriateness of replacing all existing means of evidence gathering with a new instrument based on the mutual recognition principle with a view to developing some basic minimum standards of fundamental rights and guaranteeing the effectiveness of the right to a fair trial also during the course of criminal investigations. This paper ends with some proposals for further legislation.

Keywords EIO, Legal remedies • Evidence gathering • Executing state • Issuing state • Recognition, execution and transfer of an investigative measure

Contents

1 Introduction 112
2 The Rules on Legal Remedies: From the EEW to the EIO 112
3 Challenging the Substantive Grounds for the EIO 113
4 Effects of Legal Remedies and Their Impact on Fundamental Rights 115
5 The Protection of Third Parties 116
6 Concluding Remarks 117
References 118

A. Arena (✉)
Department of Law, University of Messina, Piazza Pugliatti Nr. 1, 98100 Messina, Italy
e-mail: alexaren@virgilio.it

S. Ruggeri (ed.), *Transnational Evidence and Multicultural Inquiries in Europe*,
DOI 10.1007/978-3-319-02570-4_9, © Springer International Publishing Switzerland 2014

1   Introduction

In April 2010 seven Member States drew up a proposal for a Directive regarding the European Investigation Order.[1] The EIO seeks to establish a complete system for obtaining evidence in cross-border cases, trying to facilitate the lawful gathering, safeguarding and admissibility of any type of evidence relevant to an alleged offence. This addition to the range of mutual recognition instruments represents a further development of criminal cooperation among Member States.

This paper analyses the issue of legal remedies against an EIO. The study aims to ascertain the legal problems and practical deficiencies of the proposed regulation from the perspective of its impact on the rights of the individuals involved in such investigative procedures.

2   The Rules on Legal Remedies: From the EEW to the EIO

In order to extend the principle of mutual recognition to the field of evidence gathering among the EU Member States, in 2008 the Council adopted a Framework Decision on the European Evidence Warrant (hereafter, FD EEW). This legal instrument contains an articulated regulation on legal remedies. Indeed, remedies must be available in the executing State, even if the substantive reasons for the EEW may only be challenged in the issuing State. Moreover, both States must grant remedies equivalent to those applicable to purely domestic proceedings and are subject to obligations regarding time limits and the facilitation of proceedings.[2] According to the FD EEW, States have the discretionary power to provide for remedies with a limited object and restrict legal remedies to those cases on which the execution of an EEW entails the use of coercive means. Furthermore, Article 18 provides that actual and effective remedies must be guaranteed (with a reference to Article 13 ECHR).[3]

The issue of legal remedies against the EIO is regulated under Article 13 of the draft Directive. However, in the original text of the proposal the provisions regarding legal remedies were insufficient, in that they only required the cooperating authorities to make legal remedies accessible to interested parties in accordance with national law. This main principle was applicable both to the issuing and the executing State. This unsatisfactory regulation gave rise to numerous human rights concerns. Indeed, even if all Member States have their own legal remedies under their domestic laws, the rules on remedies differ considerably amongst Member States, may apply at different stages of proceedings and may also have different impacts on these proceedings. The regulation set forth in the original proposal was

---

[1] Interinstitutional File: 2010/0817 (COD), COPEN 115 EJN 12 CODEC 363 EUROJUST 47.

[2] Peers (2011), p. 714.

[3] Vervaele (2009), p. 159.

deficient even in situations where no legal remedy is available in the executing State, either because its national law does not provide for informing the individual of the investigative measure prior to its execution, or because the investigative measure must be carried out at an early stage of the procedure. It was thus necessary to address these failings by modifying the text of the proposal to ensure fair process also pending an investigation.

In the course of the Council examination, however, the regulation of Article 13 was considerably widened and new provisions on legal remedies introduced. The aim of this short paper is to ascertain whether the new approach can ensure a proper balance between the need for efficiency and the protection of the rights of the individuals affected by the investigative measure in relation to the *whole transnational procedure.*

3 Challenging the Substantive Grounds for the EIO

Following the approach of the FD EEW, paragraph 3 of Article 13 of the draft Directive provides that the substantive reasons for issuing the EIO may only be challenged in an action brought before a court in the issuing State. This provision, which reflects a typical approach to dividing tasks between the cooperating authorities,[4] may lead to unfairness. The main problem arises when defendants are citizens of, or are resident in, a country other than that of the relevant proceedings. In such cases they will have to defend themselves in a foreign country, facing further expenses and the difficulties of dealing with a legal system they are not familiar with.[5]

In relation to such difficulties, however, a step forward in EU legislation has been made thanks to the Directive 2010/64/UE on the right to interpretation and translation in criminal proceedings.[6] Indeed, the provisions on the rights of interpretation and translation require that Member States take concrete measures to ensure that the interpreting and translation services provided meet the quality

---

[4] Schomburg et al. (2012), pp. 1ff.

[5] Therefore a proposal has recently been made to entrench jurisdiction not in the State where the crime was committed, but in the State where the defendant has their substantial interests (such as citizenship or permanent residence) in order to ensure a judgment of criminal liability on the basis of a knowable criminal provision. See Ruggeri (2013a), §§ 4.2.2.1 and 4.2.2.2. This proposal has been developed above in Ruggeri, Part IV, Sect. 3.1.

[6] The Directive 2010/64/UE provides that language assistance must be free and adequate, timely, in the native language or in another language well-known by the person concerned, should also cover communications between defendant and his lawyer, and should be contestable both in terms of adequacy and completeness. In particular, Article 3 provides that Member States must ensure that suspected or accused persons who do not understand the language of the proceedings concerned are, within a reasonable period of time, provided with a written translation of all documents which are essential to ensure the exercise of defensive rights and the safeguard and the fairness of the trials.

required and request those responsible for the training of judges, prosecutors and judicial staff involved in criminal proceedings to pay special attention to the particularities of communicating with the assistance of an interpreter so as to ensure efficient and effective communication. For these reasons, Article 2 of this Directive requires that interpreting be of a quality sufficient to safeguard the fairness of the proceedings, in particular by ensuring that suspected or accused persons are aware of the case against them and are able to exercise their right of defense.[7] Notwithstanding this, harmonization has been achieved at a minimum level and the linguistic comprehension of investigative activities, which is of essential importance in judicial cooperation, is still very differently regulated in the domestic legislations of EU Member States.[8]

Furthermore, to ensure the effectiveness of the action aimed at challenging the substantive grounds for the EIO, due information must be ensured about the possibilities for seeking legal remedies. In this regard, Article 13(4) PD EIO proposal requires information to be provided when legal remedies "*become applicable.*" This provision fails to clarify when this might be. To be sure, information should be provided once a decision is made to give effect to the request so that it is clear that the duty to inform the affected parties lies with the executing authority *prior* to the gathering of evidence. However, this should not mean that affected persons are not informed at all. Thus, if there are then any reasons to preserve confidentiality, it should be ensured that, once the evidence has been gathered and secured, the affected persons are informed that they can seek legal remedies.

Against this background, we should analyze whether and how the Directive 2012/13/EU on the right to information in criminal proceedings can improve the rights of the individuals affected by the EIO. According to this Directive, Member States must ensure access at least to all material evidence in the possession of the competent authorities, whether for or against suspects or accused persons, to those persons and to their lawyers. Access must be granted in due time to allow the effective exercise of the right of defense and at the latest upon submission of the grounds for the charge to the judgment of a court. Any refusal of such access must be weighed against the defense rights of the suspected or accused person, taking into account the different stages of the criminal proceedings. Restrictions on such access should be interpreted strictly and in accordance with the principle of the right to a fair trial under the ECHR and with the ECtHR case law.[9] The main failing of this regulation is that the Directive does not provide for any remedy in the event of the competent authority's refusal to exhibit the requested documents. Moreover, it should be assessed whether the rules of the 2012 Directive, which relate to *domestic* criminal proceedings and the proceedings for the execution of an EAW, might be applied extensively to transnational investigative procedures under the EIO.

---

[7] Rafaraci (2012), pp. 338f.

[8] Ruggieri (2013b).

[9] ECtHR, Decision of 13 October 2009, *Dayanan v Turkey*, Application No. 7377/03; ECtHR, Decision of 6 January 2010, *Fernandez-Huidobro v Spain*, Application No. 74181/01.

Yet, the main concern arising from the scheme of the division of labors is that it can make it difficult for individuals affected by investigative measures to challenge the substantive grounds for issuing the EIO.[10] In this regard, a coordinated action of the cooperating authority is of essential importance since it would provide the interested parties with all relevant information, which is necessary to bring about an effective remedy.[11]

4   Effects of Legal Remedies and Their Impact on Fundamental Rights

The issue of information is strictly linked to the effects of legal remedies and their impact on individual rights. In this regard, a distinction should be drawn between different situations, based on the moment when the person becomes aware of the execution of the investigation measure concerned, as follows:

a) The first situation concerns cases where the law of the executing State allows for the interested party to be informed prior to the execution of the measure and to challenge the decision to execute the measure before its execution. In many countries, this is the case of the taking of a blood sample or the compulsory examination of a witness. In such cases, the remedy will probably impact on whether or not the measure will be executed. It is worth observing that Article 11(4) provides the Member States with a certain margin of flexibility, since the measure must be executed within 90 days after the decision on the recognition and execution has been taken. Article 11(6) also provides the possibility to postpone execution even further.

b) The second situation concerns cases where the law of the executing State allows for the person to be informed of the measure only during or after its execution. The person may therefore challenge the measure only during or after recognition of the EIO and execution of the investigative measure. This may include for example the search of premises where there is a seizure of evidence under Italian law.[12] In this case, the question arises whether or not the transfer of the evidence sought should be postponed pending the outcome of the legal remedy. This question is not expressly addressed in the Directive and the solution therefore depends on the national law of the executing State. According to Article 12(1), evidence must be transferred without undue delay. However it can be reasonably argued that a pending remedy is a legitimate reason to delay the transfer of the evidence if the remedy has suspensive effect under national law.

---

[10] Schünemann, Part IV, Sect. 1.2.1.

[11] Peers (2011), p. 13.

[12] EU Council opinion 18918/11.

c) The third situation concerns cases where the law of the executing State does not provide for any duty of information about the investigative measure or allows the suspect to be informed only at a later stage. This may be the case of wiretaps, in that, depending on the national systems concerned, the person will not be informed at all, or will only be informed after the investigation has been completed. In most cases, the possibility of challenging the investigative measure will be accessible only after evidence has been transferred to the issuing State and therefore the remedy will be exercised in the issuing State. It may, however, happen that the remedy had already been exercised in the executing State. In this case, the most problematic issue is no longer the suspension of execution/transfer but the impact of the remedy exercised in the executing State on the relevant proceedings. This specific issue is addressed in paragraph 5a PD EIO, which provides for the prior verification of two situations: (1) either the exercise of a remedy leads to the conclusion that the EIO should not have been recognized, for example because of a ground for refusal; (2) or the EIO should have been executed but there was some irregularity in the way the evidence was collected according to the national law of the executing State.

In the light of this, further concerns derive, in my view, from the scheme of the division of labors. Not only does it make it difficult to challenge the substantive reasons for issuing the EIO but it also gives rise to problems of coordination of the remedies in the cooperating countries. Thus, Article 13(5b) requires the issuing State to "*take into account*," in accordance with national law, a decision taken in the executing state after transfer of evidence that a request should not have been recognized. This does not seem to be a proper approach. To be sure, where a legal remedy is raised, there should be no transfer until a decision is taken in relation to it. This provision may, therefore, be amended by providing for either the suspension of the investigation measure or the transfer of evidence gathered (depending on the stage at which the legal remedy is pursued) until a decision has been reached. These changes might help avoid the risk of unlawful use of evidence in the issuing State. On the other hand, it should not be overlooked that the provision of a suspensory tool would affect the speed of the transnational investigation. For this reason it would be more appropriate to consider a solution that allows the issuing State to provide parameters balancing the efficiency of the transnational procedural and the protection of rights, in particular those of the accused person, with coordinated action of the cooperating authority. This solution seems more proper and capable of maintaining the flexibility of the text of the proposal.

5 The Protection of Third Parties

Another shortcoming of the proposed regulation on legal remedies relates to the protection of the rights of third parties involved in the execution of the EIO. Surprisingly, there is no reference in Article 13 to an action that anyone other than an accused or suspect may bring to protect his or her rights. Therefore, in order to complete the defensive system, it would be appropriate to introduce a tool also for third parties. Member States should, therefore, take necessary measures to ensure that any interested party, including bona fide third parties, have legal remedies to protect their legitimate interests, against the recognition and execution of the EIO. This aspect is important to ensure compliance with the principles outlined by the case law of the ECtHR and to allow for effective protection to persons whose legal positions could be adversely affected by the execution of an EIO.

On the other hand, these amendments of Article 13 should be addressed in order to bring the proposal in line with other EU instruments. Thus, Article 8(2) of the Framework Decision 2006/783/JHA regarding confiscation orders includes as grounds for refusal the fact that, under the legal system of the executing State, enforcement is prevented by the rights of the parties involved, including those of third parties acting in good faith (for example, when attempts are made to confiscate a specific property transferred to a third party acting in good faith). Through this measure, this Framework Decision aims at compensating third parties for any deprivation of their fundamental right to be heard in the criminal proceedings resulting in the issuing of an order to confiscate some of their property. The executing court must determine to what extent the existence of rights was taken into consideration by the issuing authority at the time of the confiscation order, since the executing authority cannot review the merits of the decision it has to enforce.[13]

6 Concluding Remarks

The issue of legal remedies highlights the importance of finding a balance between the need for efficient transnational inquiries and the protection of individual rights. In this regard, the enhancement of the rules on legal remedies is to be welcomed. However, Article 13 still displays several shortcomings and should be amended though further guarantees starting with the approach of the FD EEW. Indeed, comparing Article 13 of the EIO proposal with Article 18 EEW, it is worth noting that the rules on legal remedies have been significantly weakened.[14] In light of this, a new approach should be sought to achieve a proper balance between the need for efficient transnational investigations and the protection of the fundamental rights of the individuals affected by the proposed instrument.

---

[13] Gascón Inchausti (2012), p. 263.

[14] Comment of the Meijers Committee, 9 June 2011.

References[15]

Gascón Inchausti F (2012) Mutual recognition and transnational confiscation orders. In: Ruggeri S (ed) Transnational inquiries and the protection of fundamental rights in criminal proceedings, A study in memory of Vittorio Grevi and Giovanni Tranchina. Springer, Heidelberg, pp 261–267

Peers S (2011) EU justice and home affairs law. Oxford EU Law Library, pp 712–716

Rafaraci T (2012) The right of defence in EU judicial cooperation in criminal matters. In: Ruggeri S (ed) Transnational inquiries and the protection of fundamental rights in criminal proceedings, A study in memory of Vittorio Grevi and Giovanni Tranchina. Springer, Heidelberg, pp 332–343

Ruggeri S (2013a) Concorrenza tra potestà punitive, conflitti transnazionali di giurisdizione. Il contributo della comparazione giuridica al diritto penale transnationale orientato ai diritti della persona. La legislazione penale (in press)

Ruggieri F (ed) (2013b) Criminal proceedings, languages and the European Union. Springer, Heidelberg (in press)

Schomburg W, Lagodny O, Gleß S, Hackner T (2012) Einleitung. In: Schomburg W, Lagodny O, Gleß S, Hackner T (eds) Internationale Rechtshilfe in Strafsachen. C.H. Beck, München, pp 1–50

Vervaele JAE (2009) Il progetto di decisione quadro sul mandato di ricerca della prova. In: Illuminati G (ed) Prova penale e Unione europea. Bononia University Press, Bologna, pp 153–160

---

[15] The chapter contributions contained in this book have been quoted with the only reference to the Author's surname, the Part in which the contribution is contained and the number of the paragraph concerned.

The Defendant's Rights in the Hearing by Videoconference

Alessandra Grio

Abstract This chapter examines the issue of hearing by videoconference, laid down in Article 21 of the EIO draft proposal.

The main aim of this study is to analyse the proposed regulation in light of the procedural guarantees which must be granted to the defendant in the case of hearing by videoconference.

The main question from the perspective of the defendant is whether examination by videoconference allows the defendant's right to a defence can be effectively respected.

The protections of the right of suspected and accused persons in criminal proceedings is a fundamental challenge of the Union, which is essential in order to maintain mutual trust between Member States and public confidence in the European Union within the AFSJ pursuant to Article 67 TFEU.

Keywords Hearing by videoconference • Privilege against self-incrimination • Right to a defence

Contents

1	Introductory Remarks	120
2	The Hearing of the Defendant by Videoconference	120
3	Critical Perspectives on the Defendant's Right of Defence	121
4	Defensive Rights in Examination by Videoconference	122
	4.1 Foreword	122
	4.2 The Privilege Against Self-incrimination and the Guarantee Against Pressures on the Moral Freedom of Expression and Thought	123
5	Conclusions	125
	References	125

A. Grio (✉)
Department of Law, University of Messina, Piazza Pugliatti No. 1, Messina, Italy
e-mail: grio.alessandra@gmail.com

S. Ruggeri (ed.), *Transnational Evidence and Multicultural Inquiries in Europe*,
DOI 10.1007/978-3-319-02570-4_10, © Springer International Publishing Switzerland 2014

1   Introductory Remarks

The proposal of the directive regarding the European Investigation Order aims to establish an overall system for obtaining evidence in cross-border cases. It represents a further step in the evolution of the mutual recognition agenda and the enhancement of criminal cooperation among member States. It also represents a break with the traditional mechanism of mutual legal assistance.

Chapter IV of the for the EIO Directive Proposal is dedicated to acts of investigation that require specific regulation, borrowed mainly from the Convention on mutual assistance between Member States of the EU in 2000 and the Protocol of 2001.[1]

The reason for this choice lies in the need to "provide more details than the general system,"[2] also providing some "additional reasons for refusal"[3] related to the different and specific activity whose performance is required.

In this paper I shall focus on the hearing of the defendant by videoconference, as laid down in Article 21 of the EIO draft proposal. In terms of the modes and guarantees to be granted to participants, the structure of this provision reflects the contents of Article 10 of the 2000 Convention. The main aim of this study is to analyse the proposed regulation in light of the procedural guarantees which must be granted to the defendant.

2   The Hearing of the Defendant by Videoconference

The first issue which deserves to be examined is concerned with the grounds for refusal. In the hypothesis under consideration the grounds for refusal—supplementing the general grounds provided for under Article 10(1a) PD EIO—regard the defendant's failure to give prior consent (to accept videoconferencing) and the non-compliance of videoconferencing methods with the fundamental principles of the law of the prosecuting State.

The protection of the rights of suspected and accused person in criminal proceedings is a fundamental challenge of the Union, which is essential in order to maintain mutual trust between the Member States and public confidence in the European Union within the AFSJ pursuant to Article 67 TFEU.

---

[1] Protocol established by the Council in accordance with Article 34 of the Treaty on European Union, the convention on mutual assistance in criminal matters between the Member States of the European Union.

[2] Accompanying Document to the Proposal for a Council Directive regarding an European Investigation Order in criminal matters, Detailed Statement, 9288/10 ADD 2, COPEN 117 EJN 185 CODEC 384 EUROJUST 217, p. 17.

[3] *Ibid.*

Technological innovations have now extended the reach of the court hearing. This has permitted the remote participation of the defendant. It is essential that the examination of the defendant by videoconference, while having advantages in terms of procedural economy, does not preclude the exercise of his defensive rights.

On the other hand, remote participation via video conferencing not only satisfies objectives of procedural economy, but also helps reduce the time of the hearing and the risks associated with the frequent movement of prisoners who are defendants in numerous lawsuits pending in different locations. It thus also helps avoid the frequent postponements of court hearings, due to the defendant's inalienable right to participate in each proceeding.

3   Critical Perspectives on the Defendant's Right of Defence

The main question linked to the perspective of the defendant is whether examination by videoconference allows the defendant's rights of defence to be effectively respected. In fact, the personal and aware participation of the defendant in the trial from a remote location, being different from the physical location in the courtroom, does not allow him, as would normally be the case, to have full knowledge of the events occurring in the hearing or effectively perceive the behaviour of the protagonists, both of which are conditions essential to ensuring full understanding of the dynamics of the proceedings and the deployment of the most appropriate defensive strategy. Moreover, remote participation is not the same as attendance at the hearing in person, since it does not allow the same full actuation of the right of defence even when there is a linkup capable of transmitting the most faithful of images in real time.[4] The defendant still has an incomplete knowledge of the trial documents and a fragmentary vision of the debate, preventing him from appreciating it in all its nuances.

It is no coincidence that in the Italian legal system doubts have been expressed about the constitutional legitimacy of Articles 1 ff. of Law no. 11 of 7 January 1988 (relating to remote participation in proceedings of a defendant in custody) with reference to Articles 3, 10, 24 and 27 of the Italian Constitution. In judgment no. 342 of 14 July 1999, the Constitutional Court rejected the assumption that only the physical presence of the defendant at the hearing could create the conditions such as to effectively guarantee the right of defence, thus declaring the question of legitimacy to be unfounded. The Court reiterated that what was needed for the purposes of constitutional compliance was the guarantee that the defendant effectively took part in the trial personally and in an informed manner, and that this was assured by the adequacy of the technical means to meet the above requirements.

---

[4] Russo (2009), p. 4.

Article 21 PD EIO, on the other hand, does not regulate in detail the procedure for conducting the defendant's examination by videoconference (for example, Italian legislation seems to deal in more detail with the organizational aspects related to use of the remote connection). However, we should remember that the use of technology ("Hearing by videoconference or other audio-visual transmission"), always functional to the achievement of objectives of procedural economy, does not mean that we can ignore the problems related to the inadequacy of the technical means used and the dysfunctions that in practice can occur when using audiovisual equipment.

In short, there have for some time been calls for an efficient and effective protection of defensive rights in transnational proceedings where the use of technical tools is involved.[5]

4 Defensive Rights in Examination by Videoconference

4.1 Foreword

Article 21 PD EIO does in fact lay down "minimum" guarantees to protect the person to be examined by videoconference, but remains silent on issues that I believe should instead be expressly regulated. Among these is the defendant's right to submit a total *recusatio respondendi* (*ius tacendi*), the privilege against self-incrimination (understood as an exception to the criminally punishable duty to tell the truth), the right not to be questioned (understood as the right of the defendant to entirely refuse dialogue with the prosecuting authority)[6] and, more generally, the lack of pressure on moral freedom and expression of thought.

It is precisely the lack of any effective protection beyond "minimum guarantees" that highlights the complex problem of protecting fundamental rights. These deficiencies have been pointed out both by various non-governmental organizations (Justice, Fair Trials Abroad) and by the EU Agency for Fundamental Rights, in its Opinion of the 14 February 2011 on the EIO proposal,[7] particularly with regard to the presumption of innocence, the right not to be obliged to incriminate oneself, and the right to remain silent.

Doubtless the EIO can impinge on several fundamental rights. And although in the field of transnational enquiries the ECtHR has not actually declared that violations related to activities in the investigation stage contravene the Convention, since they can be compensated for in judgment on the basis of an overall

---

[5] In this sense cf. Gleß (2006), pp. 115f.

[6] Amodio (1974), p. 408; Patanè (2006).

[7] Opinion of the European Union's Agency for Fundamental Rights on the draft Directive regarding the European Investigation Order, http://fra.europa.eu/fraWebsite/research/opinions/op-eio_en.htm, p. 12.

assessment,[8] it should be recognized that the guarantees of a fair trial apply to criminal proceedings in their entirety, including the pre-trial investigation stages.

The role of fundamental rights during examination by videoconference is different to that found in investigative activities aimed at affecting—by limiting them—specific individual rights, such as property, secrecy of correspondence, etc. It rather concerns the conduct of the examination, which must be carried using means that respect specific defensive guarantees.

Article 21 should thus include a detailed provision establishing the rights to be guaranteed to the defendant during remote examination. Since for the defendant, exercising the right to a adversarial hearing means exercising the right to defend himself, the law must adequately satisfy the defensive needs of persons subjected to criminal proceedings.

4.2 The Privilege Against Self-incrimination and the Guarantee Against Pressures on the Moral Freedom of Expression and Thought

With specific regard to the "privilege against self-incrimination," this right must be expressly guaranteed to the defendant during remote examination and, in my opinion, should be explicitly included in Article 21 PD EIO.

Historically, the privilege against self-incrimination, originally circumscribed within the narrow confines of the prohibition of forcing the defendant to testify against himself, has gradually become wider-ranging in scope, to the point that it now recognizes the actual freedom of non-cooperation.[9]

The methods for protecting the right to remain silent depend not only on the changing definition of the balance between individual freedom and the repressive requirements of state authorities, but also on the tendency of criminal procedure towards the accusatory or inquisitorial.

Thus, in the Italian legal system, the recognition of the right to silence expresses a procedural model that takes into account the protection of the right not to be questioned that, at least during examination in court, sees the examination of the defendant as a voluntary option and prohibits the prosecuting authority from forcing the defendant to submit to examination. The full development of the potential of the rule *nemo tenetur se detegere* may in fact be found in a procedural model of an accusatory nature and in the concept of public order that hinges around the individual, and that does not subject the individual to state power.

Moreover, the irresistible affirmation of the principle *nemo tenetur se detegere* suffers from the hard-to-shrug-off conception rooted in common sense whereby, on the one hand, the innocent defendant has no interest in remaining silent, but rather

---

[8] ECtHR, 27 June 2000, *Echeverri Rodriguez v The Netherlands*, Application No. 43286/98.
[9] Zuckerman (1989), p. 855.

in "demanding the right to speak," while on the other hand, the choice to be silent is considered *per se* contrary to common sense and to ordinary ethical rules.[10]

The Italian code of criminal procedure, which tends towards the accusatory, clearly establishes the way to view the role of the defendant in the trial, combining the rule whereby the defendant's decision to speak must necessarily be voluntarily with the principle of personal responsibility that characterizes the adversarial system. In the various phases of criminal proceedings we see a variety of ways in which the defendant's knowledge is acquired and, correlatively, different ways to guarantee the right to remain silent. In the course of preliminary investigations we see on one hand questioning characterized by coercion, and on the other, the suspect's right to refuse to answer any questions. The "strongest model" of the protection of the right not to cooperate is seen in examination in court, where we find a comprehensive guarantee of the right not to be questioned, to the point that the defendant is actually exempted from appearing before the judge to explain his unwillingness to be examined. If the defendant agrees to be examined, the entire process is based on the principle of personal responsibility, a principle that, on one hand, sees the examination as conscious choice made by the party, and on the other hand attributes the defendant with the responsibility for the possible prejudicial consequences of his choice to undergo examination.

The European Court also tends to incorporate in the constitutional concept of due process that right to silence that according to the European Court is at the heart of a fair trial. Consistent case law has established that, when assessing whether the right to fair trial has been violated, the European Court of Human Rights "must [. . .] satisfy itself that the proceedings as a whole were fair."[11]

In the context of the right to silence, the distinction between the right not to answer the questions, and the prohibition for the judge to evaluate negatively the silence of the defendant seems to be deeply rooted.

The Court rules out in principle a violation of the rules of a fair trial on condition that the non-collaboration of the defendant is clearly, considering the circumstances of the case, in itself indicative.[12]

---

[10] Foschini (1956), p. 384, who considers that it is in the interest of the defendant to give "the most comprehensive demonstrations of his innocence."

[11] ECtHR, Decision of 26 September 1996, Miailhe v. France, Application No. 18978/91, § 43.

[12] ECtHR, Decision of 6 June 2000, A*verill v UK*, Application No. 36408/97. In the case in point, the questions focused on overwhelming evidence against the applicant that clearly required explanation on the part of the latter, viz. the discovery on his body of traces of the gloves and balaclava used for the murder. The *Rules of Court* establish, in this regard, a model of instruction: "However you may draw such a conclusion against him only if you think it is a fair and proper conclusion, and you are satisfied about three things: first, that when he was interviewed he could reasonably have been expected to mention the facts on which he now relies; second, that the only sensible explanation for his failure to do so is that he had no answer at the time or none that would stand up to scrutiny . . .; third, that apart from his failure to mention those facts, the prosecution's case against him is so strong that it clearly calls for an answer by him . . . 4. (Add, if appropriate:) The defence invites you not to draw any conclusion from the defendant's silence, on the basis of the following evidence (here set out the evidence. . .). If you think this amounts to a reason why

The gnoseological perspective adopted by the European Court highlights the ambiguous meaning of the self-defensive choices of the defendant, neutralizing that aura of suspicion that surrounds the decision to remain silent and preventing the defendant's conduct from being interpreted in a distorted way, such as in terms of the paradox of a liar who "if he speaks, lies; and if he is silent, has something to hide."[13]

The consecration of the right to silence acknowledges the defendant's inviolable personal sphere, which not even the search for truth may invade.

With this in mind, Article 21 should be, as mentioned earlier, supplemented by the inclusion of a detailed provision regarding the rights to be guaranteed to the defendant in remote examination. But that is not all. In my opinion, Article 21 should also express the principle whereby in the course of the hearing by videoconference, use may not be made, even with the consent of the person questioned, of methods or techniques such as to affect the freedom of self-determination or to alter the defendant's mnemonic or evaluative capacities [principle guaranteed for instance in Articles 64(2) and 188 of the Italian CCP]. This is not just due to significant concerns regarding the reliability of the results achievable using such means, but above all, due to a need to protect the moral freedom of the person.

5 Conclusions

The privilege against self-incrimination and the principle whereby in the course of the hearing by videoconference use may not be made, even with the consent of the person questioned, of methods or techniques such as to affect the freedom of self-determination or to alter mnemonic or evaluative capacities, should—in my opinion—be explicitly guaranteed in Article 21 of the proposal for a EIO directive, for the protection of the defendant's defensive rights.

References

Amodio E (1974) Diritto al silenzio o dovere di collaborazione? Rivista di diritto processuale 408–419
De Cataldo Neuburger L, Gulotta G (1996) Trattato della menzogna e dell'inganno. Giuffrè, Milano
Foschini G (1956) Sistema del diritto processuale penale, vol I. Giuffrè, Milano
Gleß S (2006) Beweisrechtsgrundsätze einer grenzüberschreitenden Strafverfolgung. Nomos, Baden-Baden

---

you should not draw any conclusion from his silence, do not do so. Otherwise, subject to what I have said, you may do so." The criteria of relativization may be represented by the degree of coercion exercised on the defendant, as well as the relative weight of the evidence against him.

[13] De Cataldo Neuburger and Gulotta (1996), p. 201.

Patanè V (2006) Il diritto al silenzio dell'imputato. Giappichelli, Torino
Russo C (2009) Videoconferenze, Diritto di difesa, standards tecnici previsti dalla legge. Nota a: Cassazione penale, 10/04/2008, n. 28548, sez. I. Cassazione penale 12:4768–4777
Zuckerman AAS (1989) Trial by unfair means. The report of the working group on the right of silence. Crim Law Rev 855–865

The EIO Proposal and the Rules on Interception of Telecommunications

Simona Arasi

Abstract In the new European regulatory framework aimed at jurisdictionalizing mutual recognition procedures and introducing simplified relationships, the goal of the mutual admissibility of evidence should characterize the trial stage in the strict sense but also the pre-trial stage. We are looking for "minimal rules for a statute on means of gathering evidence".

The object of this study is a means of gathering evidence that has great potential to harm the private sphere: telecommunications interceptions. The regulation of this tool is to be found in Articles 27b et seqq. PD EIO, but is a source of some considerable perplexity. Firstly, there are questions as to whether the rights violated by the use of the aforementioned instrument fall within the rights disciplined in Article 17 PD EIO and what prevails in the balance between legal truth and right of defence. Moreover, some procedural doubts arise about who is the actively legitimate subject, as well as some terminological doubts, on the meaning of "relevance," and some practical ones, if the high costs involved are included in the reasons for refusal.

The present paper aims at a survey of the system in the PD EIO, highlighting obscure points and regulatory gaps. Finally, taking into account the fragmentation of legal rules, we try to provide an exegetical aid to operators called to move within the complex rules, with regard to the solution of application problems.

Keywords Costs • Interceptions of telecommunications • Jurisdictionalization • Means of gathering evidence • Mutual recognition • Relevance • Right of defence • Trial truth

S. Arasi (✉)
Department of Law, University of Messina, Piazza Pugliatti n. 1, Messina, Italy
e-mail: sarasi@unime.it

S. Ruggeri (ed.), *Transnational Evidence and Multicultural Inquiries in Europe*,
DOI 10.1007/978-3-319-02570-4_11, © Springer International Publishing Switzerland 2014

Contents

1   Introductory Remarks. Searching for a European Law of Evidence   128
2   Interception of Telecommunications: Specific Clauses and Doubts   129
    2.1   The Rights Violated by the Use of This Tool   129
    2.2   The Actively Legitimate Subject: "The Issuing Authority"   130
    2.3   The Requirement of "Relevance"   132
    2.4   The Enormous Costs of Interceptions   133
    2.5   Problems During the Circulation of Evidence   134
3   Concluding Remarks and Proposal   134
References   136

1   Introductory Remarks. Searching for a European Law of Evidence

From the traditional model of international judicial cooperation, essentially based on classical forms of so-called "rogatory" legal assistance law, there has been, over the years, a radical process of change in means of cooperation.[1] By combining the principle of the admissibility of evidence lawfully obtained and "circulating" in the territory of the European Union with that of its compatibility with the internal rules relating to the right to the evidence, it is hoped to achieve the inter-proceeding transfer of criminal evidence. The new European legislative framework aimed at "jurisdictionalizing" mutual recognition procedures, in order to introduce simplified and direct relationships between the judicial Authorities and to progressively restrict political authorities' powers of filtering and interdiction. In this context, the aim of the mutual admissibility of evidence doesn't concern only the trial phase in the strict sense but also the "minimal rules for a statute on the means of gathering evidence" in the pre-trial phase.

As is known, in the general theory of the trial, not only in Italy, the preliminary proceeding is decomposed mainly into three phases respectively aimed at admitting, obtaining and, finally, assessing evidence.

In addition to these distinctions, some scholars distinguish between evidence already gathered by foreign authorities (gathered statements, interceptions already carried out, things and documents previously seized and/or obtained) and evidence to be collected (witnesses to be heard, interceptions or searches to be performed, requests for data from providers, etc.).[2]

---

[1] Chiavario (2005), pp. 974ff.

[2] See, among others, Furgiuele (2012), p. 242. Cf. also Ruggeri (2013), pp. 299ff., who underlines that in all adversarial systems evidence is always a legal construction and the distinction between the evidence that, although directly available, does not already exist and the evidence that, although already existing, is not directly available without further investigation or examination appears, according to the Author, somewhat questionable. In neither case will evidence in itself be

It should remembered that the EEW allows for obtaining objects, documents and data already in possession of another Member State; it cannot, therefore, be issued to request another Member State to carry out telecommunications interceptions or hear witnesses.[3] In such circumstances it would seem necessary to use the traditional means of rogatory letters. Moreover, it is worth noting that the decision on the Prüm Treaty aims at the circulation of evidence already existing in the databases by direct access to national databases. There are no legal instruments, at a European level, which cover the gathering of dynamic evidence, traditional or atypical, which directly affect fundamental rights (personal freedom, freedom of residence, privacy, etc.), so-called "constituting evidence" in the strict sense.

2 Interception of Telecommunications: Specific Clauses and Doubts

2.1 The Rights Violated by the Use of This Tool

Articles 27b et seqq. of the EIO proposal regulate telecommunications interceptions.

The ECtHR has often pointed out the high potential of the private sphere to be harmed, and has also underlined that interference in the private sphere can be justified under Article 8(2) ECHR only if interceptions are governed by rules which are sufficiently precise to be protected against the possible arbitrariness of the public authorities.[4] The risk to avoid is that of cognitive elements entering the system which have been obtained outside any procedural context and using methods that might not be in line with internal regulations, such as the result of intelligence activities or preventive investigations.[5]

The simple application of the principle of mutual recognition, in this area, would cause a significant lowering of the barriers of intervention to the lowest common denominator, which would be, therefore, unacceptable and devoid of any practical use. The interception of telecommunications must be accompanied by "special barriers" in order not to disrupt the balance of the procedure to the damage of the concerned subjects.

The growing exchange of data, functional to the fight against organized crime, must be harmonized with the need to preserve procedural guarantees and, above all,

---

available and exist from a legal viewpoint and in both cases it will result only from procedural activity.

[3] De Amicis (2011).

[4] See, among others, ECJ, 2 August 1984, *Malone v United Kingdom*, Series A, No. 82, 7 EHRR (1985), par. 66 and ECJ, 10 March 2009, *Bykov v Russia*, no. 4378/02.

[5] Troisi (2012), p. 154.

the right of defence and the right to cross-examination.[6] It seems appropriate to point out that the PD EIO, in recital nr. 17 and in Article 1, expressly provides for the respect of fundamental rights and the principles recognized by Article 6 TFEU and the EU FRCh.

The rights of the person involved in criminal investigations now play a central place in European trial policies, thanks not only to the provisions of the fundamental charters, primarily in Articles 5 and 6 ECHR and Articles 6 and 47 EU FRCh, and in Treaties, Article 82 (2) TFEU, but also in a legislation that is gradually recognizing the need to ensure, at the European level, a high and uniform level of protection of the rights of accused persons.[7]

If the path to follow can only be that of safeguarding the fundamental principles of the system, however, the question naturally arises as to whether, in the balance between trial truth and defence rights, the inviolability of "fundamental rights" must always prevail, and if so, which rights.

Moreover, it is worth noting that there are additional difficulties arising from the legal control of investigation orders executed in a foreign country, primarily deriving from the existence of a different legal system and from the fact that the required documentation is often in a foreign language.

In addition, an extension of the scope of this instrument from the simple content of telecommunications to what recital nr. 14g defines as the "collection of traffic and location data associated with such telecommunications" means, as an immediate corollary, a potential increase in injuries to rights.

Ultimately, the approach of national lawgivers cannot be that of taking the opportunity to level down the protection of individuals; rather, the aim should be to provide extremely high standards of guarantees, in order to comply with those required by the "stricter" legal systems.

2.2   The Actively Legitimate Subject: "The Issuing Authority"

In the discipline under analysis, there lacks a definition that accurately establishes who is entitled to request an interception of telecommunications.

---

[6] Note that in the effectiveness of the investigation of the trial the oral tradition of evidence is stifled. An example is the crystallization of the extensive investigative results in the trials of organized crime harnessed by the dense network of interceptions, with the consequent transformation of the oral examination into the "recitation of a script" of the conversations intercepted.

[7] See, among others, Directive 2010/64/EU of 20 October 2010 on the right to interpretation and translation in criminal proceedings; Directive 2012/13/UE on the right to information in criminal proceedings; proposal for a Directive on the right of access to a lawyer in criminal proceedings and the right to communicate upon arrest [COM (2011) 326].

On closer inspection, we find that Article 27b uses a rather broad, ambiguous expression, "The issuing authority." This could in fact refer, not only to the judicial authority but also to the public prosecutor and to additional categories of subjects.

An extensive interpretation of this locution could be considered contrary to the conventional guarantees.[8] Firstly, the principle of equality of arms in criminal proceedings would be affected.

If the purpose is to make supranational measures available to the public prosecutor, one priority should be to similarly facilitate the presentation of the defence. It would thus be appropriate to create new opportunities for the judge to have access to the defence, since the former is familiar only, or mainly, with the material in the possession of the public prosecutor, talks to the public prosecutor who seeks his intervention in crucial moments of the investigation, and hears the defence case only after that of the prosecution.

It should be recalled that in adversarial systems, public prosecutors are required to deal with the limitations and constraints imposed by their commitment and role in the trial. Their institutional role affects their initiatives, which should always be circumscribed within legislative guidelines.

Otherwise, the approval of an additional tool to facilitate the transfer of evidence between "criminal pursuit authorities" would increase the imbalance between public prosecutor and defence, in reality already existing for the traditional instruments of judicial assistance.[9]

The pursuit of an effective equality of arms between public prosecutor and defence cannot be achieved simply by adjusting the powers of the individual parties, but hinges on the judge's position, and on the impartiality and incisiveness of his role.[10]

An extension of the powers of the public prosecutor without a simultaneous increase in those of the defence would fragment judges' functions to the point that they become incapable of curbing the procedural sovereignty of the public prosecutor.[11]

The European Union, in pursuing the creation of a European area of freedom security and justice, therefore, cannot strengthen judicial cooperation through the adoption of innovative tools without increasing and improving the procedural guarantees for the accused persons.

Some doubts also concern the type of the issuing Authority's intervention. Because interceptions of telecommunications are ad hoc acts, judicial intervention should be authorizational and the possibility of defence subsequential rather than preventive. Article 5a(3) of the proposal provides a validation procedure, that is

---

[8] See Vogel (2004), as quoted as Vervaele (2005).

[9] Cfr. *ex plurimis* Constitutional Court, Judgement 184/2009, which underlines the asymmetry between the public prosecutor's position and that of the accused, with the consequent creation of imbalance.

[10] Amodio (2012).

[11] *Ibid.*

Where an EIO. is issued by an authority referred to in Article 2(a)(ii), the EIO shall be validated, after examination of its conformity with the conditions for issuing an EIO under this Directive, by a judge, prosecutor or investigating magistrate before it is transmitted to the executing authority

2.3 The Requirement of "Relevance"

Article 27b(3)(a) requires the issuing authority to indicate in the EIO the reason why it considers a measure requested for the purposes of criminal proceedings to be "relevant".

However, some doubts arise as to how this condition of admissibility must be interpreted, that is, strictly, as absolute indispensability, or more flexibly, as simple pertinence-adequacy-importance.

It should be mentioned that there are often ambiguities even within individual jurisdictions. By way of example, if we consider the requirement of "absolute indispensability for the continuation of the investigation" provided under Article 267(1) of the Italian CCP. This apparently rigid provision leaves open various jurisprudential interpretations. On one hand, this requirement must be the specific motive, and in detail, the grounds for authorization must necessarily take into account the reasons why certain users should be intercepted, and therefore cannot omit to indicate the connection between the on-going investigation and interception.[12] On the other hand, the rule seems to be tempered by the other requirement, that is the "serious circumstantial evidence of a crime," which concerns the existence of a criminal offence and not the guilt of a particular person, meaning that it is possible to legitimately proceed with interception even if the evidence does not point to one individual in particular.[13] Indeed, the authorization decree of Article 267 of the Italian CCP can be based on any evidence of a crime, also derived from previous unusable interceptions.[14]

According to the principle of mutual recognition, the executing State should not be allowed to carry out assessments to "justify" the requested measure as a condition for its execution. The Authorities of the executing State should trust the evaluations of the issuing State and should have no opportunity to corroborate the necessity or proportionality of the applied measure.

The only motive for opposition, under the general clause contained in Article 1(3) PD EIO, would seem to be a breach by the executing State of fundamental rights or constitutional rules.[15] That said, it is hard to accept that the PD EIO requires the judicial authorities of States to "blindly" trust those of others.

---

[12] See *ex multis* Court of Cassation, Section VI, Decision of 12 February 2009, no. 12722.

[13] See *ex plurimis* Court of Cassation, Section IV, Decision of 17 October 2006, no. 42017.

[14] See, among others, Court of Cassation, Section V, Decision of 10 February 2011, no. 4951.

[15] Backmaier Winter (2010), p. 589.

The request for "blind" trust in the actions of public prosecutors or judges, regardless of whether they are national or foreign authorities, seems contrary to rules that are designed to ensure control of the methods adopted in the taking of evidence.

We must not forget that one of the functions of the defence is to verify the legitimacy of all measures taken in the course of criminal proceedings. Often this may be done only in retrospect, especially with regard to measures carried out in extra-national territory by means of judicial cooperation.

It is therefore necessary to define in more detail the meaning of "relevance" and, consequently, of any powers of assessment that may be exercised by the executing State with regard to this requirement.

2.4   The Enormous Costs of Interceptions

The use of systems installed to make interceptions inevitably involves a cost, in some cases very high, that, in accordance with Article Y, is incumbent on the executing State, except for the costs arising from any transcription, decoding, or decryption of intercepted communications that will be incumbent on the issuing State.

One wonders: could a high cost, therefore contrary to the principle of economy, constitute a reason for refusal by the executing State? And what should be done, for example, if the executing State lacks the necessary resources?

In the preparatory work (see par. 5 and Article Y)[16] the issue was addressed, with the possibility of additional solutions examined, including direct communication between the competent authorities, the extension of deadlines, the sharing of costs, etc. In particular, it had been established that the executing State, in the case of "exceptionally high" costs, could agree with the issuing Authority on the sharing of costs, or on their being covered exclusively by the issuing Authority, with the latter being able to totally or partially withdraw the E.I.O.

It is difficult, however, to clarify the meaning of "exceptionally high costs," or if there is a threshold-limit above which the costs must be qualified as such, or whether these must be assessed case by case, with reference to the resources of the executing State. And in the latter case, it is problematic to establish who should decide this threshold.

However, point 2.3. PD EIO, in highlighting the need to "continue further the establishment of a comprehensive system for obtaining evidence in cases with a cross-border dimension," hoped for "a new approach, based on the principle of mutual recognition, that also [took] into account the flexibility of the traditional

---

[16] The Working Party on Cooperation in criminal matters met on 11 and 12 January 2011 and continued the examination of the initiative for a Directive on the European Investigation Order. See Doc. 5591/11 COPEN 10, EJN 5, EUROJUST 9, CODEC 91.

system of mutual judicial assistance," requiring the creation of "a global system
[. . .] covering as far as possible all types of evidence and deadlines for enforcement
and limiting as far as possible the grounds for refusal."[17]

2.5   Problems During the Circulation of Evidence

Evidence which has been obtained in compliance with the minimum provided
guarantees can display some problematic aspects in the phase of its circulation,
such as for example its dispersion, the disclosure of its contents and loss of
authenticity.

The need for the increased exchange of information, in fact, must be guaranteed
not only by ensuring the utmost respect for privacy and abovementioned rights, but
also by developing a comprehensive strategy for the protection of data.[18]

The protection of data clearly satisfies both interests of an individual nature,
connected to fundamental demands for the protection of rights and personal freedoms, and objective-public interests, in other words, those functional to ensure that
any data gathered, stored and exchanged is inviolable and authentic (correct,
complete and up-to-date), in order to remove the risk of information circulating
whose veracity and reliability is uncertain.[19] There has even been recognized a right
to the protection of data, the processing of which reflects European policy, whereby
we have moved on from static to "procedural" privacy.[20]

The introduction of guarantees to ensure the integrity of tangible or intangible
res, collected and transmitted from one State to another, is, therefore, necessary.

3   Concluding Remarks and Proposal

In light of the foregoing considerations the introduction of a single tool shared by all
Member States to use in the search for evidence would produce some positive
effects, and must be preferred to the application of general rules to all types of
evidence.

The co-existence of several evidence gathering tools in transnational criminal
cases inspired by different approaches has led to confusion and difficulties in the
law enforcement that need to be overcome within a common area of freedom,

---

[17] Accompanying Document to the Proposal for a Council Directive regarding an European
Investigation Order in criminal matters, Detailed Statement, 9288/10 ADD 2, COPEN 117, EJN
13, CODEC 384, EUROJUST 49, § 2.3.

[18] Pisani (2011), p. 70.

[19] Rodotà (1997), p. 470.

[20] See, among others, Allegrezza (2010), pp. 61ff.

security and justice. This situation may also jeopardize the success of the recent instruments based on the principle of mutual recognition, since due to their limited sphere of application, Member States will often prefer to avail themselves of the traditional tools of mutual legal assistance, which present the advantage of offering only one channel for the obtaining of evidence.

It is an instrument of effective and significant impact on the operational level but that, doubtless, may be amended in many ways, not least in terms of the need for a better balance between the scope of the purpose assigned to the new model of "euro-order" and the protection of procedural rights of persons affected by the rapid and simplified "circulation" of investigative measures, with a view to strengthening the principles of legality of the evidence-gathering proceedings and effectiveness of judicial guarantees. In other words, within a European judicial area based on a high level of protection of fundamental rights enshrined in the Charter of Nice, as formally incorporated in Article 6(1) of the Lisbon Treaty, the strengthening of the tools of mutual acknowledgement is vital, as is the harmonization of the normative framework of the requirements and conditions of mutual admissibility of evidence between Member States, as determined by the European Board of Tampere and subsequently reaffirmed in Article 82(2)(a) TFEU.

A greater harmonization in the preliminary proceeding stage would, probably, produce some positive outcomes, not only facilitating the admissibility of evidence, but also helping the defence review the legality of the evidence gathering itself. It is also necessary to establish the rules on how evidence should be evaluated or may be considered admissible in each State, in the observance of minimum guarantees, in other words, the criteria for determining when evidence must be considered non-receivable/inadmissible because it has not respected certain minimum requirements.[21]

It has been noted that the notion of "admissibility," though widely used at European level, remains rather vague. In domestic criminal procedures, the admissibility stage, although sometimes appearing to coincide with the collection of some item of evidence, usually precedes the latter stage, as only evidence already admitted may be taken. But the meaning to be given to "admissibility" at a European stage is not clear. In other words, whether this notion concerns the decision on the admission of evidence preceding the order for obtaining evidence abroad or the admission stage following the taking of evidence once it arrives in the home State.

It must be emphasized that neither the Commission's proposal nor the original draft of the PD EIO dealt with the issue of the preventive admissibility of evidence, thus leaving this control exclusively to the domestic authority requesting assistance

---

[21] The principle of mutual recognition of decisions in criminal matters, in particular in its aspirations for a European transfer of evidence by using the "admissibility of evidence throughout Europe", is obviously modelled on the rules of the free movement of citizens. However, the principle of the free movement of goods and services cannot plainly be applied to the area of intergovernmental transfer of evidence, because the "import" of evidence touches the rights of the accused in a fundamental way. See Hecker (2013), p. 276.

pursuant to its own law. In the original draft proposal no provision required the issuing authority to check beforehand the necessity and proportionality of the measure and the admissibility of the requested measure under *lex fori* in a comparable case, as preconditions for the issuance of the EIO.[22]

The variety of the possible combinations of procedural instruments of different national origins would create a confusing and incoherent universal legal construction. If the rule of law is to be afforded any consideration, such a universal legal construction cannot be seen as a suitable model for a European Criminal Procedure Law.[23]

The aim, in fact, is to replace, in relations between the European Member States, the existing cooperation, conventional or not, and the research and evidence-gathering instruments, with a new and more flexible "horizontal" model, testable by almost all of the most important investigative measures. In order to achieve this objective it will be necessary to balance the need for the transmigration of evidence and the essential standards of constitutional guarantees derived from individual Charters and from the ECHR.

In summary, the text of the PD EIO is generally positive, particularly in terms of its capacity to facilitate and accelerate the request for and execution of available evidence in other Member States. A tool used for the request for almost all types of evidence is more efficient than the EEW, that is predictably of little use due to its limited scope. However, looking at the position of the accused persons, in some points the EIO seems to ignore that evidence obtained in a foreign country cause additional difficulties for the defence and, consequently, inequality of arms between the parties in criminal proceedings.

References

Allegrezza S (2010) Critical remarks on the Green Paper on obtaining evidence in criminal matters from one member state to another and securing its admissibility. Zeitschrift für die international Strafrechtsdogmatik 569–579. www.zis-online.com

Amodio E (2012) Il diritto di difesa tra equilibri formali ed equilibri sostanziali. www.penalecontemporaneo.it

Backmaier Winter L (2010) European investigation order for obtaining evidence in the criminal proceedings. Study of the proposal for a European directive. Zeitschrift für die internationale Strafrechtsdogmatik 580–589. www.zis-online.com

Chiavario M (2005) Cooperazione giudiziaria e di polizia in materia penale a livello europeo. Rivista italiana di diritto e procedura penale 48:974–989

De Amicis G (2011) Limiti e prospettive del mandato europeo di ricerca della prova. www.europeanrights.eu

Furgiuele A (2012) Le prove formate fuori dal giudizio. Giappichelli, Torino

Hecker B (2010) Europäisches Strafrecht, 3rd edn. Springer, Heidelberg

---

[22] For further details see Ruggeri (2013), pp. 287ff.

[23] In this sense Hecker (2010), § 12 para. 65ff.

Hecker B (2013) Mutual recognition and transfer of evidence. The European evidence warrant. In: Ruggeri S (ed) Transnational inquiries and the protection of fundamental rights in criminal proceedings, A study in memory of Vittorio Grevi and Giovanni Tranchina. Springer, Heidelberg, pp 269–278

Pisani M (2011) Problemi di prova in materia penale. La proposta di direttiva sull'Ordine Europeo di Indagine. Archivio penale 3:1ff

Rodotà S (1997) Persona, riservatezza, identità. Prime note sistematiche sulla protezione dei dati personali. Rivista critica del diritto privato 583–601

Ruggeri S (2013) Horizontal cooperation, obtaining evidence overseas and the respect for fundamental rights in the EU. From the European Commission's proposals to the proposal for a directive on a European Investigation Order: towards a single tool of evidence gathering in the EU? In: Ruggeri S (ed) Transnational inquiries and the protection of fundamental rights in criminal proceedings, A study in memory of Vittorio Grevi and Giovanni Tranchina. Springer, Heidelberg, pp 279–310

Troisi P (2012) La circolazione di informazioni per le informazioni penali nello spazio giuridico europeo. Cedam, Padova

Vogel JR (2004) The European evidence warrant. A new legal framework for transnational evidence gathering in criminal matters. As quoted as Ijzerman A. (2005) from the CATS portfolio: the European evidence warrant. In: Vervaele JAE (ed) European evidence warrant: transnational judicial inquiries in the EU. Intersentia, Antwerp, p 1

The EIO Proposal for a Directive and Mafia Trials: Striving for Balance Between Efficiency and Procedural Guarantees

Paola Maggio

Abstract PD EIO could mark a turning point in the development of "European criminal procedure."

The Proposal will obtain evidence in cross-border cases and is particularly suitable for investigations on the subject of international organized crime. From the long gestation period and the contents of the Proposal emerges, however, the difficulty of making a balance between the investigation of crimes and the guarantees of the individuals involved.

The use of collected of evidence from different legal systems is often an overly neglected aspect. Doubt surrounds the regulation of banking instruments, the rules on wiretapping, and all provisions for undercover investigations.

Keywords Balances • Efficiency • Mafia cases • PD EIO • Procedural guarantees

Contents

1 The PD EIO in a Broader Framework 140
2 EIO and Absence of Trust 142
3 Lights and Shadows of the Proposal 143
4 Past and Future 148
References 149

P. Maggio (✉)
Department D.E.M.S., Law School, University of Palermo, Via Maqueda No. 172, Palermo, Italy
e-mail: paola.maggio@unipa.it

S. Ruggeri (ed.), *Transnational Evidence and Multicultural Inquiries in Europe*, 139
DOI 10.1007/978-3-319-02570-4_12, © Springer International Publishing Switzerland 2014

1   The PD EIO in a Broader Framework

The proposal for a Directive on a European Investigation Order (PD EIO) aims at introducing a more unified and general legal regulation for obtaining evidence in cross-border cases than the current MLA instruments.

In this context, investigation into transnational "Mafia cases" deserves particular attention. Especially the delicate balance between efficiency and effectiveness of judicial cooperation and human right's protection imposed by minimum standards in evidence gathering.

With this objective, the PD EIO has to set-up "a framework" that considers recent legislative European measures and the most efficient implementation of existing instruments (for example EEW) to maintain the highest level of respect for human rights.

The underlying backdrop for this approach focuses on the freezing of assets, concrete issues of proportionality, respect for the Roadmap for Strengthening Procedural Safeguards, and the Directive on Interpretation and Translation. The Directive on the right to access to a lawyer, and the directive on confiscation of the proceeds of crime have also great importance.[1]

International expansion of organized crime has mainly been directed towards all European Countries. We need to pay constant attention to all the various aspects inherent to a multi-dimensional perspective. This objective cannot be pursued abstractly, but focusing intently on each individual standard or institution, with full respect for human rights and for the trial guarantees of the suspected. For this reason, we should place EIO in a broader framework.

In this context, it is noteworthy that in September 2011 the European Commission emphasized that the criminal law of the European Union, flanked by principles of subsidiarity and proportionality, must be oriented towards maximum respect for human rights,[2] including interventions in organized crime.

A new Resolution[3] tries to combat organised crime, and to encourage Member States to strengthen their judicial authorities and police forces on the basis of the best experiential outcomes, including comparing the legislation and resources designed to support their activities, and to assign adequate human and financial resources to that purpose. It calls on the Member States to pursue a proactive approach to investigation, draw up national plans to fight organised crime, and provide for central coordination of activities through appropriate specific structures, taking their cue from the most successful experiences of some Member States. The Resolution of 25 October 2011 specifies that all measures to counter organised crime have to fully respect fundamental rights, and to be proportionate to the pursued objectives. The achievement of these objectives is of essential importance

---

[1] COM/2012/085 final—2012/0036 (COD) (12 March 2012). See Maugeri (2012), pp. 180ff.

[2] COM(2011) 573 final (20 September 2011).

[3] European Parliament Resolution (25 October 2011) on organized crime in the European Union (2010/2309 INI); Alfano and Varrica (2012), p. 4.

in a democratic society, in accordance with Article 52 EU FRCh, without unduly restricting the freedom of individuals, as enshrined in the ECHR, the EU FRCh, and the constitutional principles common to the Member States.

In short, Europe has suggested the following needs: a greater public awareness towards this type of phenomena[4]; the autonomous treatment of organized crime to terrorism; the offense of participation in a "criminal organization"; the provision of a crime of Mafia association with particular attention to the crimes in the environmental sector. Behind these indications, there is a widespread dissemination of criminological knowledge of organized crime in the European context, and of the economic interests of mobsters to such an extent that the future regulations will aim to prevent companies, linked to organized crime or "Mafia," to participate in public tenders or contracts.[5]

The repression of the authors is accompanied by "understanding" the damage suffered by the "victims" with a financial support for their business (paragraph 43), and with considerable interest to the witnesses and their families. This approach includes the creation of a European fund aimed at the protection and assistance of victims and witnesses of Justice (paragraph 12).

It is a more functionalist approach that aims at countering illegal wealth; the discovery and repression of these serious crimes is a clear goal of the European Union. The massacre of Duisburg, in 2007,[6] demonstrates the ability of "branching" of the 'Ndrangheta, and the need to conduct investigations in other European countries. The phenomenon of criminal globalization, inspired by the "lex maxima of profit."[7]

Since the expansion of organized crime has mainly been directed towards European countries, we have to pay attention to all the various aspects inherent to a multi-dimensional perspective.

---

[4] Institution of a special committee on the dissemination of criminal organisations which operate across borders, including mafias, one of whose aims will be to investigate the extent of the phenomenon and the negative social and economic impact it has throughout the EU, including the issue of the misappropriation of public funds by criminal organisations and mafias and their infiltration into the public sector; commission carefully to monitor the transposition by the Member States of the EU directive on the protection of the environment through criminal law, to ensure that it is done promptly and effectively; the establishment of an EU forum of associations of victims' families; eradicating entrenched mafia-style organised crime in the EU strengthen both the role of civil society and partnerships between civil society and the judicial system and the police.

[5] One Commission, in cooperation with Europol and Eurojust, conducted a study by June 2013 to assess the negative impact of transnational organised crime in the European Union; calls on Europol to draw upon a thematic OCTA on the threat posed by the presence of mafia-type criminal organisations in the EU by 2012 (point 16).

[6] On 15 August 2007, six men belonging to the 'Ndrangheta clan were shot dead in their cars near the train station of Duirsburg in western Germany. Italian court, July 2011, sentenced the ringleader of the massacre Giovanni Strangio and other seven people to life terms for their role in the violent mob feud that culminated in the Duirsburg slayings. It was important collaboration between the Italian and German authorities during the investigation.

[7] Pisani (1998), p. 703.

I therefore consider it necessary to include this proposal for a directive in line with the European criminal policies contrasting the organized crime, as I believe it is essential to track consistency (inconsistency?) with respect to such sources.

It is also interesting to validate the compatibility of the PD EIO with the powers of the European Public Prosecutor.[8] Article 86 TFEU needs a "codification" of a European criminal procedure. The regulations shall determine the

> general rules applicable to the European Public Prosecutor's Office, the conditions governing the performance of its functions, the rules of procedure applicable to its activities, as well as those governing the admissibility of evidence, and the rules applicable to the judicial review of procedural measures taken by it in the performance of its functions.[9]

It is, therefore, a regulatory approach that goes far beyond the realm of mere harmonization, since it is not limited to ensuring compatibility between heterogeneous acts, but it embodies the elaboration of common rules for investigative measures of the European Public Prosecutor available in all European countries.

PD EIO extends "horizontally." It can, in fact, be applied during the investigative stage of the case, and during trials and hearings. For this specific reason, it is necessary to assess its impact and compatibility within different criminal procedure models present in the EU. This implies the possibility for diverse regulatory strategies to manoeuvre with obvious respect for the underlying principles of the system, without altering the framework of the procedures. At its core, the flexibility of certain rights and certain guarantees has been justified in balancing conflicting calls for security and efficiency.[10]

Within this ideal frame, my analysis will focus on: data protection, most appropriate definition of "investigative measures," judicial control and legal remedies, grounds for refusal to execute, immunity, transfer of persons in custody, and finally, costs and resources.

2 EIO and Absence of Trust

The PD EIO represents a further bold departure from the norms of traditional, mutual legal assistance. It also goes further than the mutual recognition initiatives in existence.

The mutual recognition model in the criminal justice field has encountered problems. First of all total absence of trust. For example, the European Arrest

---

[8] See Allegrezza (2008), pp. 3882–3883; Balsamo and Recchione (2010), p. 3620.

[9] Ruggieri (2007), p. 551; Bargis (2004), p. 745; Lanzi et al. (2002), p. 3.

[10] Sayers (2011) p. 3: "unfortunately, the PD EIO appears to be a myopic measure lacking in foresight or perspective. In detaching itself from the lessons learnt from the mutual recognition journey to date, and by ignoring the move to strengthen procedural protections"; Daraio (2013), p. 579.

Warrant (EAW) and the mutual recognition instruments for freezing of evidence and assets, for confiscation orders, for financial penalties, and for evidence warrants, for custodial penalties, and for alternative sentences, as well as decisions on pre-trial bail demonstrate this situation. It is a schizophrenic situation: there is a great interest in requests for cooperation, because they guarantee independence of the countries; instead, when switching to the plane of harmonization, European states show a great "fear" of losing power and autonomy in these areas.

The creation of structures and devices with uniform legal rules is not easy.[11] The practice shows an intervention of EU law on the procedural level too narrow in the areas of the judicial cooperation and of the basic principle of mutual recognition. There are practical difficulties of investigative coordination and exchanges of acts contained in evidence. In absence of trust, it is very important to establish minimum procedural standards of individual protection,[12] save for the belated return to the procedural safeguards agenda with the Swedish Presidency's Roadmap published in 2009.[13] The Stockholm Programme confirmed its commitment to developing such standards.[14] The question is: has PD EIO produced real safeguards for these instances? A genuine area of mutual trust for such mechanisms of cooperation requires the understanding of the varied context in which such instruments will operate, and awareness that mutual legal-assistance protections exist for the main purpose to protect sovereignty and to regulate the effects of diversity among systems.

The Directive is suffering from an original defect. It focuses on research and training of evidence and disregards terms of admission (or exclusion) of the evidence gathered in the different European legal proceedings. Schemes usability evidence are often very different from each other. The proposal is not interested in following the logical procedural rules for the implementation of the measures and does not take into account the minimum characters that testing must possess in order to be usable and be able to move freely within Europe.[15]

3 Lights and Shadows of the Proposal

European bodies greeted positively[16] the simplification of the procedure using standard forms, which are valid at all stages of the proceedings. Similarly, it is worth emphasizing the enhancement of the principle of mutual recognition of

---

[11] Melillo (2006), p. 272, hops some type of vertical cooperation; Moscarini (2011), pp. 635ff.

[12] Sayers (2011), pp. 12ff.; Marchetti (2011), pp. 164–165.

[13] Council of the European Union, Resolution of 30 November 2009 on a Roadmap for strengthening procedural rights of suspected or accused persons in criminal proceedings, OJ C 295/1, 4.12.2009.

[14] During European Council, Stockholm Programme, Italian government officially suggested to introduce a true "principle of availability" of evidence open to procedural rights of the defense.

[15] Pisani (2011), p. 935.

[16] Eurojust opinion on EIO of 4 March 2011, pp. 1 f.

judicial decisions of the authorities of the Member States, in place of the "political" nature of the traditional request for assistance. Finally, it is praiseworthy that the shorter timeframes for the implementation of the measures allow significant acceleration of procedures. In my opinion, it is very important that the improvement of the Proposal will be in accordance to the EU FRCh and the constitutional principles of the individual Member States.

The right to a fair trial can include pre-trial measures, so that Article 6 protections should be factored into the PD EIO. This incorporates being notified of criminal charges, and having access to an interpreter free of charge in certain circumstances, with this respect explicit reference should be made to the Directive on Interpretation and Translation. The EU FRA has commented on the relevance and importance of such protections of the right to a fair trial and has also noted the need to ensure access to a lawyer, and if necessary, legal aid during an investigation. The PD EIO set out in the form provided for in Annex shall be translated by the competent authority of the issuing State into the official language or one of the official languages of the executing State.

The progress of the PD EIO should be tied to the development of the Roadmap; there should be specific protections in relation to video and telephone conferencing, including access to a lawyer, the recording of proceedings and the right to challenge the evidence and equivalent protections for the presumption of innocence.

In particular, the Italian legislation (Art. 147 and 147bis of the Rules Implementing the CCP) established the protection for witnesses, the presence of the lawyer, and the visibility of the person. In this direction, it is important to safeguard the rights that the hearings of witnesses, "crown witnesses," or other people benefiting from special protection measures. Picture or likeness image of themselves should not be shown during the trial.[17]

If witnesses or suspects are interviewed, they should be tape-recorded, have access to legal advice, and there should be provisions on the retention of this evidence.

Evidences gathered should be used for a defined purpose and should be subject to clear data protection and confidentiality protections.

I believe that the term "investigative measure" should be defined by reference to what it includes as well as what it excludes. It is inadmissible to use criminal investigative measures in administrative, civil, taxation and other cases. Criminal investigative measures can affect human rights to a large extent, businesses, and citizens legitimate interests, and therefore, they are appropriate only for most serious offences—crimes. These measures should be specifically limited to investigations with a cross-border element, with this term being clearly defined.[18]

---

[17] Amendment nr. 169 to Article 21 by Rosario Crocetta (AM Com Leg Report).

[18] The EU FRA confirms that data protection with unlimited discretion leads to legal uncertainty. Thus, it is essential that the term "investigative measure" be defined, because the purpose for using the data needs to be clearly stipulated to ensure it is being used appropriately. See Opinion of the European Union's Agency for Fundamental Rights on the draft Directive regarding the European Investigation Order, http://fra.europa.eu/fraWebsite/research/opinions/op-eio_en.htm.

However, the freezing of instruments and proceeds of crime seems to be excluded as, in accordance with Article 29(2), the Directive (only) applies among the Member States to the freezing of items of evidence in substitution to the corresponding provisions of Framework Decision 2003/577/JHA, on the execution in the European Union of orders freezing property or evidence. Whereas there may be a justification for excluding confiscation of assets from the purport of the Directive, the exclusion of the freezing of assets could entail negative consequences[19]: bank information (*e.g.*, information on the amount of money on a bank account) would be covered by the Directive. Freezing of the amount of money on that bank account would be exclusively covered by Framework Decision 2003/577/JHA. Hence, it would be necessary to issue two different forms (under two different legal regimes) to achieve the desired result. One could argue that this approach—in two steps—has the advantage of allowing the issuing authority to assess the material gathered before issuing a freezing order.

This method may not be appropriate in organized crime cases, where there is a high risk of dispersion of assets derived from crime. Furthermore, the issuing of a separate form—in addition to MLA request—to obtain the freezing of assets appears to be one of the reasons why practitioners show little interest in applying Framework Decision of orders freezing property or evidence.

Moreover, it might be difficult in practice, at least at the beginning of an investigation, to distinguish among evidence, instruments and proceeds of crime, as the same asset could be classed under all these heads. Thus, as far as freezing orders are concerned, the new instrument offers an opportunity to replace Framework Decision 2003/577/JHA and to set up a unique, coherent, and comprehensive legal regime in this field which would apply to both evidence and assets.

With respect to judicial control and legal remedies, the proportionality[20] test should be linked to what would be issued in the issuing state and not what could be issued. In the proposal the control of the proportionality requirement for the issuing and the executing state is in accordance in particular with Article 48 and 52 of the EU FRCh. Furthermore, where an executing authority has reasons to believe that the conditions in Article 5a(1) have not been met, it may consult the issuing authority if an explanation has not been given in the PD EIO. Following the consultation, the issuing authority may decide to withdraw the PD EIO or to maintain the PD EIO, which will then be executed according to this Directive.

Legal assistance, with legal aid where necessary in the interests of justice, should be available for challenges.

In my opinion legal remedies ensure an effective right by any interested party, but at the same time also ensure that they will not be used as purely a delaying mechanism, or as a way to hamper the effectiveness of the investigations that

---

[19] Eurojust Opinion on EIO, 4 March 2011, p. 6.

[20] Bachmaier Winter, Part III, Sect. 4, considers that the wording and systematic of the PD EIO can be further improved, especially with regard to the possible grounds of non-recognition and non-execution of the European Investigation Order.

justified the request. Legal remedies shall be available for the interested parties in accordance with national law. The substantive reasons for issuing the PD EIO can be challenged in an action brought before a court of the issuing or executing State.

The grounds for refusal to execute should be more clearly and consistently set out. It is not a simple reference to the invasive acts.

Many doubts are raised about the concept of immunity. In fact, there is no common definition of what constitutes an immunity or privilege in the European Union, and the precise definition of these terms is therefore left to national law, which may include protections for medical and legal professions, but should not be interpreted against the obligation to abolish certain grounds for refusal in Article 7 of the 2001 Protocol to the ECMACM between the Member States of the European Union. This may include as well, even though they are not necessarily considered as privilege or immunity, rules relating to freedom of the press and freedom of expression in other media.

Regarding the transfer of persons in custody, the term "custody" should better be defined. Prisoners in provisional detention generally have greater rights. There is a need to guarantee consistency of treatment from one country to another.

An absence of consent would not necessarily block a transfer, so explicit protections should be created and factored into refusal grounds, *e.g.* owing to proportionality, human rights grounds, or the protection of vulnerable suspects. On the one hand, this clause could in fact block the effectiveness, on the other hand it could seriously jeopardize the rights of the suspect.

Before executing the PD EIO, the person concerned shall be given the opportunity to state their opinion to the executing authority on the temporary transfer. Where the executing State considers it necessary, in view of the person's age or physical or mental conditions, he shall be given access to legal representation. The opinion of the person shall be taken into account when deciding to execute a PD EIO. I consider it necessary to reach a better definition of this point.

The proposal includes the possibility of interception. This choice will determine serious problems of jurisdiction[21] and probably engage Eurojust in the settlement of disputes between States. The invasive activity will have to take into account the discipline of the requested State.

It must also be considered the injury of privacy and freedom of communication and correspondence with the guarantees ready Article 8 ECHR, as interpreted by the ECtHR.[22]

Some problems arise in maintaining the position of undercover investigations (covert investigations) in the text of the Directive, in order to replicate the Convention on mutual assistance between the EU Member States of May 2000, which, however, dictated a discipline geared to cooperation between states and not based

---

[21] Ruggeri (2013), pp. 305–306.

[22] ECtHR, Decision of 7 June 2007, *Dupuis v Francia*, Application no. 1914/02, § 49; ECtHR, Decision of 17 July 2003, *Craxi v Italia*, Application no. 25337/94, §§ 80 f.

on the principle of mutual recognition of judicial decisions. In fact, this is a typical activity of police.

A comprehensive data protection directive is required, covering all aspects of criminal and police investigations.[23] The FRA confirms that data protection with unlimited discretion leads to legal uncertainty.[24] The Stockholm Programme referred to the protection of personal data as a "political priority." There is a need for specific work to set standards to be implemented. Personal data processed when implementing this Directive should be protected in accordance with Council Framework Decision 2008/977/JHA of 27 November 2008 on the protection of personal data processed in the framework of police and judicial cooperation in criminal matters, and with the principles laid down in the 1981 Council of Europe Convention for the Protection of Individuals with regard to Automatic Processing of Personal Data.

We need a balancing between two conflicting interests: the investigation on criminal offences and the protection of the individual. Clear commitment to protecting privacy rights should be articulated based on the requirements of the ECtHR case law. However, specific safeguards are required to protect professional or investigative secrecy.

Cost is a very complex issue. At present, the executing state will bear the cost of execution, save for explicit provisions that enable costs to be shared. This may invite overuse and abuse, as states may be less careful about applying for measures if there are no cost implications. Had better than all expenses arising from an investigation request, with a view of obtaining evidence, will be shared in equal parts between the issuing and the executing States, unless, in concrete cases, they have previously agreed on a different distribution of costs. In opinion of Eurojust,[25] the transfer to the issuing State of part or all the costs arising from the execution of the PD EIO should be limited to "extraordinary" costs, i.e., not those resulting from the execution of investigative measures that are usually requested (hearings, house searches, bank information, etc.).

Obtaining information from banks presents many critical aspects. Some amendments are required when an offence is punishable by a penalty involving deprivation of liberty, or a detention order of a maximum period of at least 2 years in the issuing State, or if the execution of such a measure would contravene the European Charter of Fundamental Rights or the constitutional principles of the executing State.[26]

---

[23] The recommendations of the EDPS should be adopted. These include guaranteeing the accuracy of evidence (*e.g.*, in relation to translations), the security of data and investigative security with electronic systems. The EDPS also recommends the creation of consistent professional standards and internal procedures to ensure the protection of individuals with regard to the processing of personal data and accountability systems. These recommendations require the application of adequate resources.

[24] See EU FRA Opinion, above, fn. 18.

[25] Eurojust Opinion on EIO, 4 March 2011, p. 12.

[26] *Amendment nr. 55 by Rosario Crocetta (Am Com Leg Report)*.

At the same time, many European countries have pointed out that limiting the requests for information from banks only against persons (legal or natural) subjected to a process or a criminal investigation is not convincing.[27] This choice, in fact, excludes the area—wide and relevant—of information on the ownership of reports when the coordinates are known but not the holders; prominent investigative reports entertained by people not investigated/charged; investigations to be carried out in proceedings against unknown persons.

The sector of economic activity is just that in which the Mafia shows its "criminal abilities."

4 Past and Future

The current slow pace in the final stages of approval of the Proposal for a Directive demonstrates how the extraordinary Potential of this tool are still important to many European countries. The fear of losing sovereignty and independence in criminal investigations is the background in which the instrument took its first steps.

European legislation will strike a fair balance between society's need for protection against crime and the interests of suspected and accused persons, a balance based on thorough investigation of facts and consideration of the views of all parts of the spectrum. Granted that such a proposal would not be enacted immediately or universally, and ought not to be enacted uniformly, they would nevertheless set workable standards for the police and afford useful guidelines for judges.

My final impression is that Europe is still looking for a balance between the fight against organized crime and respect for human rights. Acting as a guide in this complex situation is the requirement of the ECHR regarding the criminal trials. The manner in which they are applied in practice will determine whether or not the requirements of the ECHR are actually observed. Having regard to the way in which the ECtHR interprets and applies the ECHR in specific circumstances[28] may thus provide a useful guide when it comes to interpreting and applying the new Proposal. The relevance of the ECHR on criminal justice should not be overlooked since the rights and freedoms which it guarantees, and also sets limits on, is the main scope of criminal law and criminal procedure.

---

[27] Observations of Italian delegation about the Proposal 13.12.2011.

[28] For example, about confiscation, ECtHR, Decision of 10 Mai 2012, *Soc. Sud Fondi v Italy*, Application no. 75909/01, § 61 f., Italy has to restore the situation as a total elimination of the consequences of the measure.

References

Alfano A, Varrica A (eds) (2012) Per un contrasto europeo al crimine organizzato e alle mafie. La risoluzione del Parlamento Europeo e l'impegno dell'Unione Europea. Giuffrè, Milano

Allegrezza S (2008) L'armonizzazione della prova penale alla luce del Trattato di Lisbona. Cassazione penale 3882–3893

Balsamo A, Recchione S (2010) La costruzione di un modello europeo di prova dichiarativa: il "nuovo corso" della giurisprudenza e le prospettive aperte dal Trattato di Lisbona. Cassazione penale 3620–3639

Bargis M (2004) Il pubblico ministero nella prospettiva di un ordinamento europeo. Rivista italiana di diritto e procedura penale 745–788

Daraio G (2013) La circolazione della prova nello spazio giudiziario europeo. In: Kalb L (ed) Spazio europeo di giustizia e procedimento penale italiano. Giappichelli, Torino, 579–581

Lanzi A, Ruggieri F, Camaldo L (2002) Il pubblico ministero europeo. Cedam, Padova

Marchetti MR (2011) Dalla Convenzione di assistenza giudiziaria in materia penale dell'Unione europea al mandato europeo di ricerca delle prove e all'ordine europeo di indagine penale. In: Rafaraci T (ed) La cooperazione di polizia e giudiziaria in materia penale nell'Unione europea dopo il Trattato di Lisbona. Giuffrè, Milano, 135–167

Maugeri AM (2012) La proposta di direttiva UE in materia di congelamento e confisca dei proventi del reato: prime riflessioni. www.penalecontemporaneo.it. Accessed Aug 2013

Melillo G (2006) Il mutuo riconoscimento e la circolazione della prova. Cassazione penale 265–273

Moscarini P (2011) Eurojust e il pubblico ministero europeo: dal coordinamento investigativo alle investigazioni coordinate. Diritto penale e processo 635–641

Pisani M (1998) Criminalità organizzata e cooperazione internazionale. Rivista italiana di diritto e procedura penale 703–725

Pisani M (2011) Problemi di prova in materia di indagine penale. La proposta di direttiva sull'ordine di indagine europeo. Archivio penale 925–957

Ruggeri S (2013) Horizontal cooperation, obtaining evidence overseas and the respect for fundamental rights in the EU. From the European Commission's proposal to the proposal for a Directive on a European Investigation Order: towards a single tool of evidence gathering in the EU? In: Ruggeri S (ed) Transnational inquiries and the protection of fundamental rights in criminal proceedings, A study in memory of Vittorio Grevi and Giovanni Tranchina. Springer, Heidelberg, 279–310

Ruggieri F (2007) Il pubblico ministero europeo. In: Rafaraci T (ed) L'area di libertà, sicurezza e giustizia: alla ricerca di un equilibrio fra priorità repressive ed esigenze di garanzia. Giuffrè, Milano, 551–584

Sayers D (2011) The European Investigation Order travelling without a 'roadmap'. CEPS 1–27. http://ceps.eu. Accessed Aug 2013

European Investigation Orders and Non-repeatability of Evidence in Cross-Border Cases: The Italian Perspective

Diego Foti

Abstract The aim of the present study is to analyse how the regulation of the new European Investigation Order (EIO) may operate in the event of non-repeatability of evidence in cross-border cases. This issue will be analysed from the perspective of the impact of the proposed instrument on the defendants' right to confrontation and their right to a defence in criminal proceedings.

Keywords Criminal proceedings • European Investigation Order • Fundamental rights

Contents

1 Introduction 152
2 Italy as an Issuing State 152
   2.1 Orders Aiming at Executing an Investigative Measure 152
   2.2 Orders Aiming at Gathering of Evidence Already Carried
       Out by the Executing State 154
3 Italy as an Executing State 155
   3.1 Receipt of Order Aimed at Conducting an Investigative Non-repeatable Measure 155
   3.2 Order Addressed to the Italian Authority to Obtain Evidence Already Gathered . . 157
4 Conclusions 157
References 158

D. Foti (✉)
Department of Law, University of Messina, Piazza Pugliatti no. 1, Messina, Italy
e-mail: dfoti@unime.it

S. Ruggeri (ed.), *Transnational Evidence and Multicultural Inquiries in Europe*,
DOI 10.1007/978-3-319-02570-4_13, © Springer International Publishing Switzerland 2014

1 Introduction

The development of EU legislation in the field of obtaining evidence from other Member States has received a crucial boost through the initiative aimed at the adoption of a Directive of the European Parliament and of the Council regarding the introduction of a European Investigation Order (hereafter EIO).

The fundamental objective of the proposed instrument is to overcome the deficiencies and legal lacunas of the MLA system by facilitating the exchange of evidence between Member States for the purposes of criminal or administrative proceedings which potentially could require criminal investigations.

For this purpose, it is noteworthy that, by means of a European Investigation Order, it will be possible for EU Member States to obtain not only evidence already obtained in the pending procedure in the executing State, but also that used in the investigations in other Member States.[1]

This is a significant phase in view of the implementation of the Stockholm Programme, which, along the lines of Article 82(1)(a) TFEU, calls for a new approach aimed at introducing a comprehensive tool of gathering almost any type of evidence in the EU area.

The purpose of this study is to analyse how the new EIO could operate in the event of non-repeatability of either measure or requested evidence. The issue of non-repeatability of evidence is of particular delicacy under Italian procedural law as it constitutes the subject of specific regulations concerned with the admissibility at trial of the results of investigative measures conducted either in the pre-trial phases of the same proceedings or in different proceedings. For these reasons, I shall conduct my analysis from the viewpoint of Italian law with the aim of underlying the implications the new instrument may have for the Italian legal system. For this purpose I shall focus on some of the most relevant issues namely those relating to the protection of the right to confrontation and, more generally, the right to an effective defence.

2 Italy as an Issuing State

2.1 Orders Aiming at Executing an Investigative Measure

Here the problem arises in relation to the so-called "original non-repeatability of evidence," i.e. where there is certainty of the non-repeatability at the time when the

---

[1] The proposal of the Directive has been submitted to the European Union Council, in its first version, on June 3, 2010, Council of the European Union, Brussels, 29 April 2010, 9145/10, Interinstitutional File: 2010/0817 (COD), COPEN 115; CODEC 363; Eurojust 47; The European Investigation Order travelling without a 'roadmap'. CEPS 1–27; EJN 12. For a critical analysis of the Proposal, see Bachmaier Winter (2010), p. 580; Sayers (2011), pp. 1ff.; De Amicis (2010), pp. 1ff.; Pulito (2010), pp. 381ff.

investigative measure is carried out. If the measure at issue took place in Italy, it would be necessary to follow the procedures provided for by the Italian legal system for the protection of the right to a defence. These procedures entail a detailed system of warnings to the suspect and to his lawyer and their participation in the implementation of the measure at issue.[2]

On the basis of the aforementioned issue, one might wonder whether evidence can be obtained by means of the EIO pursuant to the formalities provided for by Article 360 of the Italian CCP on the so-called "*accertamento tecnico irripetibile.*" Of course this is just an example; such issues can arise in relation to a large number of measures under the Italian CCP, taking into consideration the complex nature of the preliminary investigations under Italian law and the admissibility of their results in the trial phase.[3]

In this regard, it is noteworthy that Article 8(2) PD EIO provides that the executing Authority shall follow the procedures and formalities expressly indicated by the ordering Authority. Moreover, paragraph 3 of the same Article allows the issuing State to indicate one or more "authorities" to assist at the execution of the EIO by supporting the competent authority of the executing State. This provision does not, however, mention any form of participation by private parties and their defence.

Although this argument may seem to lead to a negative answer, it seems appropriate to choose an interpretation that may be more in line both with the principles of the EU FRCh, as required by the same PD EIO [Art. 1(3)], and the fundamental principles of the Italian Constitution. In light of this, it seems to me that the Prosecutor, where it needs an investigation entailing the participation of the defence also because of the non-repeatability of the same measure, requires foreign authorities to fulfil specific formalities, which include, *e.g.*, appropriate notice to the concerned parties and their lawyers in order to allow for the measure being carried out with the participation of such subjects.

Otherwise, the application of the new rules of the proposed Directive would result in an infringement of the principles laid down in Articles 24 and 111 of the Italian Constitution. Along with the respect for criminal defence rights, further-more, the fundamental principle of equal treatment would be disregarded since defendants' rights would have different protection depending on whether the measure is carried out by national authorities in the context of domestic procedures or by the Italian authority in response to an order of investigation issued by a foreign authority.[4]

Such a solution would still allow for the achievement of the main objective of the proposed Directive, namely obtaining evidence to be used in an ongoing procedure

---

[2] Giostra (2001), p. 4; Tonini (2000), p. 1338; Ubertis (2003), p. 2096.

[3] Lozzi (2012), p. 358.

[4] On the need to avoid discrimination on the basis of national or international character of the criminal investigation, see Vogler, "The European Investigation Order: Fundamental Rights at Risk?", Part II.

in the issuing State.[5] This result would be frustrated if respect for the fundamental principles of domestic law led to inadmissibility of the evidence taken overseas.[6]

2.2   Orders Aiming at Gathering of Evidence Already Carried Out by the Executing State

In relation to the case in which the EIO aims to obtain a piece of evidence already gathered abroad, the Italian legal system has severe legal lacunas as there is no instrument specifically aimed at achieving this result. To be sure, movement of evidence in such cases is particularly problematic even within the confines of national procedures, especially in relation to cases of non-repeatability of an item of evidence requested for the purposes of other proceedings.

The only means of doing so is provided by Article 238 of the Italian CCP. However, this proves problematic due to a complex and unsatisfactory regulation. Thus, paragraph 3 of the afore-mentioned Article allows for

obtaining the documentation of measures that are not repeatable. If the measure has become unrepeatable due to unexpected facts or circumstances, evidence may be collected only in the case of unforeseeable facts or circumstances.

Such provision entails serious difficulties with regard to both the movement and the collection of evidence within national proceedings,[7] due to the complexity of the assessment of the non-foreseeability of the non-repeatable investigation, an assessment that is closely tied to the so-called "*incidente probatorio*," a procedure aimed at obtaining evidence in the pre-trial stages.[8] Due to the link with this national procedure, this assessment would, of course, be extremely difficult, if not impossible, in relation to evidence gathered by non-repeatable means in other countries, since many criminal justice systems do not provide for similar procedures.

To be sure, a specific rule concerned with transnational procedures is contained in Article 78 of the Rules Implementing the CCP, which deals with the gathering of evidence in the possession of foreign authorities. In this context, paragraph 2 of this

---

[5] Obtaining evidence for the its use at trial is the key objective of the proposed Directive in accordance with the Stockholm Programme, which, in paragraph 3.1.1, calls for the formation of "a comprehensive system for obtaining evidence in cases with a cross-border dimension, based on the principle of mutual recognition." The Stockholm Programme—An open and secure Europe serving and protecting citizens (2010/C 115/01).

[6] On the influence of the European law in the light of the case law of the European Courts on the Constitution in the field of judicial cooperation, see Pollicino and Rando (2013), §§ 4–5.

[7] Rombi (2001), p. 363.

[8] On the practical application of Article 238(3) CCP cf., among others, Cass. pen, Sez. VI, 11 July 2002, No. 30797; Cass. pen, Sez. I., 20 June 2006, No. 23571; Cass. pen., Sez. VI, 13 October 2005, No. 41186.

Article deals with the collection of evidence gathered abroad through non-repeatable investigative measures of the police, which may be obtained and admitted into the trial file only with the consent of the parties, or after the testimonial examination of the author of the activity itself, also by means of letters rogatory.[9] However, due to its limited scope of application, which relates only to police investigations, this provision does not seem to provide a comprehensive solution to the problem of obtaining the results of non-repeatable investigative activities carried out overseas.

On the other hand, the regulation provided for in the text of the PD EIO agreed in the Council in December 2011 is certainly incomplete in this regard.[10] Whereas Article 10(1) provides for general grounds for refusal of the execution of the order, paragraph 1a of the same Article contains a list of investigative activities to which such ground apply. Amongst these cases, we should mention the case of information or evidence already held by the executing authority under the condition that it might be obtained if it had been in compliance with the law of the executing State. In such case, there is no reference to whether these pieces of evidence are the result of coercive measures or not, nor to whether they are the result of repeatable or non-repeatable activities. Nor can the executing authority have recourse in these cases to another investigative measure pursuant to Article 9 PD EIO due paragraph 1a. Even admitting that the evidence already held by the foreign Authority has been obtained in compliance with the law of the executing State, the problem arises in the event of subsequent non-repeatability of the investigative means.

In summary, both Italian procedural law and the proposed EIO Directive fail to draw due attention to individual guarantees in the case of evidence already gathered in other Member States through non-repeatable investigative activities.

3 Italy as an Executing State

3.1 Receipt of Order Aimed at Conducting an Investigative Non-repeatable Measure

In this case, the problem is characterized by a different logic than those examined until now, given that the issuing State will have to establish the terms of the investigation order according to the needs it aims to satisfy.

To start with, we should consider the eventuality of the EIO aiming at a non-repeatable investigative activity being carried out in the framework of

---

[9] For the evaluation of the application of Art. 78, implementing provisions CCP, see Calvanese (2003); Cantone (2013), p. 624.

[10] A general agreement was reached in the Council on 21 December 2011. Council of the European Union, Brussels 21 December 2011 18918/11. Interinstitutional File 2010/0817. COPEN 369, 217 Eurojust; EJN 185 CODEC 2509.

administrative proceedings. The case is relevant from Italian viewpoint, since Italian law requires the fulfilment of the formalities of criminal procedural law once administrative investigations lead to a suspicion of guilt.[11] A problematic case dealt with by the Rules Implementing the Italian CPP relates to the so-called "*attività ispettive e di vigilanza*" in the context of which suspicion of guilt arises, as well as in the case of analysis of samples (*analisi di campioni*), whenever no review is legally admitted. In such cases, evidence can be admitted into the trial file due to the non-repeatability of the investigation on condition that the rules of the CCP have been applied and there have been the required warnings aimed at protecting the concerned parties' right to a defence of.[12]

Thus, it can happen that, in the framework of an investigation requested on the basis of an EIO, the investigative authority needs to carry out such an activity. In this case, the question arises as to whether the guarantees provided by the Italian code must be applied, regardless of whether the issuing authority has requested it.

In order to properly answer this question, we should start with some preliminary considerations. The main aim of the EIO is to enhance judicial cooperation among States through a new way of providing mutual recognition in the field of transborder investigations. Moreover, it is noteworthy that, where the requested formalities entail the risk of infringement of fundamental rights under the law of the executing State, the executing authority will be entitled to refuse the execution. As has been noted, the same applies where the investigation entails in itself a violation of the fundamental rights of the law of the executing State, although amongst the grounds for refusal there is none specifically corresponding to the general provision of Article 1(3).

In light of this, one might wonder whether the executing State should carry out the EIO at all, or is entitled either to reject it or to carry it out in accordance with its law. From the viewpoint of Italian law, the national authority would have to face the alternatives either of acting in accordance with the formalities requested through the EIO or of complying with the procedures set out under Article 223 of the Rules Implementing the CCP.

Doubtless, the need to grant the people involved in such investigations their defence guarantees following the emergence of a suspicion of guilt, as well as the need to ensure the their participation in activities of a certainly non-repeatable nature, can be deemed as expressions of fundamental principles of the Italian legal system, i.e., the right to an effective defence and the so-called "*principio del contraddittorio nella formazione della prova*," enshrined respectively in Articles 24 and 111(4) of the Italian Constitution.

In the light of this, the authority of the executing State should thus be entitled to refuse the execution of the investigation order or to execute it according to its fundamental principles.

---

[11] Art. 220 of the Rules Implementing the Italian CCP.

[12] Ubertis (1992), p. 428. On the subject, see also Court of Cassation, Section III, Decision of 9 July 2002, No. 38857.

3.2 Order Addressed to the Italian Authority to Obtain Evidence Already Gathered

This last case may seem to be the least problematic. As noted above, it is possible for the executing authority to refuse the recognition of the EIO only when a fundamental principle of the national legal system has been violated. This event seems, however, to be unlikely to happen as the request aims here at obtaining a piece of evidence already collected through an investigation carried out according to the rules of the procedural code of the executing State. In this case, the issue of admissibility of evidence will have to be assessed only in the issuing State according to the limitations laid down by its law.

Although this solution is in line with a typical division of labour logic, it does not seem to take fully into account the need to consider the individual as a subject of international judicial cooperation in criminal matters.[13] A useful solution might be, in my view, to introduce into in the draft proposal an additional ground for refusal where, regardless of the lawfulness of the collection of evidence in the executing State, the executing authority considers that the movement of evidence would manifestly entail the risk of violation of the fundamental principles of the law of the issuing State. As an example, we could consider the case of evidence gathered in the State A in the context of administrative proceedings in compliance with its national administrative law but in respect of which it is known that the State B requests that evidence to use it in a criminal process, thus leading to a breach of the fundamental principles of its own law.

4 Conclusions

This study has analysed some of the questions concerned with the collection of evidence through non-repeatable investigative means, by focusing on the main practical and theoretical problems related to this complex topic.

Doubtless, the need to respect the fundamental rights not only of the accused in national criminal proceedings but also of all the individuals involved in transnational criminal procedures calls for more decisive action by European law to enhance international cooperation without lowering the standards of protection of the most vulnerable people in respect of domestic procedures.

---

[13] On the need for protection of the individual as a subject of international cooperation, see Eser et al. (2002).

References

Bachmaier Winter L (2010) European Investigation Order for obtaining evidence in the criminal proceedings. Study of the proposal of a European directive. Zeitschrift für die internationale Strafrechtsdogmatik 9:580–589

Calvanese E (2003) La cooperazione giudiziaria in material di sequestro (Nota a Cass. sez. unite 16 aprile 2003, n. 21420). Cassazione Penale:3894–3900

Cantone R (2013) Sub art. 238 disp. att. c.p.p. In: Lattanzi G, Lupo E (eds) Codice di procedura penale, Rassegna di giurisprudenza e di dottrina, 3rd vol. Giuffrè, Milano, pp 609–625

De Amicis G (2010) L'ordine europeo di indagine penale. www.europeanrights.eu

Eser A, Lagodny O, Blackesley C (2002) The individual as subject of international cooperation in criminal matters. Nomos, Baden-Baden

Giostra G (2001) Contraddittorio (principio del) (dir. proc. pen.). Enciclopedia giuridica Treccani, Agg. X

Lozzi L (2012) Lezioni di procedura penale. Giappichelli, Torino

Pollicino O, Rando G (2013) Judicial cooperation and multilevel protection of the right to liberty and security in criminal proceedings. The influence of European Courts' case-law on the modern Constitutionalism in Europe. In: Ruggeri S (ed) Transnational inquiries and the protection of fundamental rights in criminal proceedings, A study in memory of Vittorio Grevi and Giovanni Tranchina. Springer, Heidelberg, pp 85–110

Pulito L (2010) La circolazione della prova penale in Europa dopo il Trattato di Lisbona. Giustizia penale I:381–388

Rombi N (2001) Circolazione probatoria e diritto al contraddittorio. In: Tonini P (ed) Giusto Processo. Nuove norme sulla formazione e valutazione della prova. Cedam, Padova

Sayers D (2011) The European Investigation Order travelling without a 'roadmap'. CEPS 1–27. http://ceps.eu. Accessed Aug 2013

Tonini P (2000) Il contraddittorio: diritto individuale e metodo di accertamento. Diritto penale e processo 1388–1399

Ubertis G (1992) L'utilizzazione dibattimentale di prelievi ed analisi di campioni. Cassazione penale 428–457

Ubertis G (2003) Giusto processo e contraddittorio in ambito penale. Cassazione penale 2096–2103

Part IV
Cross-Border Criminal Inquiries in Europe: Solution Models and Human Rights Challenges

Solution Models and Principles Governing the Transnational Evidence-Gathering in the EU

Bernd Schünemann

Abstract It is undeniable that there is a need for effective transnational criminal proceedings including the possibility of gathering evidence abroad and using it before domestic courts. However, transnational proceedings pose specific threats to defence rights, which must be addressed in the relevant instruments. This article discusses several solution models and whether they can secure the principles allowing for a fair trial and maintain the balance between prosecution and individual rights. The traditional mutual legal assistance treaties focus on the States' interest in effective cooperation, and the new mutual recognition approach in the EU provides for an even closer collaboration between State authorities. Neither model solves the specific issues of defence rights in cross-border cases. The alternative model of transnational procedural unity allows for effective transnational proceedings while securing defence rights on an institutional level.

Keywords Criminal procedure • Defence rights • Double criminality • Effective criminal investigation • Evidence • Fair trial • International cooperation • Mutual recognition

Contents

1 Governing Principles 162
    1.1 Effective Criminal Investigation and Prosecution 162
    1.2 Fair Trial/Defendant's Rights 163
    1.3 Double Criminality 165
    1.4 Legitimate Grounds for Jurisdiction 166
2 Traditional Mutual Legal Assistance (MLA): Requests Between Sovereign States 166
3 Federalist Models 167
4 Mutual Recognition 168

B. Schünemann (✉)
Juristische Fakultät, Ludwig-Maximilians-Universität München, Prof.-Huber-Platz Nr. 2, Munich, Germany
e-mail: bernd.schuenemann@jura.uni-muenchen.de

S. Ruggeri (ed.), *Transnational Evidence and Multicultural Inquiries in Europe*,   161
DOI 10.1007/978-3-319-02570-4_14, © Springer International Publishing Switzerland 2014

5   The Principle of Transnational Procedural Unity 173
6   Conclusion 177
References 177

1   Governing Principles

1.1   *Effective Criminal Investigation and Prosecution*

Any transnational gathering of evidence follows the need for effective criminal investigation and prosecution. Obviously, criminals may act abroad or flee from criminal proceedings. This is, as has often been emphasized,[1] particularly true in the EU since border controls have been abolished at least in the Schengen area.[2] In short, it has been acknowledged that facing transnational crime, criminal justice cannot be strictly confined to national territories.

1.1.1   Possibility of Evidence-Gathering Abroad

In particular, potential evidence may lie in foreign countries. Be it that the murder suspect has fled the country with the weapon, that a witness lives abroad, or that a wiretap in another State may provide crucial information: it is almost self-evident that criminal justice authorities need to access evidence that lies in foreign countries.

1.1.2   Admissibility of Such Evidence Before Domestic Courts

But, more crucially, any piece of evidence must be fit to be used in the criminal proceedings. Generally, evidence must be gathered in a certain way, following legal rules, for it to be admissible during a trial. This requirement follows directly from the rule of law principle. Since the procedural rules and, in particular, the rules on evidence, vary considerably from one State to another, difficulties necessarily arise when evidence is gathered under another procedural law. This issue is often dealt

---

[1] Böse (2003), pp. 233, 237; Harms and Knauss (2011), pp. 1479, 1488; Heard and Mansell (2011), p. 353; Heger (2007), pp. 547–549; Satzger (2012), § 8 para. 23; Schünemann (2006a), pp. 344, 360.

[2] Agreement of 14 June 1985 between the Governments of the States of the Benelux Economic Union, the Federal Republic of Germany and the French Republic on the gradual abolition of checks at their common borders (printed in the EU OJ L 239/2000, pp. 13–18), implemented in 1995 and incorporated into EU law (with an opt-out for the UK and Ireland) by the Amsterdam treaty signed on 2 October 1997.

with in a pragmatic way. For example, the German Federal Court considers that "foreign" evidence may be admissible in German proceedings even if it has been gathered in accordance with foreign rather than German procedural law; as a compensation, the judge shall consider this fact when appreciating the evidence and, where necessary, give lesser credit to such "tainted" evidence.[3]

But another approach is imaginable: instead of gathering evidence according to the law of the State where it lies (*locus regit actum* principle), it can be done following the law of the State that runs the proceedings (*forum regit actum* principle).[4] This way, the admissibility problem would disappear. Such a solution is envisaged in various legal instruments on mutual legal assistance.[5]

1.2 Fair Trial/Defendant's Rights

Until now, I have only addressed the needs of criminal proceedings from the perspective of the judicial authorities. As it is generally admitted—at least in theory—the defendant's right to a fair trial is applicable, regardless of whether evidence is collected in the prosecuting State or abroad.[6] In practice, however, this proves to be the issue most difficult to address. I will mention the core principles that can be inferred from the fair trial principle for the trans-national gathering of evidence, and base myself on the assumption that the right to a fair trial cannot be denied or even truncated just because proceedings have a trans-national dimension.

Fundamentally, any national criminal procedure law provides for a comprehensive and coherent set of rules that balances the interests of effective prosecution and the safeguarding of the defendant's rights. But when cases become trans-national and actors from different countries apply (and combine) specific rules from different legal orders, it is a challenge for the actors involved—legislators, courts, other authorities—to ensure that the trial, as a whole, fulfils the requirements of a fair trial.

---

[3] BGHSt 2, 300, 304; OLG Hamm DAR 1959, 192, 193; for critique see Sommer (2003), pp. 351 et seqq.; Gleß (2003), pp. 131 et seqq.; see also Roxin and Schünemann (2011), § 24 para. 39, § 46 para. 34.

[4] Gleß (2006), pp. 106 et seqq.; 416; Gleß (2004), pp. 679, 683; Gleß (2008), p. 917; see also the proposed Article 4 of the Programme on European Criminal Justice, pp. 263, 269 and Schünemann (2006a), p. 359; Resolution D 2 of the Preparatory Colloquium (Section IV) of the XVI Congress of the *Association Internationale de Droit Pénal*, cited by Vogel (1998), pp. 974, 983.

[5] See for example Art. 4(1) EUCMACM of 29 May 2000 (OJ C 197/1) and, in civil matters, EU Regulation 1206/2001 (OJ L 174/1).

[6] See Schomburg et al. (2012), para. 112 et seqq.; Gaede (2003), pp. 845–874; ICTR, Judgment Kajelijeli v. The Prosecutor, judgment of 23 May 2005, ICTR-98-44A-A para. 220; ECHR, Judgment Stojkovic v. France and Belgium (App. No. 25303/08).

1.2.1 Legal Remedies

The right to an effective remedy (as Article 13 ECHR puts it) is a fundamental aspect of the rule of law. Any individual whose rights are violated must be able to assert this violation before a "national authority." To be more precise, this right must be given to anyone whose rights *could* be violated, and the "authority" in question will generally have to be a court.[7] This seems easy in principle, but raises some delicate questions when measures are ordered by one State, but executed by another State and, again, have effects in the ordering State, namely when evidence is collected abroad to be used in criminal proceedings. In such a case, where the authorities of (at least) two States share the responsibility for invasive measures, it may become unclear before which courts these measures should be challenged.

Often, as we will see, remedies will be split between the courts of the States involved, depending on whether they pertain to the substantive reasons of the measure or the way it is carried out. Such a solution is inacceptable from the point of view of the right to an "effective remedy", for a number of reasons: first, it puts upon the defendant the burden of determining the competent court and finding legal advice in a foreign country. Second, such a splitting jeopardizes the comprehensive appreciation of the measure by the judge, since he is not allowed to scrutinize it as a whole. Third, since the procedural laws vary considerably between States, remedies may apply at different stages of proceedings. Therefore, it could happen that a remedy against the substantive reasons for a measure is inadmissible both in the executing State and, at the same time, in the requesting State, if this State's procedural law provides for remedies at later stages of proceedings only.

1.2.2 Ability to Challenge Evidence

Concerning evidence in particular, it is a fundamental right of the defendant to challenge it before the judging court. In the context of trans-national evidence gathering and shared responsibility for the related measures, two main issues must be addressed: first, the material criteria that determine whether evidence is admissible—should they be drawn from the law of the sentencing State or from the law of the State that collected the evidence? Or should there be a specific set of rules for "trans-national evidence?"

Second, the mere geographical distance between the place of the trial and the place where evidence is collected may prevent the defendant from challenging it. For example, a defendant in pre-trial custody facing the statements of witnesses gathered in a foreign State is unable, at the stage of the trial, to confront these witnesses.

---

[7] In the case of non-judicial authorities, the "effectiveness" of remedies questionable, see Grote and Marauhn (2006), Kap. 20 margin No. 56; ECHR, judgment Silver et al., A 61, para. 113 (b).

At any rate, the right to challenge evidence is a crucial piece of the "equality of arms" between the prosecution and the defence and must be secured in all criminal proceedings.

1.3 Double Criminality

Another traditional cornerstone of trans-national criminal proceedings is the double criminality principle. It has been, historically, linked to State sovereignty,[8] and therefore some authors consider it to become increasingly obsolete in an "ever-closer Union."[9] But on the contrary, we have to revisit it from a modern perspective, taking fully into account individual rights. From this point of view, the principle *nulla poena sine lege* must be respected in trans-national proceedings. It requires that nobody be punished for an act that was not clearly established as a criminal offence prior to the act. While it can hardly be denied that the execution of a foreign sentence is a "punishment" and therefore demands double criminality,[10] it is controversial whether this applies to other acts of legal assistance as well, especially the gathering of evidence. Coercive measures like arrest warrants have traditionally been subject to a double criminality requirement,[11] while plain measures of evidence gathering sometimes haven't.[12] I don't have time to address the issue thoroughly at this point, but would like to stress out that such measures are, by definition, carried out for the purpose of criminal proceedings, which therefore constitute the only possible justification for these measures.

From this point of view, it would be contradictory for a State to deem an act not punishable while at the same time contributing to its punishment. Therefore, at least where the offense is strongly linked to the requested State, the requirement of double criminality must also apply to evidence gathering measures. In order not to

---

[8] Via the principle of reciprocity between sovereign States, see Schomburg et al. (2012), § 2 IRG para. 2; Grützner (1969), pp. 119–124; Böse (2012), § 81 para. 13; Vogel (2001b), Vor § 1 para. 74; Wilkitzki (1991), Vor § 59 para. 7. Others consider it merely as a means to avoid conflicts between States, see Vogel and Burchard (2009), § 3 para. 20; Jescheck (1969), pp. 73–80; see also the judgment of the High Court of Australia of 27 November 1985, Riley v. The Commonwealth, 159 CLR 1.

[9] Schomburg et al. (2012); Böse (2003), *loc. cit.*; Ligeti (2005), p. 95; Schomburg (1995), pp. 1931, 1934 fn. 38; Vogel (2001a, b), pp. 937–942; Andreou (2009), pp. 57–181; Mavany (2012), p. 120.

[10] See Schünemann and Roger (2010), pp. 515, 520 et seqq., reply by Böse (2010a), pp. 607, 609 et seqq., response by Schünemann (2010), pp. 735, 739 et seqq.; Satzger (2006), pp. 395, 407.

[11] See Art. 2(1) of the 1957 European Convention on Extradition; Art. 3(1)(e) of the 1983 Convention on the Transfer of sentenced Persons; Art. 2(1) of the 1978 Extradition Treaty Germany–USA.

[12] See Art. 59 et seqq. of the German Act on International Cooperation in Criminal Matters: Art. 66 (2)(1) contains a double criminality requirement only for the handing over of objects; Art. 2 of the 1959 European Convention on Mutual Assistance in Criminal Matters contains no double criminality requirement, while Art. 1(4) of the 2003 MLA Treaty Germany–USA explicitly waives it.

foster exorbitant criminal jurisdiction by foreign States, the same should apply when the act is not or only weakly linked to the requesting State.[13]

1.4 Legitimate Grounds for Jurisdiction

In principle, the aforementioned issue of extensive criminal jurisdiction must be addressed at a prior stage, when it comes to determining whether a State is entitled at all to investigate on a certain behaviour that *could* turn out to be a criminal offence. But since that would require a stringent legal instrument missing in the EU, the requirement of legitimate jurisdiction needs to be acknowledged at least as an underlying principle of, and an imminent bar to mutual legal assistance.

2 Traditional Mutual Legal Assistance (MLA): Requests Between Sovereign States

I will now address the most relevant solution models in theory and practice.

1. Historically, the need for effective criminal prosecution in trans-national cases has long been addressed by what we call, in general terms, mutual legal assistance. In this model, sovereign States grant each other assistance on terms they set forth at their discretion, without interfering with each other's proceedings.[14] From this follow two main aspects of the MLA model: the considerable leeway for both States involved, and the lack of consideration for the individual targeted by legal assistance measures.
2. Technically, the rules for legal assistance may be enshrined in national law or, more frequently, in bi- or multilateral treaties between States. For the specific area of the European Union (and beyond), we can mention the 1959 ECMACM and the 2000 EUCMACM that have been ratified by (almost) all Member States.[15]

---

[13] Therefore, this criterion, used in a disputable way in the Federal Constitutional Court's decision on the European Arrest Warrant (of 18 July 2005, English version available at http://www.bundesverfassungsgericht.de/entscheidungen/rs20050718_2bvr223604en.html, para. 86; for critique see Schünemann 2005, pp. 681 et seq.), could be relevant in the field of "plain" or "small" mutual legal assistance, i.e. the collection and exchange of evidence.

[14] Andreou (2009), p. 43; Braum (2005), pp. 681, 683 et seqq.; Lagodny (1987), pp. 27 et seqq., 55 et seqq., *passim*; for remainders of the State-oriented approach with little consideration for individual rights see the comparative findings in Eser et al. (2002).

[15] European Convention on Mutual Assistance in Criminal Matters of 20 April 1959, CETS/SEV No. 30; Convention of 29 May 2000 Established by the Council in Accordance with Article 34 of the Treaty on European Union, on Mutual Assistance in Criminal Matters between the Member States of the European Union, EU OJ C 197/1.

As I said, the traditional MLA model leaves the involved States the greatest leeway: each State is sovereign in the design of its MLA rules, and may or may not commit itself in international conventions; even then, such agreements are binding only under international law, not in the national legal order. The same goes for the application of MLA rules in a specific case: the State in which the proceedings take place may request and, subsequently, use evidence more or less at its discretion; the requested State gathers information following its own rules (*locus regit actum* principle) and, even where it is bound by a treaty, has extensive and widely discretionary grounds for refusal.

3. Of course, the international conventions have gradually narrowed down the involved State's discretionary powers. But basically, being historically rooted in an era prior to strict individual rights considerations, the MLA model does not consider the individual as a subject, but merely as the object of the cooperation between sovereign States. Hence the extensive grounds upon which a State may refuse cooperation do not necessarily have a subjective counterpart that would benefit the individual. This is what *Lagodny* has dubbed the "2-dimensional model."[16] Meanwhile, legal reasoning has brought forward the "3-dimensional model" that considers the individual as a fully-fledged party in MLA proceedings and stresses out his subjective rights. However, MLA still remains deficient on the aspects of the fair trial principle I mentioned earlier. In particular, it does not provide for a balance in the process of gathering evidence as well as in the use of such evidence during a trial. Although recent conventions have achieved some progress—for instance, the 2000 EU convention provides at least for an optional *forum regit actum* rule[17]—they still do not solve the fundamental issues. The crucial problem of the admissibility of evidence is left to the States to regulate, so that German courts for example can follow the "pragmatic" approach ("*Beweiswürdigungslösung*") I have mentioned above. This means that evidence gathered in accordance with the law of the requested State, but not with German procedural law, may be used in a German trial, although nothing ensures that such proceedings would fulfil the requirements of a fair trial.

3 Federalist Models

On the contrary, there are federalist models according to which one State can simply exercise its power on another State's territory but is permanently bound to its own safeguards. Among European countries, the former Swiss system can be considered a characteristic example.

While they are all bound by the same Federal constitution, each canton (State) had created its own peculiar law on criminal procedure, while there was a federal

---

[16] Lagodny (1987), pp. 27 et seqq., 55 et seqq.; Schomburg et al. (2012), para. 2, 98 et seqq.; See also Murschetz (2007), pp. 312 et seqq.

[17] Art. 4(1).

law only applying to some specific cases. Although this model has to date become obsolete,[18] I will describe its characteristics[19] as a promising model for judicial cooperation between EU member states while prosecuting abroad but applying their own law.

First, there was a detailed set of federal rules that determine which canton has jurisdiction over a specific case. These rules basically followed the territoriality principle, but there were very differentiated rules for cases that were linked to more than one canton. Nevertheless, the authorities involved might also agree on a different attribution of jurisdiction, and the person concerned could not invoke a right to be tried by the court determined following the legal criteria.

Once jurisdiction had been attributed, the competent authorities of one canton were entitled to execute investigative measures and gather evidence on the territory of another canton, under their domestic law (*forum regit actum* rule). This was, in principle, a straightforward way to ensure that the proceedings were governed by one single, coherent set of rules and should provide for a fair trial. But, notably, the competent authorities might also request the authorities of another canton to gather evidence, following the traditional MLA model mentioned above. In this case, the law of the executing canton was applied (*locus regit actum* principle), and the flaws of MLA recurred. Even worse, the choice between the two options was a discretionary one for the competent authority, so that the menace of *forum shopping* arose: the authorities might choose one option over the other purposefully to circumvent the rights of the individual concerned.

Thus, although the federalist model has decisive advantages, it requires not only some legal unity (as provided by a federal constitution), but also specific and stringent rules which, in the case of Switzerland, were devaluated by the discretionary powers given to the authorities.

4   Mutual Recognition

The mutual recognition (MR) model invented by EU authorities (now enshrined in Article 82 TFUE) can be described as a step toward automatic trans-national execution of evidence requests, but without a common constitution or stringent rules on such a "trans-national procedure."

1. This principle has been derived from the concept of common market.[20] There it states that a commodity that has been put into circulation in one member state

---

[18] The new (single) Swiss Criminal Procedure Code (*Schweizerische Strafprozessordnung*) of 5 October 2007 (Bundesblatt [BBl.] 2006 1085) came into force on 1 January 2011 (Bundesratsbeschluss of 31 March 2010).

[19] See Gleß (2001), pp. 419 et seqq.; Wohlers (2004), pp. 51 et seqq.

[20] Where it has been established by the Court of Justice's case law, see the judgments *Dassonville* (8/74) and *Cassis de Dijon* (120/78) and the following Commission white paper, COM (85) 310

can also be imported and sold in other member states. Applied to the field of criminal justice, the principle of mutual recognition turns from liberal to author- itarian effects and leads to the consequence that the criminal law system of one member state can be executed in all other member states. So it tends to enable the most punitive criminal law system to be executed in all of Europe,[21] which is an apparent contradiction to the last resort principle.[22] The crucial and most radical legal product of mutual recognition has been established by the European Arrest Warrant that compels member states to extradite even their own citizens irrespective of double criminality and without any serious judicial control.[23]

2. Similarly to a federalist model, mutual recognition follows a top-down approach, meaning it is established on a superior level—in this case, at the supranational level of the European Union. However, the Framework Decisions (FD) that have been adopted before the treaty of Lisbon must be examined critically. They are considered binding for the Member States,[24] although they have been adopted only by government representatives in the Council and therefore, *stricto sensu*, do not belong to the supranational *acquis*. And from a substantive point of view, precisely because they constitute inter-governmental agreements, it is questionable whether they can bind national legislators. From the perspective of German constitutional law, the Federal Constitutional Court has ruled that

[d]ue to the fact that democratic self-determination is affected in an especially sensitive manner by provisions of criminal law and criminal procedure, the corresponding basic powers in the treaties must be interpreted strictly – on no account extensively -, and their use requires particular justification.[25]

Technically, this entails that

[f]rom the perspective of German constitutional law, the necessary degree of democratic legitimation via the national parliaments can only be guaranteed by the German

---

final, p. 18. It has been proclaimed "cornerstone of judicial cooperation" at the Tampere European Council in 1999, see the Programme of measures to implement the principle of mutual recognition of decisions in criminal matters of 15 January 2001, OJ C 12/10.

[21] For details see Schünemann (2003a), pp. 185, 187; Schünemann (2003b), p. 472; Schünemann (2003c), pp. 344, 348; Schünemann (2003d), pp. 116, 120; Kaiafa-Gbandi (2006), pp. 317, 326.

[22] Schünemann (2003d), pp. 116, 119 et seqq.; see also Hackner et al. (2006), pp. 663, 668; on the principle of last resort (*ultima ratio*) in general see Roxin (2006), § 2 para. 97 et seqq.; Roxin (2005), pp. 135 et seqq.; from my own point of view see Schünemann (2003e), pp. 133 et seqq.; Schünemann (2006b), pp. 18 et seqq.

[23] Framework Decision 2002/584/JHA of 13 June 2002 on the European Arrest Warrant (FD EAW) (OJ L 190/1), see Nestler (2004), pp. 332, 340; Salditt (2003), pp. 136, 137; Schünemann (2005), p. 681; Schünemann (2007), pp. 265, 271 et seqq.; Wehnert (2003), pp. 356, 358.

[24] Without even questioning their legitimacy, see for example Satzger (2012), § 8 para. 24; Satzger (2009), pp. 297, 305; Hecker (2010), § 4 para. 30, § 8 para. 55.

[25] Judgment of the Second Senate of 30 June 2009 (2 BvE 2/08 et al.), available in English at http://www.bundesverfassungsgericht.de/entscheidungen/es20090630_2bve000208en.html, para. 358.

representative in the Council exercising the Member States' rights set out in Article 82 (3) and Article 83(3) TFEU only on the instruction of the German Bundestag.[26]

This means that, even under the new regime of the Lisbon Treaty with the European Parliament acting as a legislator, it is only because the so-called handbrake set out in Article 82(3) TFEU allows national Parliaments to block a proposal incompatible with "fundamental aspects of its criminal justice system" that EU instruments on criminal procedure comply with democratic requirements. While the "handbrake" itself does not apply to mutual recognition proposals, the general requirements of strict interpretation and parliamentary precedence set out by the Court do. From this it follows that, a fortiori, since the former framework decisions have been taken without any decisive participation of the European Parliament, it would have been necessary that the democratically elected national parliaments be involved in the legislative process. Since this has not been the case and government representatives cannot give orders to the legislator, framework decisions must be considered not binding upon the Member States.[27]

However, they have been and are still being transferred into national law and therefore, as a matter of fact, they are determining the cooperation between Member States in criminal matters. Basically, the mutual recognition instruments shift the nature of this cooperation from requests between sovereign States to compulsory orders given by an authority of one State to another State's authority. Hence the possibilities to refuse cooperation are narrowed down to a few exceptions provided for in the framework decision's exhaustive enumeration. Furthermore, judicial review in the executing State is limited, and the traditional double criminality requirement is widely abolished.[28] This shift is confirmed by a change of vocabulary: instead of "requesting" and "requested" States, the mutual recognition instruments mention "issuing" and "executing" States or authorities. Note that the mention of "authorities" indicates that it is intended that the judicial authorities cooperate directly with one another, without the medium of State diplomacy.

---

[26] *Ibid.*, para. 365.

[27] Schünemann and Roger (2010), pp. 515, 516 et seq.; Schünemann (2010), pp. 735, 737 et seq.; *contra* Böse (2010b), p. 607; see also Schünemann (2003d), pp. 116, 120; Schünemann (2005), p. 531; Schünemann (2003a), p. 185; Schünemann (2003b), p. 472; Schünemann (2004), p. 200.

[28] The reduction of judicial review follows as an implicit consequence from the recognition of a foreign measure (Satzger 2008, pp. 15, 32 et seq.) and is explicitly mentioned in some instruments, for example in Art. 11 FD 2003/577/JHA on freezing orders (OJ L 196/45), Art. 9 FD 2006/783/JHA on confiscation orders (OJ L 328/59), Art. 18 para. 2 FD 2008/978/JHA of 18 December 2008 on the European Evidence Warrant (OJ L 350/72) (see also Roger 2010, pp. 27, 40 et seq.); this Framework Decision was also the first to generally abolish the double criminality requirement for certain measures (Art. 14, see Roger 2010 pp. 38 et seq.); other instruments have suppressed it for certain (broad) categories of offenses, as Art. 2(2) FD EAW; Art. 10 FD freezing orders (above); Art. 5(1) FD financial penalties (see also Schünemann and Roger 2010, pp. 515, 520 et seq.).

3. In the field of evidence gathering, the relevant instrument at the moment is the 2008 Framework Decision on the "European Evidence Warrant (EEW) for the purpose of obtaining objects, documents and data for use in proceedings in criminal matters."[29] As the long name indicates, it covers only existing items, so that trans-national evidence gathering remains a patchwork, other investigative measures as wiretapping, interviews, etc. still following the 2000 MLA Convention. Also, it should be noted that the framework decision has not been implemented in all Member State and might be rendered obsolete by the further developments, namely the European investigation order, which is still "under construction."[30] But we can consider it as an example of what the mutual recognition model means for the gathering of evidence.

The EEW, according to Article 1 of the Framework Decision, "shall be a judicial decision issued by a competent authority of a Member State with a view to obtaining objects, documents and data from another Member State for use in proceedings referred to in Article 5," which means criminal proceedings or administrative proceedings that might be tried by a criminal court. This means that a non-judicial authority could issue an EEW that the executing state would then have to recognise and execute, even if under the law of that State, only a judge could order such a measure. Article 11(4) allows the executing State to refuse the execution in this case, but on a discretionary basis and only as far as it would require search or seizure. Article 7 holds that the requested objects, documents or data must be "necessary and proportionate" for the purpose of proceedings and it is required that they could be obtained "in a comparable case" in the issuing State, "even though different procedural measures might be used." This provision may aim to secure that evidence can be used at a later stage of proceedings, but it is not stringent enough to assure the admissibility, especially because it spares the exact conditions under which the evidence is gathered.

According to paragraph 2, "these conditions shall be assessed only in the issuing State in each case," which is the problematic core of the MR approach. The EEW shall be recognised "without any further formality" and be executed in the same way as in a national case [Art. 11(1)].

So the applicable law is still, basically, that of the requested (or: executing) State (*locus regit actum* rule). But, notably, Article 12 holds that: "The executing authority shall comply with the formalities and procedures expressly indicated by the issuing authority unless otherwise provided in this Framework Decision and provided that such formalities and procedures are not contrary to the fundamental principles of law of the executing State." So the issuing authority has the option to have the *forum regit actum* rule applied, which could solve the

---

[29] See fn. 28.

[30] Initiative of seven Member States regarding the European Investigation Order, Interinstitutional File 2010/0817 (COD), see the (latest) general approach of the Council of 21 December 2011, document 18918/11, and Esser (2011), pp. 1497, 1508 et seq.; on recent developments see the minutes of the fifth EU-colloquium in Bonn by Ronsfeld (2012), p. 636.

issue of hybridisation of procedural laws. But since it is only optional, nothing ensures that the forum principle will be applied. On the contrary, the issuing authority could choose to apply it or not for tactical reasons, in order to use the most permissive rules available in the concrete case, thereby reducing the rights of the individual concerned. More generally, the optional forum principle poses a serious threat to legal certainty regarding the applicable procedural law.

4. Also, as I mentioned before, models that provide for a—more or less—automatic execution of a decision issued by one State on the territory of another State require some degree of legal unity that, despite the common values embodied by the European convention on human rights and the EU charter of fundamental rights, is still lacking in the EU. The "high level of confidence between the Member States" proclaimed by politicians is not based on actual trust in each and every criminal justice system in the EU; even the recital nr. 8 of the framework decision on the EEW recognizes that this confidence (still) must be "promoted." Last but not least, it is not the prosecution authorities that need to trust each other, but the citizens of the EU that must be able to trust the proceedings they face. In this respect, there is a need for a set of stringent and intelligible rules, and the mutual recognition approach leaves way too many aspects of the proceedings unregulated, including the admissibility of evidence gathered in a hybridised procedure.

In particular, these ad-hoc "partial European procedural laws," as *Wolter* has dubbed them, hardly address the protection of the rights of the defendant in a fair trial, which I mentioned earlier as a core principle of trans-national evidence gathering. It is not ensured that the defendant (or any other person subject to a measure) can exercise his rights—in particular, legal remedies against the EEW are split between the issuing State (for substantive reasons) and the executing State (for the circumstances of the execution) (Art. 18). But these are not easy to separate, for the different aspects and stages of evidence gathering are but part of an integral system. To mention only the simplest example: the rightfulness of the execution of a measure supposes that it has been legally ordered. So how can one effectively challenge a coercive measure before a court that has no power to examine whether the order itself was legal—while the courts of a foreign State that have this power are out of reach for the majority of defendants? These practical barriers for the defendant have not been taken into consideration, as little as the possibility to challenge evidence. Also, the double criminality requirement has been abolished for a wide range of offences that, by the way, are defined only very vaguely. Apart from that, neither the few enumerative grounds for refusal of Article 13 nor the weak and piecemeal measures of the "roadmap on procedural rights" can re-establish the balance of proceedings where prosecutorial powers have been unleashed by the mutual recognition principle. Even the few measures aimed to improve the defendant's rights, as double defence in matters of pre-trial custody, are being targeted as too far-reaching by the Council.

5. To sum up, the mutual recognition model aims to provide for an effective execution of foreign procedural decisions, but in the particular case of evidence

gathering, this is subject to the admissibility in the trial, which is not secured. In any case, it opens the door to the EU-wide execution of the most punitive criminal law systems and potentially the lowest procedural rights standards.

5   The Principle of Transnational Procedural Unity

1. In order to address these issues while at the same time ensuring the effectiveness of criminal proceedings, a group of scholars, including myself as their organiser, have drafted a "Programme for European Criminal Justice" in 2006, with financial support from the European Commission's AGIS programme.[31] It relies on three major aspects: the determination of one single State responsible for conducting the proceedings, European institutions, namely Eurojust and a new agency, Eurodefence, and, last but not least, specific safeguards for the most intrusive measures.

   The focal point of our proposal were transnational criminal proceedings concerning criminal offences the prosecution of which involves several EU member states. In such a case, an early concentration of powers must occur in such a way that one state is exclusively responsible for the investigation and the trial (the "model of trans-national procedural unity"). Significantly, this is in the defendant's own interest, but also in the interests of procedural economy. In order to capture all conceivable cases of conflict, the term has to be defined broadly and should thus not be limited to crimes touching upon several states, but should also include criminal proceedings with either investigatory demands or the need for intrusive measures in more than one state. If several states have jurisdiction, a concentration of power in one state should occur as soon as possible. This would, concurrently, establish that it is that state's criminal law and procedure that apply. We posited that only one single procedural law would be applicable in every single case, rather than accepting the creation of a hybrid criminal procedure on the basis of the model of mutual recognition.

2. The concentration of the proceedings in one single Member State requires, of course, clear rules on the attribution of jurisdiction. In this respect, we proposed a flexible two-step model (First step: formal criteria with a fixed order of preference; Second step: the ability to depart from these criteria depending upon the focal point of the alleged offence). Naturally, this steps back from the ideal of an automatic and therefore never manipulable assignment of power. It is, however, compared to the present legal reality (where the accused poten- tially faces several proceedings in different member states) still advantageous to the accused, and there are no practicable alternatives to it: where there are various acts, various places in which the harm results and various defendants in several member states, as is typical of trans-national offences, the limit of a

---

[31] See Schünemann (2006a), pp. 255 et seqq.

predetermined distribution of power becomes apparent. Logically, amongst several in theory equally qualified member States, the State in which most of the evidence is located and where therefore the actual logical focus of the proceedings is situated, must be selected as the investigating state. In the case of trans-national offences with their numerous links that would ordinarily justify a nation's exercise of its jurisdiction, an inflexible regulation would in many cases likely not even be conceptually possible. A one-sided reliance upon one aspect (e.g. the place where the act occurs) would always raise the risk of the proceedings being conducted in a state that only exhibits a more or less coincidental nexus to the total "offence-construct." This would often make a concentrated and procedurally efficient investigation, which is in the interest of all involved, impossible. Especially in the case of offences where the act occurs far from the place where the harm results, this criterion may prove inadequate and, from the point of view of procedural economy, downright useless, in particular when the violation of the legal interest intended by the accused occurs in another state. Putting aside the fact that the need for prevention is generally greatest where the violation of the legal interests occurs, the place where the act occurs may, in a Europe that is characterised by freedom of movement, often be the result of sheer chance, for instance if someone posts a fraudulent letter somewhere during a trip through several member states. The required need for flexibility is not simply borne out of considerations of expediency, since the aim of determining the truth and thus that of achieving material justice can be best accomplished in the jurisdiction in which, for example, most of the evidence is located and in which, therefore, the investigative steps can be conducted quickly and successfully.

3. The **procedural solution**, proposed by the alternative proposal, deserves preference over a rigid assignment of power based upon abstract, formal criteria. It is also in the interests of the prevention of abuse and manipulation. The core of this solution is to be found in the participation of **Eurodefence**, a new institution that would secure the rights and interests of the defendant in trans-national proceedings. It would consist in two strictly separate divisions, one to support the defence during the trial, the other—perhaps more important—to safeguard the defendant's interests from the beginning of trans-national proceedings, when he is still unaware of the charges. Its role would include representing the rights of the defendant in the attribution of jurisdiction. This "legal protection" division would ensure that, on the one hand, legitimate interests of the accused can be articulated at an early stage and, on the other hand, factually inappropriate considerations on the part of the prosecutorial authorities involved can be highlighted.

4. The next question is in which way the designated investigating State can conduct trans-national investigations or execute intrusive measures. Depending on the extent of the intrusion we proposed different levels of protection, which would be highest in the case of pre-trial custody (it being the harshest intrusive measure) and lowest in the case of simple investigatory measures, such as a questioning. Here we stressed the importance of a Copernican revolution: Any

facilitation of the Europe-wide prosecution of crimes as compared to the status quo can only be legitimate if, at the same time, European law is used to ensure that protective measures are also strengthened to the level that can be realised in Europe.

In particular, we proposed two innovative measures that involve the use of modern technology for the protection of the defendant's rights—rather than, as usually, just to increase the intrusive potential of prosecuting authorities at the expense of the defendant. For if the individual States gain an increase in the scope of their prosecutorial powers, so as to include the entire territory of the EU, they must accept, in return, the level of protection and balancing that should necessarily be available within a true area of freedom and justice and thus as mandated by the goals of the EU. We have therefore expressly integrated two technical measures into our proposals, which, given the present state of today's industrial society, impose lower demands than the introduction of the typewriter once did, and which take on a key role in fair criminal proceedings. However, these measures are being blocked—despite or perhaps rather because of that fact—cum ira et studio by the courts in many European States and certainly in Germany. The first is the obligatory videotaping of all questioning that takes place during investigations; the other is the replacement of pre-trial detention by electronic control measures—the key word is tagging. Of course, these techno-logical innovations, the almost Archimedic importance of which cannot be doubted by anyone familiar with the criminal process, deal with the general problem of fairness in criminal proceedings, particularly at the national level. However, if Europe is opening, as it were, Pandora's national box for all of Europe to see, it must necessarily add safety mechanisms without which modern criminal proceedings simply cannot be considered legitimate. While today modern technology is being employed almost exclusively for the purpose of expanding the State's access and for the intensification of the surveillance of its citizens, it should actually be a matter of course in a true area of freedom, security and justice that the possibilities offered by modern technology be utilised also and particularly for the protection of the legitimate interests of the accused and more generally for enhancing the ascertainment of truth.

5. At the time when our proposal was written, the EU certainly did not have the power to take such measures, so that it would have taken an international agreement to enact it. Under the Lisbon treaty, however, Article 83 paragraph 2 of the TFEU enables the EU to adopt "minimum rules" to facilitate mutual recognition. From the perspective of balanced proceedings, the proposed mea-sures could be seen as a "minimum" necessary to legitimate the trans-national expansion of prosecutorial powers—at least, such an interpretation would not bend the wording of the treaty more than the Court of justice is used to doing.

6. For the key issue of intrusive measures during the investigation, a three-step concept was proposed in Article 4(4) of the Programme, which grades the protective, safety measures according to the intensity of the intrusive measures. Hence, it is necessary to differentiate between pre-trial detention, the seizure of property of significant value, the use of under-cover investigators and other

intrusive measures. In the case of other intrusive measures, the only limitation is the ordre public of the legal system of the executing state, since it cannot be expected to execute measures that would violate its own principles. In a case where property of significant value is seized or where undercover investigators are employed, the "principle of most favourable treatment" applies, that is, only such measures as are permissible in both legal systems may be carried out. In the case of undercover investigators the reason is that their use is extremely delicate and such operations lie at the outer border of the rule of law. Their use can only be imposed upon the executing state if it is permitted according to its legal system. In the case of the seizure of property of significant value, the main issue is the protection of the defendant, because this type of seizure (in contrast to the obtaining of evidence) is often aimed at strangling the defence and is thus extremely dangerous to the defence. The defendant can rest assured that his assets, which are located in the executing state, can only be seized according to principles applicable in that state. Moreover, he can rest assured that any pressure against him in the criminal proceedings can only be applied to the extent permissible according to that state's principles. The "principle of most favourable treatment," however, must remain an exception according to our model's basic concept of "trans-national procedural unity." Application of the principle as a general rule would not make sense, because—like the principle of mutual recognition imposed by the EU today, although with the opposite result—it would also create a hybrid criminal procedure that does not exist anywhere in this form. Since the EU represents a unified space for the purpose of criminal policy due to the freedom of movement within its territory, and since many EU regulations—as for instance the rampant subsidies—have an undoubtedly crime-inducing effect, the prosecution of trans-border offences already faces unique challenges. For this reason, the alternative concept may not under any circumstances paralyse the necessary prosecution of criminal offences. Note that I haven't talked about admissibility—this is because when the gathering of evidence follows the sentencing State's law, admissibility is a strictly national issue (and hence for the transnational legal instrument: a non-issue).

7. Of course such a far-reaching expansion of criminal justice systems onto the territory of other Member States require measures to ensure that the defendant can adequately exercise his rights. This is another aim of the aforementioned agency Eurodefence. On one hand, the "legal protection" division can be involved in investigative measures, in particular covert measures as wiretapping or the deployment of undercover investigators. On the other hand, the "support" division is meant to help arrange defence contacts, coordinate the defence in the involved States, provide information and financial support. All in all, such an institution could secure the necessary balance between investigative powers and the rights of the defence, thereby achieving the aim of the "3-dimensional model" mentioned before and securing the fair trial principle that is essential especially for the strongly integrated models.

What's more, it would do so without affecting the effectiveness of the proceedings, so that the proposed model of transnational procedural unity addresses the flaws of traditional mutual legal assistance while securing a fair trial.

6 Conclusion

A model for transnational gathering of evidence must allow for effective criminal proceedings while safeguarding defence rights and providing for a fair trial. The old MLA model was deficient in both regards, while the new MR approach only solves—if at all—the effectiveness problem. This applies to the EEW considered here, but a fortiori to the further-reaching EIO (see the detailed assessment in this volume). Since the subject of my speech includes "solution models," I have seized the opportunity to sketch out the model of transnational procedural unity, which, regardless of political feasibility, might serve as an example for a practical realisation of the conflicting principles governing the transnational evidence gathering.

Acknowledgement The author wishes to express his sincere gratitude to *Benjamin Roger*, Maître en Droit, for his essential and indispensable cooperation.

References

Andreou P (2009) Gegenseitige Anerkennung von Entscheidungen in Strafsachen in der Europäischen Union. Nomos, Baden-Baden

Böse M (2003) Das Prinzip der gegenseitigen Anerkennung in der transnationalen Strafrechtspflege der EU – Die "Verkehrsfähigkeit" strafgerichtlicher Entscheidungen. In: Momsen C, Bloy R, Rackow P (eds) Fragmentarisches Strafrecht. Peter Lang, Frankfurt am Main, pp 233–250

Böse M (2010a) Die Entscheidung des Bundesverfassungsgerichts zum Vertrag von Lissabon und ihre Bedeutung für die Europäisierung des Strafrechts. Zeitschrift für internationale Strafrechtsdogmatik 76–91

Böse M (2010b) Der Rechtsstaat am Abgrund? Zur Skandalisierung des EU-Geldsanktionengesetzes. Replik auf Schünemann/Roger, *ZIS* 2010, 515. Zeitschrift für internationale Strafrechtsdogmatik 607–613

Böse M (2012) § 81 IRG. In: Grützner H, Pötz PG, Kreß C (eds) Internationaler Rechtshilfeverkehr in Strafsachen, 3rd edn. C.F. Müller, Heidelberg

Braum S (2005) Das Prinzip der gegenseitigen Anerkennung. Historische Grundlagen und Perspektiven europäischer Strafrechtsentwicklung. Golddammer's Archiv für Strafrecht 681–699

Eser A, Lagodny O, Blakesley C (2002) The individual as subject of international cooperation in criminal matters. Nomos, Baden-Baden

Esser R (2011) Auswirkungen der Europäischen Beweisanordnung auf das deutsche Strafverfahren. In: Heinrich M, Jäger C, Schünemann B et al (eds) Strafrecht als Scientia Universalis – Festschrift für Claus Roxin zum 80. Geburtstag. De Gruyter, Berlin, pp 799–817

Gaede K (2003) Nullum judicium sine lege: Die völkerrechtliche Bindung eines gemeinschaftsrechtlichen Sonderstrafverfahrens an das Potential der Europäischen Konvention für

Menschenrechte und Grundfreiheiten. Zeitschrift für die gesamte Strafrechtswissenschaft 115:845–879

Gleß S (2001) "Aus 29 mach 1" – die jüngsten Bemühungen um die Vereinheitlichung des Strafverfahrensrechts in der Schweiz. Zeitschrift für die gesamte Strafrechtswissenschaft 113:419–426

Gleß S (2003) Die "Verkehrsfähigkeit von Beweisen" im Strafverfahren. Zeitschrift für die gesamte Strafrechtswissenschaft 115:131–150

Gleß S (2004) Zum Prinzip der gegenseitigen Anerkennung. Zeitschrift für die gesamte Strafrechtswissenschaft 116:353–367

Gleß S (2006) Beweisrechtsgrundsätze einer grenzüberschreitenden Strafverfolgung. Nomos, Baden-Baden

Gleß S (2008) Beweisverbote bei Fällen mit Auslandsbezug. Juristische Rundschau 317–326

Grützner H (1969) Aktuelle Probleme der Auslieferung. Zeitschrift für die gesamte Strafrechtswissenschaft 81:119–124

Grote R, Marauhn T (2006) Konkordanzkommentar zum europäischen und deutschen Grundrechtsschutz. Mohr Siebeck, Tübingen

Hackner C, Schomburg W, Lagodny O, Gleß S (2006) Das 2. Haftbefehlsgesetz. Neue Zeitschrift für Strafrecht 12:663–669

Harms M, Knauss P (2011) Das Prinzip der gegenseitigen Anerkennung in der Strafrechtssetzung der EU. In: Heinrich M, Jäger C, Schünemann B et al (eds) Strafrecht als Scientia Universalis - Festschrift für Claus Roxin zum 80. Geburtstag. De Gruyter, Berlin, pp 1479–1496

Heard C, Mansell D (2011) The European arrest warrant: the role of judges when human rights are at risk. New J Eur Crim Law 2:133–147

Hecker B (2010) Europäisches Strafrecht, 3rd edn. Springer, Heidelberg

Heger M (2007) Perspektiven des Europäische Beweissicherung - Perspektiven der strafrechtlichen Zusammenarbeit in Europa. Zeitschrift für internationale Strafrechtsdogmatik 547–556

Jescheck H-H (1969) Gedanken zur Reform des deutschen Auslieferungsgesetzes. In: Études en l'honneur de Jean Graven. Georg, Genève, pp 75–89

Kaiafa-Gbandi M (2006) Recent developments in criminal law and rule-of-law deficits. In: Schünemann B (ed) Ein Gesamtkonzept für die europäische Strafrechtspflege/A programme for European criminal justice. Carl Heymanns, Köln, pp 317–332

Lagodny O (1987) Die Rechtsstellung des Auszuliefernden in der Bundesrepublik Deutschland. Max-Planck-Institut, Freiburg i. Br.

Ligeti K (2005) Strafrecht und strafrechtliche Zusammenarbeit in der europäischen Union. Duncker & Humblot, Berlin

Mavany M (2012) Die europäische Beweisanordnung und das Prinzip der gegenseitigen Anerkennung. C.F. Müller, Heidelberg

Murschetz V (2007) Auslieferung und Europäischer Haftbefehl. Springer, Wien

Nestler C (2004) Europäisches Strafprozessrecht. Zeitschrift für die gesamte Strafrechtswissenschaft 116:332–352

Roger B (2010) Europäisierung des Strafverfahrens – oder nur der Strafverfolgung? Zum Rahmenbeschluss über die Europäische Beweisanordnung. Goltdammer's Archiv für Strafrecht 27–43

Ronsfeld P (2012) Tagungsbericht: Europa – Hochspannung zwischen Eingriffs- und Beschuldigtenrechten. 5. EU-Strafrechtstag, Bonn, 14.9.-15.9.2012, Strafverteidigervereinigung NRW e.V. Zeitschrift für internationale Strafrechtsdogmatik 636–640

Roxin C (2005) Rechtsgüterschutz als Aufgabe des Strafrechts? In: Hefendehl R (ed) Empirische und dogmatische Fundamente, kriminalpolitischer Impetus, Symposium für Bernd Schünemann zum 60. Geburtstag. Carl Heymanns, Köln, pp 135–150

Roxin C (2006) Strafrecht. Allgemeiner Teil I. Beck, München

Roxin C, Schünemann B (2011) Strafverfahrensrecht. Beck, München

Salditt F (2003) Doppelte Verteidigung im einheitlichen Raum. Strafverteidiger 136–137

Satzger H (2006) The European assumption of enforcement. In: Schünemann B (ed) Ein Gesamtkonzept für die europäische Strafrechtspflege/A programme for European criminal justice. Carl Heymanns, Köln, pp 395–408

Satzger H (2008) Das Strafrecht als Gegenstand europäischer Gesetzgebungstätigkeit. Kritische Vierteljahresschrift 17–38

Satzger H (2009) "Schwarze Kassen" zwischen Untreue und Korruption – Eine Besprechung des Urteils BGH – 2 StR 587/07 (Siemens-Entscheidung) – Neue Zeitschrift für Strafrecht 297–306

Satzger H (2012) International and European criminal law. Beck–Hart–Nomos, Munich

Schomburg W (1995) Strafrecht und Rechtshilfe im Geltungsbereich von Schengen II. Neue Juristische Wochenschrift 1931–1936

Schomburg W, Lagodny O, Gleß S, Hackner T (2012) Einleitung. In: Schomburg W, Lagodny O, Gleß S, Hackner T (eds) International cooperation in criminal matters, 5th edn. C.H. Beck, München, pp 2–50

Schünemann B (2003a) Europäischer Haftbefehl und EU-Verfassungsentwurf auf schiefer Ebene – Die Schranken des Grundgesetzes. Zeitschrift für Rechtspolitik 185–189

Schünemann B (2003b) Europäischer Haftbefehl und gegenseitige Anerkennung in Strafsachen. Zeitschrift für Rechtspolitik 472

Schünemann B (2003c) Die Rechte des Beschuldigten im internationalisierten Ermittlungs-verfahren. Strafverteidiger Forum 344–351

Schünemann B (2003d) Bürgerrechte ernst nehmen bei der Europäisierung des Strafverfahrens! Strafverteidiger 116–122

Schünemann B (2003e) Das Rechtsgüterschutzprinzip als Fluchtpunkt der verfassungsrechtlichen Grenzen der Straftatbestände und ihrer Interpretation. In: Hefendehl R, von Hirsch A, Wohlers W (eds) Die Rechtsgutstheorie: Legitimationsbasis des Strafrechts oder dogmatisches Glasperlenspiel? Nomos, Baden-Baden, pp 133–154

Schünemann B (2004) Fortschritte und Fehltritte in der Europäisierung der Strafrechtspflege. Goltdammer's Archiv für Strafrecht 193–209

Schünemann B (2005) Die Entscheidung des Bundesverfassungsgerichtes zum Europäischen Haftbefehl: markiges Ergebnis, enttäuschende Begründung. Strafverteidiger 681–685

Schünemann B (2006a) The foundations of transnational criminal proceedings. In: Schünemann B (ed) Ein Gesamtkonzept für die europäische Strafrechtspflege/A programme for European criminal justice. Carl Heymanns, Köln, pp 344–361

Schünemann B (2006b) Rechtsgüterschutz, ultima ratio und Viktimodogmatik – von den unverrückbaren Grenzen des Strafrechts in einem liberalen Rechtsstaat. In: von Hirsch A, Seelmann K, Wohlers W (eds) Mediating Principles: Begrenzungsprinzipien bei der Strafbegründung. Nomos Verlagsgesellschaft, Baden-Baden, pp 18–35

Schünemann B (2007) Die Implementation des europäischen Haftbefehls in Polen und Deutsch-land im Vergleich – Eine kritische Skizze aus deutscher Sicht. In: Joerden JC, Szwarc AJ (eds) Europäisierung des Strafrechts in Polen und Deutschland – rechtsstaatliche Grundlagen. Duncker & Humblot, Berlin, pp 265–277

Schünemann B (2010) Noch einmal: Zur Kritik der rechtsstaatlichen Bresthaftigkeit des EU-Geldsanktionengesetzes, des europatümelnden strafrechtlichen Neopositivismus und seiner Apologie von Böse. Zeitschrift für internationale Strafrechtsdogmatik 735–741

Schünemann B, Roger B (2010) Die Karawane zur Europäisierung des Strafrechts zieht weiter. Zur demokratischen und rechtsstaatlichen Bresthaftigkeit des EU-Geldsanktionengesetzes. Zeitschrift für internationale Strafrechtsdogmatik 515–523

Sommer U (2003) Die Verwertung von im Ausland gewonnenen Beweismitteln. Strafverteidiger Forum 351–356

Vogel J (1998) Thema IV: Internationale Zusammenarbeit in Strafsachen. Zeitschrift für die gesamte Strafrechtswissenschaft 110:974–984

Vogel J (2001a) Abschaffung der Auslieferung? Kritische Anmerkungen zur Reform des Auslieferungsrechts. Juristenzeitung 937–943

Vogel J (2001b) Vor § 1 IRG. In: Grützner H, Pötz PG, Kreß C (eds) Internationaler Rechtshilfeverkehr in Strafsachen, 3rd edn. C.F. Müller, Heidelberg

Vogel J, Burchard C (2009) § 3. In: Grützner H, Pötz PG, Kreß C (eds) Internationaler Rechtshilfeverkehr in Strafsachen, 3rd edn. C.F. Müller, Heidelberg

Wehnert (2003) Europäischer Haftbefehl. Strafverteidiger Forum 356–360

Wilkitzki P (1991) Vor § 59 IRG. In: Grützner H, Pötz PG, Kreß C (eds) Internationaler Rechtshilfeverkehr in Strafsachen, 3rd edn. C.F. Müller, Heidelberg

Wohlers W (2004) Strafverfolgungskompetenzen im Bundesstaat. In: Schünemann B (ed) Alternativentwurf Europäische Strafverfolgung. Carl Heymanns, Köln, pp 51–74

Criminal Evidence and Respect for Fair Trial Guarantees in the Dialogue Between the European Court of Human Rights and National Courts

Richard Vogler

Abstract This chapter examines the growing phenomenon of "transjudicial dialogue" between judges in different national jurisdictions and judges in the international courts. It takes the European Court of Human Rights (ECtHR) as an example of an international court which has engaged actively in such dialogue, reviewing the communications between judges of this court and those of the UK Supreme Court in their respective judgements in the cases of *Al-Khawaja* [2011] and *R v Horncastle* [2009], respectively. It concludes that such communications do not erode but instead support the individuality and distinctiveness of judicial systems and, by encouraging knowledge and mutual respect between courts, improve the quality of judgements.

Keywords Caselaw • Cosmopolitan • European Court of Human Rights • Hearsay evidence • Judicial dialogue • Right to confrontation • Transjudicial • UK Supreme Court • Witnesses

Contents

1 Introduction 182
2 The Global Community of Judges 182
3 The European Court of Human Rights in Dialogue 183
4 Confrontation with the UK Courts 185
5 The Response of the UK Courts 187
6 Dialogue and Resolution 189
7 Conclusion 190
References 191

R. Vogler (✉)
Sussex Law School, University of Sussex, Flamer BN1 9QQ, UK
e-mail: R.K.Vogler@Sussex.ac.uk

1   Introduction

The creation of the new, transnational crime-fighting measures which are being considered in this volume requires us to think very hard about the nature of the protective regimes which we have in place across Europe. For the first time we must re-analyse criminal procedure in each of our countries from the standpoint of supranational human rights norms.[1] Some would argue that the procedural jurisprudence of the ECtHR in conjunction with the EU Stockholm Process, is evolving a network of Federal procedural rules for Europe. And the sooner, so it is argued, the better. The right, for example, under Article 6(3)(d) ECHR for the accused "... to examine or have examined the witnesses against him" must mean the same thing and be protected by exactly the same basic procedures in Messina as in Manchester. Without this safeguard, the international transfer of evidence should not be permitted.

However, I will argue in this short paper that there are alternatives to the convergence approach and that the homogenisation of European criminal evidence procedures is not the only way to defend our fundamental rights against the onslaught of the new European Criminal Investigation Directives. The alternative which I want to discuss, is dialogue.

2   The Global Community of Judges

Legal scholarship over the last decade has explored the concept of a global community of judges, sharing the same great project for the international entrenchment of human rights norms.[2] In this enterprise judges step outside the authoritarian hierarchies of their national jurisdictions and engage in direct horizontal dialogue with their colleagues in courts in other countries and in the international tribunals. This "transjudicial dialogue"[3] is a recent, internet-driven phenomenon, encouraged by the free availability of judgements online and increased knowledge of the English language. International judicial conferences, international publications and institutional contacts have all played a role in this shared professional enterprise. As Slaughter puts it, these dialogues are enlivened by "personal contacts, persuasive authority and peripatetic litigants."[4] They are also a consequence of the historic global shift (particularly noticeable in the common law world through the development of the Bangalore principles between 1981 and 1988) from a dualist system of law, where international human rights norms are seen as a separate and discrete sphere of "international law," to a monist one where they are part of

---

[1] Roberts and Hunter (2012), p. 2.

[2] Baudenbacher (2003).

[3] Slaughter (1994).

[4] Slaughter (2003), p. 219.

domestic law.[5] Justice L'Heureux-Dubé of the Canadian Supreme Court has claimed that "[m]ore and more courts, particularly within the common law world, are looking to the judgements of other jurisdictions, particularly when making decisions on human rights issues."[6] This is a shared project and an important one since, as Slaughter argues, how else, except through these conversations, "do we build a world under law?"[7] But dialogue implies not only building consensus but also conflict and disagreement and a secondary purpose of my paper is to examine how, in these early days of global judicial dialogue, these inevitable conflicts over ideas about evidence can be managed through cooperation.

3   The European Court of Human Rights in Dialogue

This issue is particularly important in Europe where, under the influence of the ECtHR, so it is argued, a Kantian cosmopolitan legal order is slowly emerging[8] which obliges officials in all countries to respect the same fundamental rights of all persons within their jurisdiction.[9] This is being achieved by a court in transition from the status of international tribunal to one with some kind of supranational constitutional role based on its a strong ideological purchase on the domestic legal orders of member states.[10] But the position of the ECtHR in relation to these domestic orders cannot be characterised merely as the normal "constitutional" summit of a pyramid of judicial authority. On the contrary, the relationship is a much more complex and pluralist one, based on an "open architecture" which allows different countries to react in different ways to judgements. This is heterarchy rather than hierarchy and must be organised through accommodation, rather than conflict.[11]

As Keller and Stone Sweet have pointed out, there is a wide variety of different approaches amongst European judiciaries to Strasbourg jurisprudence.[12] Some judiciaries have been very reluctant to engage. The priority of national autonomy and the adequacy of existing national human rights protections have long been asserted by the German and Austrian Constitutional Courts, particularly in their early caselaw. The Italian Constitutional Court, the Irish and British courts and the French higher courts until the 1990s have all expressed similar views and as a

---

[5] Waters (2007).

[6] Cited in Slaughter (1994), p. 194.

[7] *Ibid.*, p. 219.

[8] Bjorge and Andenas (2011).

[9] Stone Sweet (2012).

[10] Krisch (2008), p. 184.

[11] *Ibid.* Also, Costa JP, The Relationship Between the European Court of Human Rights and National Constitutional Courts. Lecture, 15 February 2013, Cambridge University.

[12] Stone Sweet and Keller (2008); see also Anagnostou (2010).

result, their traditional response to interference from Strasbourg was hostile. By contrast, judiciaries in countries emerging from dictatorship have looked to the ECtHR for ideological support and adopted a much more accommodating and even submissive attitude. Examples might be the Spanish Constitutional Tribunal in its early jurisprudence and some Eastern European states. The Greek courts up until the 1990s, the Turkish courts until 2004 and the Russian courts until today have failed to negotiate any relationship at all.[13]

In France, during the lengthy debate over the role of Advocates-General in the *Cour de Cassation,* the courts conducted a vigorous *"dialogue des juges"* with Strasbourg by criticising and initially rejecting the ECtHR judgements, for example in the *Poitrimol*[14] and *Kress*[15] cases, before agreeing to amend the procedure complained of, after the European court had modified its approach in response.[16] A similar approach has been adopted in Germany. In its 2005 decision in the case of *Görgülü* the German Constitutional Court ruled that there was a strong presumption that judges should follow relevant decisions of the ECtHR, except in "exceptional" circumstances, namely, when "it is the only way to avoid a violation of the fundamental principles contained in the (German) Constitution."[17] One such case arose in 2009 when the ECtHR in *M v Germany,* ruled that Germany's preventive detention regime was in breach of Article 7 of the ECHR notwithstanding that 5 years beforehand, the German Constitutional Court had taken a completely different view after careful consideration of the issue. Understandably the German court refused to modify its approach, despite a series of rulings by the ECtHR finding the same violation. It was not until 2011 that it finally accepted the inevitable and agreed that the "legal situation had been changed" by the Strasbourg ruling.[18] A similar trajectory can be observed in the relationship between the Italian courts and the ECHR.[19]

Significant judicial dialogues have also taken place amongst the international courts. The relationship between the ECtHR and the European Court of Justice, after 30 years of interaction, has been described as a "friendly interplay"[20] and both the Inter-American Court of Human Rights[21] and the United States Supreme Court[22] are other close partners in dialogue. In March 2012, for example, judges of the ECtHR and the United States Supreme Court met formally in Washington for

---

[13] Stone Sweet and Keller (2008), p. 705.

[14] ECtHR, Decision of 23 November 1993, *Poitrimol v France*, Application no. 14032/88.

[15] ECtHR, Decision of 7 June 2001, *Kress v France*, Application no. 39594/98.

[16] Krisch (2008), pp. 191–196; Croquet (2011), pp. 357–358.

[17] Hoffmeister (2006); Stone Sweet (2012), p. 70; Croquet (2011), pp. 356–357.

[18] *Preventive Detention*, No. 2 BvR 2365/09 (May 4, 2011).

[19] See Tracogna (2010).

[20] Krisch (2008), p. 200; Martinico and Pollicino (2012).

[21] Bertoni (2009).

[22] de Wolf and Wallace (2009).

a "historic" colloquium.[23] But the focus here is on recent developments involving my own country and in particular a very instructive dialogue over evidence which has taken place over recent months and which seems, in my view to point the way forward. The ECHR was incorporated into UK law as recently as 1998 by the Human Rights Act of that year. Surprisingly, given that the Act requires only that courts should in general "take account" of ECtHR jurisprudence, English judges, trained in the *stare decisis* approach, have usually regarded it as authoritative and have referred to the caselaw more widely and more enthusiastically than those in almost any other European country.[24] In 2004 Lord Bingham in the House of Lords instructed English judges in no uncertain terms to "follow any clear and constant jurisprudence of the Strasbourg court."[25]

4   Confrontation with the UK Courts

This was to change. In Brighton in 2004, a practitioner in rehabilitative medicine, Imad Al-Khawaja hypnotised patients as part of their treatment. Two women claimed that during hypnosis he had sexually assaulted them, setting off a train of events which would lead to a historic confrontation between the Supreme Court of the United Kingdom and the ECtHR. The situation developed as follows. One of the women (ST), who suffered from multiple sclerosis, committed suicide for reasons unconnected with the case, after she had given a statement to the police but before the trial. The prosecution applied to have her evidence read to the jury and succeeded under the provisions of the Criminal Justice Act 2003. As a result Mr. Al-Khawaja was convicted on both counts and sentenced to 27 months imprisonment.

At the same time, another defendant, Ali Tahery, an Iranian living in London was sentenced to 9 years' imprisonment for stabbing a man in a fight. The main witness, also an Iranian, claimed to be too frightened to give oral evidence at the trial and his statement was read to the jury in his absence. On the face of it, both of these cases appear to be a flagrant breach of the ancient English "Rule against Hearsay Evidence" and the more recent right under Article 6(3)(d) ECHR that "everyone charged with a criminal offence has the following minimum rights . . . to examine or have examined the witnesses against him."

The rule against hearsay lies at the heart of the adversarial method and has been a central feature of our law of criminal evidence since at least the seventeenth century.[26] It is described by the north American scholar Friedman as:

---

[23] http://www.law.gwu.edu/News/20112012events/Pages/JudicialProcess.aspx.

[24] Krisch (2008), p. 202.

[25] *R v Special Adjudicator ex parte Ullah* [2004] UKHL, 26 at 20.

[26] See e.g. *R v Charnock* (1696) 12 St Tr 1377, col 1454.

a principle of magnificent importance, a principle first enunciated long before the development of the common law system but one that achieved full development within that system. This is the principle that a person may not offer testimony against a criminal defendant unless it is given under oath, face to face with the accused and subject to cross-examination.[27]

John Spencer calls this "eyeball to eyeball" confrontation. Not only is it a reflection of the traditional Anglo-American suspicion of the dishonest Crown witness but it also derives from the fact that all our decision-makers in criminal cases are lay people. Historically a largely illiterate jury could not be expected to read reported accounts nor to assess the relative weight of different types of evidence. Instead, their role was to evaluate all witnesses face to face in the courtroom trial. However, over the centuries the judiciary have developed a range of exceptions to the Hearsay rule so that defendants who, for example, killed the only witnesses to prevent them testifying, did not escape justice. These hearsay exceptions were codified by the Criminal Justice Act 2003 which allowed courts the discretion to admit hearsay evidence, subject to a strict regime of counterbalances, in exceptional circumstances when it felt that it was in the interests of justice to do so.

In *Al-Khawaja,* the English Court of Appeal relied on detailed consideration of the existing ECtHR caselaw in the previous case of *R v Sellick*,[28] where the main witness in a murder case was prevented from testifying because he feared reprisals. Notwithstanding that this was quite unlike the situation in *Al-Khawaja*, the Court of Appeal upheld the conviction, suggesting that the counterbalancing measures were sufficient in this case to ensure a fair trial. The ECtHR, however, did not agree. In its judgement of 20th January 2009, the fourth section of the ECtHR concluded that, since the unavailable evidence was the "sole and decisive" evidence on which a conviction was based, no amount of counterbalancing measures could prevent a breach of Article 6(3)(d):

Having considered these factors, the Court does not find that any of them, taken alone or together, could counterbalance the prejudice to the defence by admitting S.T.'s statement.[29]

Reliance on the statutory scheme laid out in the Criminal Justice Act 2003 was not sufficient and the requirements of s. 6(3)(d) were quite separate from the general requirement for a fair trial and constituted:

express guarantees and cannot be read, as it was by the Court of Appeal ... as illustrations of the matters to be taken into account when considering whether a trial has been fair.[30]

At a stroke, and in a judgement occupying 13 material paragraphs, the ECtHR had invalidated the entire scheme of limited hearsay admission established by four

---

[27] Friedman (2004).

[28] *R v Sellick* [2005] EWCA Crim 651.

[29] ECtHR, Decision of 20 January 2009, *Al Khawaja and Tahery v United Kingdom,* Applications No. 26766/05 & 2222/06, § 42.

[30] *Ibid.*, § 35.

centuries of judicial trial and error and most recently by the lengthy and meticulous deliberations of the 1997 Law Commission which had sat for 3 years and heard evidence on the subject from around the world[31] as a basis for the 2003 Act. To English eyes this looked almost as serious a blow to our distinctive traditions of criminal justice as the decision of the Chamber in *Taxquet v Belgium*. Here a group of six judges with no significant experience or knowledge of jury trial amongst them, disposed of the 1,000 year-old procedure in one paragraph, with no argument but merely asserting that jury trial was "arbitrary justice lacking in transparency" and hence in breach of Article 6.[32] Fortunately, the Grand Chamber was able to adopt a more informed approach[33] but the incident provoked a good deal of anger.

5   The Response of the UK Courts

On 16 April 2009 the United Kingdom requested that the decision of the Chamber in *Al-Khawaja* be referred to the Grand Chamber. At the same time, whether by design or accident, the opportunity was offered to the Supreme Court of the United Kingdom to engage creatively with the ECtHR in advance of the hearing by the Grand Chamber. What is important to note here is that the judgement in this case was not merely an act of national resistance, sabotage and obstruction but one of creative engagement.

Michael Horncastle and another man appealed against convictions for assault on Peter Rice in his flat near Liverpool in 2005. Unfortunately, the victim subsequently died from unrelated alcoholism and his written statement was read at trial in 2007 as the "sole and decisive" evidence. Horncastle was convicted, as were two men who had kidnapped a young woman who was too frightened to give evidence and ran away just before their trial. On both occasions the full "counterbalancing" provisions and warnings to the jury required by the 2003 Criminal Justice Act were in place.

The defendants all appealed to the UK Supreme Court, arguing that they had been convicted in flagrant breach of the *Al-Khawaja* interpretation of Article 6(3) (d) by the ECtHR. Lord Phillips, giving judgement in December 2009[34] on behalf of a unanimous Supreme Court, rose to the occasion. In 75 pages of detailed and careful argument, he respectfully pointed out the defects in the *Al-Khawaja* decision, in the light of existing ECtHR caselaw on the subject. He reviewed English and international practice and concluded that there would be rare occasions where the Strasbourg court has failed to appreciate or accommodate particular aspects of

---

[31] Evidence in Criminal Proceedings: Hearsay and Related Topics (Law Com no. 245).

[32] ECtHR, Decision of 13 January 2009, *Taxquet v Belgium*, Application no. 926/05, § 48.

[33] ECtHR, Decision of 16 November 2010, *Taxquet v Belgium*, Application no. 926/05.

[34] [2009] UKSC 14.

our domestic process and in particular the carefully "crafted code" of the Criminal Justice Act 2003 which was intended to ensure that evidence is admitted only when it is fair that it should be.[35] He endorsed the view put forward in *R v Sellick*, that Article 6 jurisprudence was developed with respect to cases tried under inquisitorial processes "without regard to such safeguards as have been built into the English process."[36] In those circumstances it was open to a domestic court to decline to follow the ECtHR, giving reasons in order to offer them the opportunity to reconsider:

> In these circumstances I have decided that it would not be right for this court to hold that the sole or decisive test should have been applied rather than the provisions of the 2003 Act, interpreted in accordance with their natural meaning. I believe that those provisions strike the right balance between the imperative that a trial must be fair and the interests of victims in particular and society in general that a criminal should not be immune from conviction where a witness, who has given critical evidence in a statement that can be shown to be reliable, dies or cannot be called to give evidence for some other reason. In so concluding I have taken careful account of the Strasbourg jurisprudence. I hope that in due course the Strasbourg court may also take account of the reasons that have led me not to apply the sole or decisive test in this case.[37]

This was an explicit challenge by Lord Phillips to open "a valuable dialogue between this court and the Strasbourg court." The Supreme Court judgement was a judicial *tour de force* of argument which contrasted sharply with the cursory 13 paragraphs of the original Strasbourg ruling and it provoked considerable debate. Lord Irving, a former Lord Chancellor offered energetic support for Lord Phillips, asserting that it was the constitutional duty of a judge "faced with an unprincipled or aberrant decision (or line of decisions) of the ECtHR, to confront the issue head on and make the case explaining why the Strasbourg Court's decision is flawed and should not be followed."[38] Others, disagreed, emphasising the "Mirror" principle that the role of the UK Supreme court was merely to anticipate a decision that the appellant would obtain at Strasbourg. As the late Lord Rodger famously put it: "*Argentoratum locutum, iudicium finitum* – Strasbourg has spoken, the case is closed."[39] Sir Philip Sales, suggested that dissent such as that demonstrated by Lord Phillips was impeding the ECtHR in its crucial work of creating "a broad congruence in the constitutional arrangements to be shared by a range of neighbouring states based on democracy, rule of law and respect for human rights."[40] The academic William O'Brien felt that on the confrontation issue, Strasbourg was right and London was wrong and hoped that "the ECtHR will refuse to back down in the face of this challenge, and reiterate in the strongest

---

[35] Para. 36.

[36] *R v Sellick* (fn.28) at [36]–[38] (Waller LJ).

[37] At 108.

[38] Irving (2012), p. 252.

[39] Hale (2012).

[40] Sales (2012), p. 266.

possible terms its existing authorities."[41] Marny Requa criticised Lord Phillips for directing his judgement exclusively towards the Grand Chamber of the ECtHR and saw the decision as a tragic "missed opportunity" for the Supreme Court to review some of the more illiberal elements of the Criminal Justice Act 2003.[42] Ian Dennis on the other hand, found the ECtHR's emphasis on the "sole and decisive" principle to be an arbitrary value preference which gave an uncritical priority to the defendant's interests.[43]

In May 2010, the Grand Chamber heard the *Al-Khawaja* case. And then followed silence. As Conor Gearty put it:

> That whole year passed and then as 2011 drifted by concern grew. Had the (Strasbourg) judges forgotten? Were they too scared to act?[44]

Clearly there were discussions behind the scenes. In March 2011 the President of the ECtHR, Sir Nicolas Bratza intervened in support of Lord Phillips. At a seminar in Edinburgh he suggested that it was "right and healthy" that national courts should continue to feel free to criticise Strasbourg judgments where those judgments have applied principles which are unclear or inconsistent or where they have misunderstood national law or practices. He announced:

> I believe that there is room for increased dialogue between the judges of the courts, both informally and through their judgments. Informally this has already occurred in the successful meetings which have periodically taken place between groups of judges of the national courts and the Strasbourg Court. But dialogue through judgments is of equal importance. Even if it is not bound to accept the view of the national courts in their interpretation of Convention rights, it is of untold benefit for the Strasbourg Court that we should have those views.[45]

6 Dialogue and Resolution

On 15th December 2011 the Grand Chamber finally broke silence and delivered its judgement. The reason for the delay at once became clear. Playing the UK Supreme Court at its own game, the Grand Chamber produced a comprehensive and detailed review of the authorities in this area, analysing the reasoning of the UK Court of Appeal,[46] the UK Supreme Court[47] and the approach adopted by common law

---

[41] O'Brian (2011), p. 94.

[42] Requa (2010), pp. 209 and 230.

[43] Dennis (2010), p. 273.

[44] Gearty C (2012) UK Constitutional Group, 9 January 2012, Al-Khawaja and Tahery v the United Kingdom, http://ukconstitutionallaw.org/2012/01/09/conor-gearty-al-khawaja-and-tahery-v-united-kingdom/.

[45] Bratza (2011), p. 511.

[46] ECtHR, Decision of 15 December 2011, *Al Khawaja and Tahery v United Kingdom*, Applications No. 26766/05 & 2222/06, §§ 51–56.

[47] §§ 56–62.

jurisdictions around the world[48] as well as its own caselaw. Having done so it conceded that in this case, London had been right and the lower Chamber had been wrong. Breach of specific Article 6(3)(d) provisions should *not* inevitably and automatically lead to a breach of the Convention notwithstanding that the evidence read to the court was the "sole and decisive" evidence. In the case of Al-Khawaja, but not that of Tahery, there were "sufficient counterbalancing factors"[49] to allow the evidence to be read out in court:

> The question in each case is whether there are sufficient counterbalancing factors in place, including measures that permit a fair and proper assessment of the reliability of that evidence to take place. This would permit a conviction to be based on such evidence only if it is sufficiently reliable given its importance in the case.[50]

It agreed that the existing safeguards in the domestic legislation were, in principle, strong safeguards designed to ensure fairness.[51] Crucially it insisted that it was important for the Court to have regard to substantial differences in legal systems and procedures, including different approaches to the admissibility of evidence in criminal trials.[52] Where such evidence was admitted, enormous care had to be taken with counterbalancing measures, particularly in "sole and decisive" cases but breach of Article 6 was not automatic. Two Judges (Sajó and Karaka) dissented, asserting that the "last line of protection of the right to defence is being abandoned in the name of an overall examination of fairness". Endorsing their dissent, Conor Gearty took the view that "on any reading it's a large-scale watering down of Article 6(3)(d)."[53]

Putting aside the rights and wrongs of the confrontation issue, it is perfectly clear that a judicial conversation significantly improved the decision-making of both courts. It turned confrontation into compromise, ensuring that both parties were satisfied with an outcome that was workable.

7   Conclusion

As indicated at the outset, many scholars see current trends in ECtHR jurisprudence as leading inevitably to the "convergence" of our European justice systems which will allow evidence to be transmitted from one jurisdiction to the next. John Jackson, for example, argues that courts such as the ECtHR and the International Criminal Court are evolving a new and entirely *sui generis* model of procedure, which he labels "participatory." This is, according to him, the "vision" which has

---

[48] §§ 63–87.
[49] § 158.
[50] § 147.
[51] § 151.
[52] § 130.
[53] Gearty (fn. 44).

been evolved over the last few years by the far-sighted judges of the ECtHR, and which is now being handed down to national jurisdictions "within and beyond the boundaries of Europe."[54] In 2012 he and Sarah Summers adopted the bold claim that criminal evidence was therefore being "internationalised."[55] Not everyone shares Jackson and Summers' enthusiasm. Just before his retirement, the distinguished Law Lord, Lord Hoffman attacked the ECtHR for trying to "aggrandise its jurisdiction" by laying down a "federal law of Europe" and by trying to erase differences between procedural regimes by interference. He cited examples, including the judgement of the lower chamber in *Al-Khawaja* of the court meddling in matters which it clearly did not understand and "teaching grandmothers to suck eggs."[56] In this view he was supported by Marc Bossuyt, the President of the Belgian Constitutional Court,[57] and many others.

It is precisely these problems that transjudicial dialogue can help to avoid. The reciprocal process which I have been describing, which as Croquet argues, could be enhanced by advisory opinions and more formalised structures for dialogue,[58] does not erode but supports the individuality and distinctiveness of our systems. It encourages knowledge and mutual respect between us. What happened in *Al-Khawaja* was clearly the failure of an attempt to homogenise evidentiary rules as a result of a conversation initiated by Lord Phillips which ultimately led to a recognition that the principles of confrontation enshrined in Article 6(3)(d) can be articulated successfully through very different modes of procedures in different countries. Further debate and yet more lively debate, can be anticipated.[59]

References

Anagnostou D (2010) Does European human rights law matter? Implementation and domestic impact of Strasbourg Court judgments on minority-related policies. Int J Hum Rights 14:721–743

Baudenbacher C (2003) Foreword: globalization of the judiciary. Tex Int Law J 38:397–404

Bertoni EA (2009) The inter-American Court of human rights and the European Court of human rights: a dialogue on freedom of expression standards. Eur Hum Rights Law Rev 3:1–26

Bjorge E, Andenas M (2011) National implementation of ECHR rights: Kant's categorical imperative and the convention. Oxford student legal studies paper no 3/2011. Oxford University, Oxford

---

[54] Jackson (2005); Jackson (2008), p. 248.

[55] Jackson and Summers (2012).

[56] Hoffmann, the Lord (2009). The Universality of Human Rights, Judicial Studies Board Annual Lecture. 19 March 2009, available at http://justice-for-families.org.uk/documents/reports/JStudiesBoardLecture0309.htm, para. 27.

[57] http://strasbourgobservers.com/2010/05/17/president-of-belgian-constitutional-court-criticizes-european-court-of-human-rights/.

[58] Croquet (2011), pp. 368–369.

[59] Hale (2012), p. 78.

Bratza N (2011) The relationship between the UK courts and Strasbourg. Eur Hum Rights Law Rev 11:505–512

Croquet NAJ (2011) The European Court of human rights' norm-creation and norm-limiting processes: resolving a normative tension. Columbia J Eur Law 17:307–375

de Wolf AH, Wallace DH (2009) The overseas exchange of human rights jurisprudence: the US Supreme Court in the European Court of human rights. Int Crim Justice Rev 19:287–307

Dennis I (2010) The right to confront witnesses; meanings, myths and human rights. Georgetown Law J 1011:255–274

Friedman RD (2004) Thoughts from across the water on hearsay and confrontation. Crim Law Rev 50:697–709

Hale B (2012) Argentoratum Locutum: is Strasbourg or the Supreme Court supreme? Hum Rights Law Rev 12:65–78

Hoffmeister F (2006) Germany: status of European convention on human rights in domestic law. Int J Constitutional Law 4:722–731

Irving L (2012) A British interpretation of convention rights. Public Law 56:237–252

Jackson JD (2005) The effect of human rights on criminal evidentiary processes: towards convergence, divergence or realignment? Mod Law Rev 68:737–764

Jackson JD (2008) Faces of transitional justice: two attempts to build common standards beyond national boundaries. In: Jackson J, Langer M et al (eds) Crime, procedure and evidence in a comparative and international context. Essays in honour of Professor Mirjan Damaška. Hart, Oxford, pp 221–250

Jackson JD, Summers SJ (2012) The internationalisation of criminal evidence: beyond the common law and civil law traditions. Cambridge University Press, Cambridge

Krisch N (2008) The open architecture of European human rights law. Mod Law Rev 71:183–216

Martinico G, Pollicino O (2012) The interaction between Europe's legal systems: judicial dialogue and the creation of supranational laws. Edward Elgar, Cheltenham

O'Brian WE Jr (2011) Confrontation: the defiance of the English courts. Int J Evid Proof 15:93–116

Requa M (2010) Absent witnesses and the UK Supreme Court: judicial deference as judicial dialogue? Int J Evid Proof 14:208–231

Roberts P, Hunter J (2012) Introduction – the human rights revolution in criminal evidence and procedure. In: Roberts P, Hunter J (eds) Criminal evidence and human rights: reimagining common law procedural traditions. Hart, Oxford, pp 1–23

Sales PJ (2012) Strasbourg jurisprudence and the Human Rights Act: a response to Lord Irvine. Public Law 56:253–267

Slaughter AM (1994) A typology of transjudicial communication. Univ Richmond Law Rev 29:99–137

Slaughter AM (2003) A global community of courts. Harv Int Law J 44:191–219

Stone Sweet A (2012) A cosmopolitan legal order: constitutional pluralism and rights adjudication in Europe. Global Constitutionalism 1:53–90

Stone Sweet A, Keller H (2008) Assessing the impact of the ECHR on national legal systems. In: Stone Sweet A, Keller H (eds) A Europe of rights. Oxford University Press, Oxford, pp 677–712

Tracogna C (2010) The influence of the ECHR jurisprudence on the national criminal procedure system. The Italian perspective: From divergence to realignment. Lex et Scientia Int J 17:85–91

Waters MA (2007) Creeping monism: the judicial trend toward interpretive incorporation of human rights treaties. Columbia Law Rev 107:628–705

Transnational Investigations and Prosecution of Cross-Border Cases in Europe: Guidelines for a Model of Fair Multicultural Criminal Justice

Stefano Ruggeri

Abstract This study analyses the issue of transnational prosecution and investigation. It starts with the premise that transborder criminal investigations and the gathering of overseas evidence cannot be adequately dealt with independently of the assignment of the power to prosecute and adjudicate cross-border crimes. The present study analyses the solutions provided by some of the main models of international cooperation and stresses that in the European scenario, characterised by an increasingly transcultural criminal law, the choice of the forum and of the applicable criminal law cannot be left to a bargaining among the competing authorities on the basis of uncoordinated national laws. The need for legal certainty requires clear rules on the assignment of the prosecutorial power that meet the requirements inherent in the essential principles of criminal law, such as *nullum crimen sine lege* and *nulla pena sine culpa*. Moreover, in a common area of freedom, security and justice, any form of discrimination among EU citizens must be avoided. The choice of the forum pursuant to these fundamental requirements is of crucial importance for establishing both the form of conducting cross-border investigations and collecting evidence overseas, and the applicable procedural criminal law.

Keywords Cross-border investigation • Human rights • Transcultural criminal law • Transnational prosecution

Contents

1 Premise 194
2 Solution Models 195
   2.1 The MLA Model 196
   2.2 The MR Model 198

S. Ruggeri (⊠)
Department of Law, University of Messina, Piazza Pugliatti No. 1, Messina, Italy
e-mail: steruggeri@unime.it

S. Ruggeri (ed.), *Transnational Evidence and Multicultural Inquiries in Europe*,
DOI 10.1007/978-3-319-02570-4_16, © Springer International Publishing Switzerland 2014

    2.3   The Model of Extraterritorial and Joint Investigations 201
    2.4   Federalist Models 203
3   Guidelines for a Model of Fair Transnational Criminal Justice 206
    3.1   The State's Power to Punish Cross-Border Offences 207
    3.2   The Assignment of the Power to Prosecute and Adjudicate Transnational Cases .. 212
    3.3   Cross-Border Investigations and Transnational Evidence Gathering 221
4   Conclusion 225
References 226

1 Premise

Investigating and prosecuting cross-border offences encompasses a number of very different situations depending on the subject and the structure of the inquiries at stake. Cross-border cases can, on an initial level, relate to *transnational offences*, i.e., to offences touching upon the interests of several countries. This circumstance may have different causes, such as the conduct being committed in the territory of various countries or the act having territorial and extraterritorial aspects, where, for example, the act has been committed by people with a citizenship other than that of the country in which it was committed and/or by people with different nationality and/or resident in different countries. In the latter cases, the definition of *multinational offence* would be perhaps more appropriate than that of *transnational* or *transborder offences*, which should be restricted to the former cases. But of course there are plenty of situations in which both these characteristics occur and one can recognise the features of a truly *transcultural criminal law*.[1] Furthermore, complex challenges are posed by internet-based crimes committed in an a-territorial space and especially by crimes committed by organisations acting in several countries.

As we will see, such cases pose, in a great part, problems of coordination among investigations conducted parallelly in more than one country against different individuals in regard to related crimes that form part of complex criminal affairs. The development in supranational legislation has, furthermore, followed the increasing recourse to enquiries conducted jointly by investigative authorities of different countries, a phenomenon that reflects the progressive shift from assistance models to new models of extraterritorial and especially joint investigations.[2] Paradoxically, however, the absence of clear rules on the assignment of jurisdiction in cross-border cases and the failure to enshrine a general ban on transnational *lis pendens* entail the risk of national investigations overlapping with each other either on the same subject or against the same individuals, or both. Moreover, there may also be cross-border aspects, in a broad sense, in investigations conducted in the context of *national* procedures, insofar as they require the collection of evidence located abroad. As we will note, the assistance models still seem to be tailored to these cases.

---

[1] Vogel (2010), pp. 1ff.

[2] Vallines García (2006), *passim*.

Against this background, the research contained in this book has followed a multilevel approach, which encompasses an analysis of the models of gathering evidence overseas, the study of the solutions offered by recent research and the increasing jurisprudential dialogues between national and supranational case law, and a critical examination of the draft Directive on a European investigation order. The purpose of this paper is to draw up, on the basis of the results of these analyses, guidelines to establish a transnational investigative procedure in line with the requirements of due process and of a human rights-oriented criminal law. To do this, I shall conduct this analysis starting with three of the questions I raised at the end of my introductory contribution on the EIO proposal, i.e.:

a) What do we mean by conducting investigations and gathering of evidence *abroad* in the *common* AFSJ?
b) In respect of what country do we conceive an investigation in *other* Member States or obtaining evidence from *other* Member States? Who will have competence to prosecute, who will investigate and who will cooperate?
c) What law, both on a substantive and procedural level, will be applied in cross-border matters?

Of course these three questions are strictly linked with each other. Therefore I shall deal with the issue of cross-border investigations starting with the assignment of prosecution. On the basis of the results of these investigations I shall then analyse the issue of the procedural and substantive criminal law to be applied to cross-border cases.

2   Solution Models

Traditionally, there was a clear division of competences in the prosecution and investigation of cross-border cases. Whereas the assignment of jurisdiction entailed the power to prosecute and adjudicate the transnational case according to *national* criminal law, investigations were carried out and evidence was obtained abroad by *foreign* authorities pursuant to their own procedural law. This approach to cross-border investigations was blurred by the involvement of authorities of the requesting country in overseas activities and the increasing rise of extraterritorial and joint investigations. Although these factors have contributed to the development of the MLA into new models aimed at achieving, albeit in different manners, forms of integration of procedural laws, Europe has failed to take similar action on the assignment of jurisdiction, which, despite the increasing role of the principle of the division of competences,[3] has remained a matter of national criminal law and, above all, of individual criminal jurisdictions.

In the light of the aim of the present paper, I shall firstly outline the developments in the relationship between the choice of the prosecutorial power and the conduction of transborder investigations by focusing on four models, i.e., the MLA

---

[3] See, among others, Satzger (2011), p. 42.

model, the MR model, the model of extraterritorial and joint investigations, and finally federalist models.

2.1   The MLA Model

The MLA model of investigative cooperation has not traditionally dealt with the assignment of jurisdiction. The failure to address this issue in the traditional international instruments of MLA is certainly due to the fact that, as noted above, this issue has been deemed to be a matter of national criminal law. This is clearly expressed by Article 1 ECMACM, according to which

> The Contracting Parties undertake to afford each other, in accordance with the provisions of this Convention, the widest measure of mutual assistance in proceedings in respect of offences the punishment of which, at the time of the request for assistance, *falls within the jurisdiction* of the judicial authorities of the requesting Party.

Nevertheless, the overlap of different uncoordinated national rules caused great uncertainty about the choice of the forum in the traditional instruments of MLA, which, in my view, has not allowed the issue of gathering of evidence overseas to be addressed in a coherent manner. Significantly, the ECMACM, unlike the provisions regarding extradition in the 1957 Convention, did not contain a ban on assistance in the case of parallel proceedings in the requested country. Furthermore, this approach entailed clear repercussions on the sphere of the defendant's rights, since it applied even where the requested assistance touched upon the goods of the defendant (*e.g.*, in cases of search and seizure) irrespective of whether they were familiar with *lex fori*.

Instead, the traditional instruments of MLA contained clear elements showing a marked preference for a territorial conception of assistance. Amongst them, we should firstly remember the territorial conception of sovereignty, which constituted one of the main grounds for refusal of assistance. Significantly, moreover, where assistance could be afforded, it was to be provided pursuant exclusively to the *lex loci*. This approach was actually strengthened in cases of intrusive measures such as search and seizure, in respect of which the ECMACM granted the contracting Parties the power to make the execution of letters rogatory dependent on the fact it was *consistent with the law of the requested State*. Moreover, whilst the ECMACM did not protect the defendant from the risk of double prosecution, it took care of the need to ensure the availability of the sought evidence for the ongoing proceedings in the requesting country.[4] Though, since the subject of these

---

[4] Two examples are noteworthy. Pursuant to Article 6(1), the requested country could delay the handing over of any property, records or documents requested, if it required the said property, records or documents in connection with pending criminal proceedings. Furthermore, According to Article 11(1)(b), the transfer of a person in custody whose personal appearance as a witness or for purposes of confrontation was applied for by the requesting country could be refused if his or her presence was "necessary at criminal proceedings pending in the territory of the requested Party."

proceedings was not specified, this approach enhanced the uncertainty about both prosecution and investigation in respect of the same offence and the same offender.

The developments of the MLA model provided stronger protection both for the defendant and for third parties. The 1990 UN MTMACM gave a clear example, in that it not only allowed the requested State to postpone the execution of the request if its execution could interfere with an ongoing investigation or prosecution in the requested State [Art. 4(3)], but it also enacted a ban on assistance in the event of *lis pendens* in the requested country, i.e., in the event of an ongoing investigation or prosecution of the same offence to which the request for assistance related [Art. 4 (1)(d)]. Nevertheless, since both the refusal and the postponement were discretionary, the requested State was empowered—for grounds that, taking into account the intergovernmental nature of the traditional MLA system, could also be of a political nature—to provide assistance *despite* the continuation of the domestic investigation or prosecution. On the other hand, the introduction in this intermediate phase of MLA of the possibility for the requesting State to require compliance with specific procedural forms of *lex fori* in the execution of the letters rogatory (Art. 6) considerably smoothened the territorial conception of legal assistance. However, the wide leeway left to the requesting State as to what procedures it could require, notwithstanding these had to be in line with the law and practice of the requested State, left complete uncertainty about the concrete form of the assistance sought in terms of the procedure of the requested investigative activity.

The jurisdictionalization of legal assistance achieved by the most advanced instruments of MLA not only could not reduce such uncertainty but also gave much greater margins to the requesting authority regarding the choice of procedures to be followed in the collection of evidence overseas, procedures that could be rejected by the requested authority only in cases of infringement of the fundamental principles of *lex loci*.[5] The enactment of this selection criterion, which mitigated the rigidity of full compliance with the law (and practice) of the requested State, entailed the great risk of hybridizing procedures that could rarely be harmonized with each other. This approach could not, however, complete the process of decoupling investigations and the collection of evidence abroad from a territorial conception of legal assistance. Furthermore, the new forms of extraterritorial and joint investigations were subject, as a rule, to the sole law of the Member State in whose territory the investigative activity was conducted.[6] Moreover, the lack of internationally agreed rules on the assignment of jurisdiction and the failure of the EUCMACM to establish rules of supplementation of the ECMACM on the management of requests for legal assistance in cases of *lis pendens* have not contributed

---

[5] For instance, see Art. 4(1) EUCMACM.

[6] Thus, Article 13(3)(b) EUCMACM states that the JIT must carry out its operations "in accordance with the law of the Member State in which it operates." Even more explicitly, according to Article 14(3) EUCMACM covert investigations must take place "in accordance with the national law and procedures of the Member States on the territory of which the covert investigation takes place."

to the establishment of a clear approach to the two core questions of transnational inquiries related to the competence for prosecution and investigation.

2.2   The MR Model

The MR model has not, since its introduction, approached the issue of overseas investigations in a consistent way. Again, the main deficiency lies, in my view, in the failure to address the issue of the assignment of jurisdiction, which has always been left to national law. Furthermore, whilst the FD EAW protected the addressee of a final judgment in *any* Member State from the risk of a deprivation of liberty aimed at a new proceeding in the issuing country, the first legislative text launched in the field of criminal evidence, albeit limited to freezing and securing evidence,[7] i.e. the FD OFPE, considerably reduced the defendant's right to avoid new proceedings for the same offence, since it left the executing authority a certain amount of leeway in rendering assistance even in cases of clear infringement of the *ne bis in idem* principle [Art. 7(1)(c)]. Equally reduced protection was granted to defendants against the risk of parallel proceedings since, unlike the FD EAW, the FD OFPE provided for the (discretionary) postponement of assistance, only for a reasonable time, where freezing or securing evidence could jeopardise an ongoing investigation, which in the absence of further indications might have the same subject as that of the relevant proceedings in the issuing State [Art. 8(1)(a)]. Concerning the form of execution of the freezing order, the FD OFPE inherited the approach of the improved MLA. However, the fact that the executing authority had to follow the requirements set by the issuing authority, albeit attenuated by the specification that these had to be restricted to those needed to ensure the validity of the evidence taken, had serious repercussions not only on the powers of the executing authority and the possibility of the proper execution of the sought measure, but also on the sphere of individual rights. Above all, this approach did not ensure the addressee of the foreign freezing order the same level of protection granted in similar domestic cases, as individuals had to undergo procedures that could diverge considerably from those established by *lex loci*, which people can legitimately trust. Significantly, some national legislation, while implementing this Framework Decision, has provided further limits aimed at avoiding the standards of protection being relaxed by the application of foreign law.[8]

---

[7] Gascón Inchausti (2007), pp. 137f.

[8] For instance, Article 695-9-14 of the French CCP, inserted by Act 570/2005, while stating that the decisions freezing pieces of evidence must as a rule be executed according to French procedural law, allows for the application of foreign law, if so requested in the certificate, within the limits of the second paragraph of Article 694-3, i.e., on the condition, under penalty of nullity, that foreign rules "do not reduce the rights of the parties or the procedural guarantees provided for by the present Code" (English translation of the French CCP with the participation of Prof. J. Spencer). On this general guarantee, laid down in the field of letters rogatory, see Lelieur (2013), pp. 402f.

These deficiencies have not been amended by subsequent EU legislation. Furthermore, not only has the first legislative instrument aimed at obtaining evidence in other Member States, i.e. the FD EEW, reproduced the approach of the FD OFPE, thus leaving the discretionary relevance both of refusal and postponement of assistance in cases respectively of *ne bis in idem* [Art. 13(1)(a)] and ongoing investigation [Art. 16(2)(a)],[9] but it has also re-introduced a typical MLA ground for refusal, which is the fact that the EEW has been issued for offences regarded under the law of the executing State as committed wholly or in a major or essential part within its territory [Art. 13(1)(f)(i)]. This territoriality requirement, which had disappeared in the first stage of the MR era, shows a clear shift towards a markedly territorial conception of transnational prosecution on the assumption that both the territorial jurisdiction and territorial criminal law provide the most adequate solution for prosecuting and sanctioning cross-border cases. This approach was not truly contradicted by the provision reproducing the combined method of gathering evidence in the executing State (Art. 12), a provision that shows a clear preference for applying the law of the issuing State. Indeed, combining the aforementioned territoriality exception with the rules on the procedures for evidence gathering can lead us to conclude that the openness towards foreign law not only concerns *procedural law* but is also restricted to those cases in which from the viewpoint of *lex loci* the act has not been committed in the territory of the executing State or has been committed within its territory only in a minor part. Thus, defendants and third parties will have to undergo a partial application of foreign law, which in the concrete case might be considerably different from local law, *due to the fact* that the offence is in great part a foreign matter only on the basis of territorial grounds.

A considerable change of approach emerged from the original draft of the EIO proposal, which, although it invoked the need to respect the fundamental principles enshrined in Article 6 TEU and in the already binding EU FRCh [Art. 1(1)], gave relevance neither to the double jeopardy rule nor to the exception of territoriality. There is no doubt that the contextual abolition of these requirements would have had immediate repercussions not only on national sovereignty but also on human rights,[10] since the individual's right not to be (further) prosecuted for the same act for which he had been definitively judged was endangered also from a domestic perspective, seeing that the peremptory wording of Article 8(1) obliged the executing authority to execute the requested measure irrespective of whether the act had been committed in its territory. Both these requirements, however, were re-introduced in the course of Council examinations and appeared in the text agreed in December 2011 amongst the grounds for refusal that potentially apply to any

---

[9] Criticism against the discretionary character of the refusal in case of *ne bis in idem* has been raised by Vervaele (2009), p. 158. Concerning the case of ongoing investigation, moreover, it is noteworthy that according to the FD EEW only a judge, court, investigating magistrate or public prosecutor of the executing State may take the decision on postponement.

[10] Peers (2010), pp. 1ff.

investigative measure, albeit in a fashion that gives rise to further human rights concerns.

Concerning the *ne bis in idem* principle, its acknowledgement does not appear to be in line with the approach of the EU FRCh, in that the existence of an investigation on an offence finally judged in another Member State still constitutes a facultative, rather than a mandatory, ground for refusal. Moreover, in order to avoid the risk of misusing the double jeopardy rule, the current text allows the execution of the EIO where it was issued against several persons but the final disposition only affects one of them, provided that the issuing authority gives proper assurance that the evidence transferred as a result of the EIO will not be used to prosecute that person. This approach appears to be somewhat contradictory and dangerous for the defendant's rights. First, this assurance relates only to a possible (further) *prosecution* in the issuing Member State, which does not extend to a criminal *investigation* against the same person, although precisely during the criminal investigations several measures can seriously threaten various rights of the defendant. Moreover, the EIO proposal establishes that, even if the consultation procedure confirms that the case has been finally dismissed with respect to a given person, the investigation order regarding them will nonetheless have to be executed. This conclusion minimizes the impact of investigative activities, which especially in cases of coercive measures produces the very effects that the double jeopardy rule aims to prevent.

Significantly, paragraph 1(f) states that assistance can be refused where the EIO was issued to obtain a coercive measure in respect of an act allegedly committed outside the issuing State and wholly or partially in the territory of the executing State, but this act does not constitute a criminal offence under *lex loci*. Also here, the approach adopted by the draft proposal seems contradictory, taking into account that refusal remains facultative in all cases. How could the executing authority decide to enforce coercive measures, which are always based on a (albeit differently construed) *fumus delicti*, where the act committed wholly or partially in its territory is not a criminal offence? Indeed, unlike the FD EEW, the EIO proposal does not allow for refusal of recognition where the EEW has been issued for offences regarded under the law of the executing State as committed wholly or in a major or essential part within its territory. This lacuna might be compensated for by a territorial conception of the procedural activities to be carried out by means of the new investigation order, a conception that is not contradicted by the possibility of authorities sent by the issuing country taking part in the investigative activities since they remain bound by *lex loci*, which provides the procedural basis of overseas investigations. On the other hand, one cannot overlook the progressive widening of the scope of application of the draft Directive, which under the draft agreed in December 2011, albeit mainly aimed at obtaining assistance by means of investigative activities conducted by foreign authorities in their territory, empowers the authorities of the issuing State to engage in law enforcement upon agreement of the executing and issuing authorities [Art. 9 (3a)]. As we have already observed, this system introduces an unprecedented system of extraterritorial enquiries *into* the MR model,[11] an innovation that should,

---

[11] Cf. Ruggeri, Introduction, above, Sect. 3.3.

moreover, be viewed in light of the reproduced openness to *lex fori* as to the procedures of investigation and evidence gathering abroad.

This approach, which makes it possible to go beyond a strict territorial view of procedural law in transnational cases, proves interesting but still gives rise to human rights concerns not only due to the failure to involve private parties[12] but also taking into account the way the combination of procedural laws is obtained. The main concerns relate to several aspects of the proposed procedure, especially the failure to define which formalities the issuing authority is entitled to request, the forced combination due to the clause of non-infringement with local law and, above all, the general conception of the procedures of the two countries, which interact as separate parts of their legal systems rather than as sources for developing an integrated procedure aimed to satisfy the needs of a transnational investigation.[13] This uncertainty regarding both the forms of the investigation and the authority entitled to provide for law enforcement entails unbearable risks for the addressee of the investigative activity, who may be exposed to more discriminatory treatment than they would be subject to in domestic cases.

2.3 The Model of Extraterritorial and Joint Investigations

Compared to the MLA model, extraterritorial enquiries constitute a relatively recent form of cross-border cooperation in the field of evidence gathering. This delay is certainly due to the strong sovereignty approach that has traditionally governed mutual assistance, which has never allowed for domestic law enforcement bodies to conduct investigations in the territory of other countries, thus limiting their participation to a vague presence in the execution of requests for assistance. It is noteworthy, furthermore, that the first forms of extraterritorial investigations were enacted in MLA texts in the same period in which radical changes occurred in the traditional request model, shifting clearly the MLA system towards the future MR model. Indeed, the first international rules on extraterritorial enquiries were introduced in the context of the MLA system.[14] An innovative approach emerged from the EUCMACM, which introduced "a new generation of extra-territorial investigations,"[15] completely unrelated to the requirement of urgency and aimed to fulfil the need to enhance horizontal cooperation in the fight against cross-border crimes requiring coordinated action. This approach

---

[12] *Ibid.*

[13] Ruggeri (2013a), p. 307

[14] In the CISA the possibility of conducting criminal investigations overseas was subject to the prior authorisation of specific investigative measures (surveillance, hot pursuit) by the host state in response to a request for legal assistance [see respectively Arts. 40(1) and 41(1)].

[15] See Klip (2012), p. 361.

provided the basis for a new way of conducting transnational inquiries that—albeit based on the request model, rather than on the order model[16]—allowed for investigative activities affecting fundamental rights[17] to be *ordinarily* carried out by the authorities of one Member State in the territory of another.

A revolutionary change took place through the introduction of a general framework for conducting investigations and gathering evidence in one or more Member States through joint activities, i.e., the setting up of joint investigation teams. Surprisingly, however, the free movement of judgements and judicial products achieved by the MR model did not lead either to establishing a free flow of law enforcement officials from one Member State to another[18] or the creation of integrated procedures aimed at satisfying the needs of the legal (constitutional) systems of the cooperating authorities. The 2002 FD JIT, dating back to the very beginning of the mutual recognition era, fully reproduced the approach of the EUCMACM, which had, unlike both instruments of improved mutual assistance and mutual recognition, established the almost strict application of the procedural law of the State in whose territory the team operates.[19] Thus, also the FD JIT, while allowing investigations by teams of officials of other Member States on national territory, adopted a markedly territorial conception of procedural law, mitigated only by providing for the possibility that members of the team other than its leader could carry out their tasks, "taking into account the conditions set by their own authorities in the agreement on setting up the team."[20]

This approach seems to be somewhat contradictory, and entails many risks both for the efficiency of cross-border prosecution and for the rights of the individuals involved in transnational inquiries. To start with, the application of *lex loci* as basis for any activity conducted by the team can give rise to a plethora of evidential laws[21] in all cases in which the team operates in the territory of more than one Member State. This solution constitutes neither an efficient nor a proper solution in a common AFSJ, since it not only multiplies the risk of incompatibility of the evidence collected with *lex fori* and therefore the risk of its inadmissibility in one or more national procedures,[22] but it can also expose individuals to similar investigative powers interfering with their rights in a possibly different manner according to

---

[16] All extraterritorial powers may, under the EUCMACM, be activated only upon request. For instance, under Article 12, "Each Member State shall undertake to ensure that, *at the request of another Member State*, controlled deliveries may be permitted on its territory in the framework of criminal investigations into extraditable offences."

[17] Both controlled deliveries and covert investigations constitute clear interferences with fundamental rights.

[18] See Klip (2012), p. 361.

[19] See respectively Art. 13(3)(b) EUCMACM. Similarly see Art. 20(3)(b) SAP ECMACM.

[20] Art. 1(3)(b) FD 2002/465/JHA. In these terms see Art. 13(3)(b) EUCMACM.

[21] Along the same lines, see Klip (2012), p. 392.

[22] It is noteworthy that the greatest resistance in Italy to the implementation of the FD JIT, which has not yet been transposed in national law, has been mainly due to concerns relating to the use at trial of the results of overseas investigations carried out by the team. On the Italian situation, see Caprioli (2013), p. 453.

the State in whose territory the team operates, thus undermining the individuals' trust in legal certainty. Uncertainty is further aggravated by the aforementioned provision that requires the members of the team to take into account the conditions established in the agreement on setting up the team, a provision that neither specifies what conditions may be required nor clarifies how these can be made compatible with *lex loci*, nor ensures that these are then fulfilled by the team during the investigations. Significantly some domestic legislation has posed legal limits on the power to agree conditions on evidence gathering in the context of joint investigation teams and in some cases the national law of the member of the team in a secondary position provides a limit to the tasks that can be required of them.[23]

Against this background, one cannot overlook the great potential of the model of joint inquiries, which has, *inter alia*, allowed for the immediate exchange of information among the authorities involved in the joint investigation.[24] Nevertheless, this model has not yet succeeded in renewing the way of investigating cross-border crimes through fair, concerted actions. The main deficiency of the JIT legislation is the incompleteness of its approach that, while bypassing the issue of assignment of jurisdiction, leaves huge leeway to the cooperating authorities in agreeing the conditions of the investigations to be carried out jointly. Upon closer examination, however, this approach remains rooted in a more territorial conception of transnational procedures than that of both the MLA and the MR models, even where the investigations require a coordinated action spread over the territory of many Member States, a solution that does not take into due account the trust both of the defendant and the addressee of the investigation in procedural law.

2.4 Federalist Models

As shown above by *Bernd Schünemann*,[25] federalist models provide a fruitful alternative to the aforementioned approaches, which deserves careful reflection also in the context of the present paper. Like other models, also this approach, applied in Switzerland before the new StPO of the Helvetic Confederation,[26] lies with the assignment of prosecution to *one* jurisdiction for *one* offence. It is, however, noteworthy that the assignment of the prosecutorial competence, unlike in any other model, also entails the power of the competent authority of a single State to investigate in the entire federal territory. This overall territorial competence

---

[23] For instance, Article 695-3 of the French CCP, inserted by Law 204/2004, provides that "French judicial police officers and agents attached to a joint investigation team may carry out operations ordered by the head of the team, over the whole of the territory of the State in which they are operating, *within the limit of the powers conferred on them by the present Code*" (English translation of the French CCP with the participation of Prof. J. Spencer).

[24] See Art. 1(9) FD JIT.

[25] Schünemann, Part IV, Sect. 3.

[26] *Ibid.*

is furthermore accompanied by the application of the sole procedural *lex fori*, starting with the assumption that also a transnational prosecution requires a single, coherent set of procedural rules.[27]

The model of "transnational procedural unity"—elaborated within a research project coordinated by *Bernd Schünemann*[28] and set forth above[29]—has in great part inherited this approach. Also here, the proposed model is based on the concentration both of prosecutorial and investigative powers in one single Member State. This result would be achieved though a prompt assignment of jurisdiction, which in cases of multiple competences of more than one State should follow a two-step approach consisting of the combination of a fixed, hierarchized order of criteria with a flexible procedural solution based upon the focal point (*Schwerpunkt*) of the alleged offence. One of the most significant innovations of this model consists of the introduction of a new institution, i.e. *Eurodefensor*, whose tasks would include representing the defendant's rights in the assignment of jurisdiction. This is a very delicate phase since, as noted above, the assignment of jurisdiction would imply the attribution to the competent authority of the power to investigate in the *whole* EU territory, i.e., in the territory of *any* Member State. Moreover, the fact that investigations and the collection of evidence follow the sentencing State's law would also make the admissibility of evidence a strictly national issue.[30]

Federalist models offer an interesting approach, whose greatest merit lies, in my view, in the coherence ensured by the assignment of prosecution to a single State and the widening of the investigative competence to the whole federal territory under a single procedural law. At the same time, the question arises as to whether the choice to link prosecution, adjudication and investigation to a single authority and a single (both substantive and procedural) law constitutes the only way to ensure coherence in *any* cross-border inquiry and, above all, as to whether this approach can properly satisfy the need for pluralism that is inherent in the most complex transnational inquiries.

Thus, especially in cases of criminal actions committed by several people with different citizenships (or resident in different countries) and consisting of a multitude of single crimes spread over the territory of several States, the solution of concentrating the prosecution in a single jurisdiction for a single offence seems to satisfy neither the need for procedural economy nor the defendant's interest in avoiding multiple prosecution.[31] Upon closer analysis, the notion of "offence" appears to be insufficient, both from an objective and a subjective viewpoint, to grasp the complexity of such phenomena, in which the concurrence of several criminal powers reveals the need for a pluralist approach that is inherent in the

---

[27] *Ibid.*

[28] Schünemann (2006b), *passim*.

[29] Schünemann, Part IV, Sect. 5.

[30] *Ibid.*

[31] In a different sense see Schünemann (2006a), p. 100.

characteristics of the concrete case and that, in my view, is therefore a value to be preserved rather than a danger to be prevented. From the defendant's viewpoint, a pluralist approach would in any way jeopardise their right not to be prosecuted by several jurisdictions as long as it can be ensured that only *one* jurisdiction deals with a single offence as allegedly committed by them. As a consequence of this, a multiple adjudication of the complex action could provide a coherent solution to the prosecution of cross-border cases according to the possibly different needs of the States involved. But also this should be viewed as an added value rather than a shortcoming.

Concerning the link between assignment of jurisdiction, adjudication and investigation of the case, it appears to me that the solution of adjudicating separately single offenders in relation to the offences of which complex criminal actions are comprised does not necessarily entail a fragmentation of the criminal law response due to a differentiated application of national *substantive* criminal laws, which in a common AFJS should no longer be seen as parts of unconnected legal systems. As has been noted, furthermore, an approximation of *procedural* criminal laws has already been achieved according to the needs of the concrete case by means of the application of foreign procedures in the execution of letters rogatory and, within the MR area, of foreign orders. And although this approach cannot result in either a general legal approximation of national criminal procedures or in the supplementation of the national legal systems they belong to, there is no doubt that it has made it possible to go beyond the traditional MLA approach, based upon a strictly national application of procedural criminal law in cross-border cases.

On the other hand, the territorial orientation both of the adjudication and the investigation, emerging from federalist models, might have repercussions on the protection of the fundamental rights of the individuals involved in transborder criminal inquiries. Concerning the distribution of powers and the adjudication of the case, the application of the substantive law of the country of the conduct (or of the consequence of the criminal action), which also here constitutes the main criterion for the choice of the forum, cannot *always* ensure that the alleged offender could have had access to the territorial criminal law, which is an essential precondition for the fulfilment of the fundamental principle *nulla pena sine lege*. Nor can this result always be achieved, in cases of complex crimes with several accomplices, by assigning the power to prosecute through the application of different criteria, such as the location of most items of evidence.[32] Following this criterion, the assignment of jurisdiction would in a great part depend on how charges are construed and preferred, and if the adjudication of the case should follow solely the substantive law of the chosen jurisdiction, this law might even be linguistically inaccessible to the offender. Similar concerns arise in the field of procedural criminal law due to the widening of the power of the competent authority to

---

[32] See Art. 2(2) of the Proposal for the Regulation of Trans-national Criminal Proceedings in the European Union containing the model of transnational procedural unity. See Schünemann (2006b), p. 6.

investigate under its own procedural law in the territory of any EU Member State. Indeed, the exercise of investigative powers over the whole EU territory does not seem to take into account the diversity of procedural legal systems and the trust of the addresses in the procedures established by their own laws. In the latter regard, why should defendants and especially suspicionless parties be subject (even after the intervention of the authority competent under *lex loci* to authorise measures of coercion) to the investigative activities touching upon their fundamental rights, carried out pursuant to procedures laid down by foreign law they could not know?

The case of interferences with fundamental rights shows, in my view, the natural limit of federalist models, which provide a very promising approach that, however, presupposes a uniform fundamental rights framework. Significantly the former Swiss model worked on the basis of a common Constitution,[33] i.e., on the basis of a uniform Charter of fundamental rights viewed from a substantive perspective. But the EU AFSJ is still far from this goal especially in the field of procedural criminal law,[34] despite the great potential of the EU FRCh. This would not, however, mean that the fundamental requirement of legal certainty could only be fulfilled by applying the territorial law of the country State in which the investigations take place,[35] a law which both the defendant and third parties may be unfamiliar with.

3 Guidelines for a Model of Fair Transnational Criminal Justice

It has been observed that the conduction of investigations and the collection of evidence *abroad* presuppose establishing which jurisdiction is empowered to prosecute and adjudicate the case. This issue has been intensively debated over recent years with specific regard to the topic of transnational conflicts of jurisdiction[36] mainly as a consequence of the fact that the Lisbon Treaty has empowered EU institutions to adopt legislative measures to prevent and solve such conflicts [Art. 82(1)(b) TFEU]. But of course the need for legal certainty, which is in the interest both of the criminal justice systems and the people involved in criminal inquiries, should require the competent forum to be established in a manner that allows conflicts of jurisdiction to be avoided in advance. Therefore, increasing attention has been paid in recent years to the need to restrict the State's power to extend its own jurisdiction and apply its own criminal law to acts committed abroad.

---

[33] Schünemann, Part IV, Sect. 3.

[34] Along the same lines, see Bitzilekis et al. (2006), pp. 250f.

[35] This was, instead, the proposal of Bitzilekis et al. (2006), p. 251, in cases of coercive means.

[36] See, among others, the results of the research projects coordinated by *Arndt Sinn*, and *Martin Böse* and *Frank Meyer*, respectively, in Sinn (2012c), and Böse et al. (2013).

This has led to a radical change of approach. From the viewpoint of international law, the traditional approach, based on the search for genuine links justifying the intervention of national criminal law,[37] not only has not succeeded in avoiding the concurrence of multiple jurisdictions but has even promoted the overlap of national criminal laws through the creation of a tangled-web aimed at avoiding negative conflicts.[38] However, concurrence may be accepted only amongst sovereign powers to punish crimes on a legitimate basis, which calls upon a drastic restriction of the power of national jurisdictions to punish cross-border cases. A new reflection on the concurrence among national jurisdictions should therefore move from what, following the well-known distinction of the Third Restatement of Foreign Relations Law of the American Law Institute from 1988,[39] is known as "jurisdiction to prescribe."[40] Thus, the power to prosecute cross-border crimes must be assigned amongst those of the countries having a legitimate right to punish transborder offences. This approach provides, furthermore, methodologically a useful basis to understand fully the topic of transborder investigations. As has been noted at the introduction of this study, the determination of what criminal law is entitled to *punish* and what criminal jurisdiction is entitled to *prosecute* transborder cases are logic preconditions to deal with cross-border investigations and the gathering of overseas evidence in a proper way. Moreover, although the choice of the forum and the power to investigate cross-border cases undoubtedly pertain to the sphere of procedural law and notwithstanding prosecution follows the investigations conducted in the pre-trial phase, in this paper I shall analyse the issue of cross-border investigations after dealing with the choice of the forum, since investigations may be initiated on the assumption that national courts have jurisdiction over the case.

3.1   The State's Power to Punish Cross-Border Offences

There is no doubt that in the current European framework the main need is not to limit but to justify the extraterritorial extension of national substantive criminal law and criminal jurisdiction in light of the limits deriving from international, constitutional and European law.[41] Whereas, however, the international principle of non-intervention in foreign affairs does not hinder the concurrence of national *Strafansprüche* based on genuine links, both constitutional and European law impose strict limits on the extraterritorial extension of the application of domestic

---

[37] See the Decision of the PCIJ in the *Lotus* case of 7 September 1927: PCIJ Series A No. 10.

[38] Böse and Meyer (2011), p. 38.

[39] American Law Institute (1988).

[40] In this sense see especially Böse (2013), pp. 75ff.

[41] This assumption is the starting point of the DFG project coordinated by *Martin Böse* and *Frank Meyer*. See Böse and Meyer (2011), pp. 337ff. Along the same lines, cf. Wörner (2013), § 4.

criminal law, i.e., among others the respect for the principles *nullum crimen sine lege* and *nulla pena sine culpa*, on one hand, and the ban of discrimination with regard to fundamental rights of EU citizens such as the right to free movement, on the other.[42]

In the former regard, it is well known that the *nullum crimen sine lege* principle, enshrined both in the ECHR (Art. 7) and the EU FRCh (Art. 49), entails qualitative requirements such as the foreseeability and accessibility of the relevant criminal law provision.[43] The foreseeability requirement is of great importance in Strasbourg's case law with regard not only to substantive[44] but also to procedural criminal law, as we will see below. Moreover, in the current multilinguistic European context and according to a modern conception of criminal law, characterised by increasing localism,[45] the application of criminal law must presuppose the possibility for a potential offender to have linguistic access to criminal law provisions. This fundamental guarantee cannot be overlooked in cross-border cases for the simple (and sometimes accidental) circumstance that a case acquires a transnational character. A qualitative extension of the *nullum crimen sine lege* principle to transborder cases emerged significantly from the discussions on the FD EAW, which raised serious concerns as to the drastic reduction of the dual criminality requirement. Credit must be given in particular to *Bernd Schünemann* for stressing the consequences of this solution, which would, in light of the characteristics of the order model, lead to the enforcement of the most punitive criminal law and the surrender of a defendant for an act that would not constitute a criminal offence or meet the requirement of legal certainty under the law of the executing State.[46] The German *Bundesverfassungsgericht* partially shared this approach in the Decision on the first German Act implementing the EAW Framework Decision, thus overruling its previous positions, based on the sufficiency of the guarantee of national (German) legal certainty,[47] and stressing the importance of the *nullum crimen sine lege* principle as an expression of the *Rechtsstaatsprinzip* aimed at protecting the citizens' trust in the orientation role of criminal law.[48] There is no doubt that the importance of these conclusions cannot be restricted to the sphere of surrender procedures, as the orientation role of criminal law towards the most sensitive values of the society logically requires that the relevant provisions may be reasonably perceived by people to prevent the legal provision of criminal law from becoming a mere fiction.[49] Moreover, the accessibility and foreseeability

---

[42] A clear analysis of these limits has been conducted by Böse and Meyer (2011), pp. 338ff.

[43] Along these lines, explicitly, see Böse (2013), p. 79.

[44] ECtHR (Grand Chamber), Decision of 17 September 2009, Kamasinski v. Austria, Application No. 9783/82, §§ 79–80.

[45] On this topic see Basile (2009), pp. 206ff.

[46] Schünemann (2003), p. 188.

[47] BVerfGE 92, pp. 325ff.

[48] BVerfGE 113, pp. 308f. See Böse (2012), para. 47.

[49] See Böse and Meyer (2011), p. 339.

of the relevant criminal law provision constitute logical preconditions to allow the defendant to be considered criminally liable according to the *nulla pena sine culpa* principle.

These observations have led to an in-depth reflection on the extraterritorial application of criminal law on the basis of criteria that do not allow for the proper respect of such fundamental requirements.[50] In particular, the extraterritorial extension of national jurisdiction on the basis of the passive personality principle and partially of the protective principle cannot ensure respect for the requirement of foreseeability of the relevant criminal law provisions, a conclusion that to a certain extent applies also to the active personality principle.[51] Furthermore, the application of the passive and the active personality principle can lead to infringing respectively the ban on discrimination and the right to free movement of EU citizens.[52]

To be sure, similar concerns also arise in relation to further international criteria and even in relation to the territoriality principle, taking into account the marked expansive tendency of substantive criminal law on the basis of an increasingly widened notion of territoriality, especially in relation to crimes with several accomplices or which are spread over the territory of several countries, in terms of the place where either the conduct or its consequence occurred.[53] In this regard, the application of the ubiquity theory proves inadequate and cannot fit the requirement of legal certainty especially in regard to the place of the consequence, taking into account that the offender might not have any possibility of having access to the law of the country of the result of his conduct. But, upon closer inspection, in a Europe characterised by the free movement of EU citizens, even the place where the act occurs "may often be the result of sheer chance."[54] Such problems become even more complicated in the field of organised crimes. Especially the failure of many legislations to define the "part" of the conduct committed in the national territory, which allows for national jurisdiction to be applied for the whole criminal action, has led to case law often extending the application of national criminal law for a criminal organisation in relation to all the alleged members of the association even if their main activities take part overseas.[55] This approach raises serious human rights concerns from the perspective of both the *nullum crimen sine lege* and *nulla pena sine culpa* principles. Thus, it is questionable that a judgement of criminal liability can be extended to people from countries in which the offence of criminal organisation does not exist as such (for instance, *Denmark*) or whose law provides

---

[50] See especially Böse and Meyer (2011), pp. 341ff.

[51] For a detailed analysis of this issue, see Böse and Meyer (2011), pp. 341ff.; Böse (2013), pp. 82ff.

[52] Cf. Böse and Meyer (2011), p. 342; Böse (2013), pp. 82f.

[53] For a comparative analysis of this tendency, see Sinn (2012a), pp. 544f.; Ruggeri (2013b), § 3.1.1.1.

[54] Schünemann, Part IV, Sect. 5.

[55] See the Italian Court of Cassation, 2nd Section, Decision of 7 April 1999, Cohau. Massimario Cassazione penale 1999 nr. 212974.

for a substantial distinction between criminal association and criminal organisation,[56] a legal distinction these people can legitimately trust.

These observations should lead to an even more radical change of approach than that of some solutions proposed in the field of conflicts of jurisdiction, which, albeit with different methods, aim at reducing the extraterritorial expansion of national jurisdiction and at strengthening the primacy of territorial criminal law.[57] This approach cannot, in my view, be shared. The compatibility of the *prosecutio transnationalis* with the *nullum crimen sine lege*[58] and *nulla pena sine culpa* principles, as well as with the respect for the freedom of movement of EU citizens and the ban on discriminating among them, should be ascertained in respect both to extraterritorial criteria and the territoriality principle. In the current European scenario, characterised both by the growth of constant activities contemporaneously in several countries and the increasing flow of people throughout Europe for very short periods, the primacy of territorial jurisdiction can no longer be justified on the basis of the State's pretension to extend unconditionally its sovereignty over all acts committed within its territorial borders[59] but can be maintained *as far as* it allows for the offender to be judged as criminally liable according to the requirements of a human rights-oriented transnational criminal law.[60] Moreover, the rigorous approach that still characterises, despite the clauses of "exculpation," the principle *ignorantia legis non excusat* entails, on the other hand, a precise duty of information on the (developments in the) criminal law system. Yet this duty can concern only those who can be deemed as substantial members of a relevant country,[61] a condition that is not restricted to those who are citizens or formally resident in a country.

This substantial concept reveals a very useful approach to define under which conditions the criminal law can be legitimately applied in transborder cases. Indeed, where the offence has been committed by a foreigner who is occasionally in the national territory, the application of local criminal law can give rise to insurmountable difficulties in terms of proving the criminal liability of the offender especially in respect of criminal law provisions which contain either elements presupposing that the offender belongs to the State's cultural context (*e.g.*, the *common* sense of decency) or legal elements implying technical knowledge of other branches of the

---

[56] See Sinn (2007), pp. 649f. Specific concerns arise in relation to the Italian legal system in cases of the so-called "external accomplices" to mafia-typed criminal organisations, a notion that, albeit frequently invoked by national case law, lacks clear legal provision and therefore does not meet the requirement of legal certainty with regard to those who are not familiar with the Italian cultural context. Cf., among others, Visconti (2003), *passim*.

[57] Along with the projects coordinated by *Arndt Sinn*, and *Martin Böse* and *Frank Meyer*, see also Biehler et al. (2003), pp. 7f.; Schünemann (2006b); Ambos (2003), § 4 para. 10 et seqq.

[58] In this regard, see Gropp (2012), pp. 41ff.

[59] For a modern reflection on the relationship between criminal law and territorial borders, see Di Martino (2006), *passim*.

[60] On the so-called *Menschengerechtes transnationales Strafrecht*, see Lagodny (2005), pp. 777ff.

[61] See, among others, Padovani (2012), pp. 242f.

national legal system.[62] The problem is further aggravated in cases of offences falling outside the field of natural criminal law, offences whose features are defined in a very different manner by national legislators. In such cases, demanding to apply the territorial law can lead to a judgement of non-liability due to a mistake of criminal law provisions and therefore to the offender's impunity.[63] To be sure, this risk cannot be ruled out in respect of the citizen who does not reside regularly (or who has never resided) in the national territory.

Against this background, the territorial law can no longer be applied in absolute terms, and it does not seem unreasonable that from a human rights perspective the *locus commissi delicti* rule should yield to a stronger link between the individual and the substantive criminal law system. In light of the aforementioned observations this link should be neither the active personality nor the law of domicile or residence *as such*, which could lead to abuses (*e.g.*, in case of domicile chosen abroad for fiscal grounds), but a criterion allowing the application of the *law of the State the offender substantially and regularly belongs to*, i.e., the criterion of the law of the country that can be considered as *substantially the offender's own country*. Significantly a similar criterion is invoked by the case law even of those countries that are strongly based on the territorial jurisdiction, such as Italy, which, albeit not admitting the *application* of foreign substantive criminal law,[64] conceives, however, the *consideration* of foreign law, thus justifying a criminal conduct constituting the exercise of a right pursuant to the offender's *law of origin*.[65] This approach promises several advantages. Far from being the expression of the anachronistic State's pretension to extend its jurisdiction to acts committed abroad by its own citizens,[66] the criterion of the country to which the offender substantially and regularly belongs should satisfy adequately the need for a judgement of criminal liability according to the *nullum crimen sine lege* and *nulla pena sine culpa* principles. Moreover, one should not overlook some practical advantages of this approach, such as that the offender could be punished on the basis of a criminal law provision he or she could realistically have access to from a linguistic viewpoint. Of course the requirement of legal certainty entails the need to define clear parameters to identify such a criterion in order to provide help in any conflictual situation.

De lege ferenda, such a solution should not entail abandoning the traditional territorial approach of national criminal laws. In the pre-trial phase, coordination will realistically involve the territorial jurisdiction as far as the defendants' identity

---

[62] For an in-depth analysis of the normative elements of criminal law provisions, see Risicato (2004), *passim*.

[63] Padovani (2012), p. 245.

[64] To be sure, the Italian CCP provides for the *application* of foreign procedures in the execution of letters rogatory in response of a request for legal assistance issued by a foreign authority under the condition that these procedures are not contrary to the fundamental principles of the Italian legal system [Art. 725(2)].

[65] See Panebianco (2010), pp. 336ff.

[66] See Böse and Meyer (2011), p. 342.

and their relationship with a country has not been clarified. Moreover, the territorial law might be maintained provided the offence has been committed by someone who can be deemed as substantially and regularly belonging to the relevant country, a situation that cannot be ruled out for the simple fact that the offender resides illegally in the national territory.[67] A closer look shows, however, that in these cases the national criminal law would not be applied on the basis of the territoriality principle but on the basis of the criterion of what is substantially the offender's own country.[68] On the other hand, this criterion might even lead to giving a new, modern significance to the territoriality principle according to the needs of the current European scenario. The primacy of territorial criminal law and the strict inexcusability of *ignorantia legis* and mistake of law were justified at a time most people regularly lived within the State's territorial borders and on the assumption that criminal law provisions could fulfil their orientation task within these borders. Nowadays, however, the territorial borders of criminal law should be re-defined in a manner that takes into account not the State's territorial borders but the capability of national criminal law to play its orientation role by reaching those who regularly and substantially belong to the State's cultural context.

3.2   The Assignment of the Power to Prosecute and Adjudicate Transnational Cases

The proposed approach might help deal properly with the assignment of the power to prosecute and adjudicate transnational cases. There is no doubt that from the perspective of procedural criminal law, the unconditional application of territorial law entails even more serious problems than those encountered in relation to the applicable substantive law and can cause insurmountable difficulties for the defendant to exercise their defence rights effectively. Whilst the territorial process, especially if conducted in the place of the result, can fulfil the need to respect the victim's interest in a local judgement, this solution offloads onto the defendant who does not belong substantially to this country the burden of facing the proceedings in a context he might be unfamiliar with. This implies further difficulties for the defendant as to the choice of and communication with the lawyer, not to mention the linguistic barriers to fully understanding procedural activities, which may jeopardise the choice of the best solution in the concrete case.[69] Furthermore, the proceedings can lead to the adoption of measures restricting personal freedom, which may contribute to accentuating the defendant's sense of isolation from their environment.

---

[67] In the same sense, with regard to *Denmark*, see Cornils and Greve (2012), p. 194.

[68] See Ruggeri (2013b), § 4.2.2.1.

[69] For an in-depth study of the linguistic problems in EU cooperation in criminal matters see, among others, Ruggieri (2013).

The European Union has in recent years addressed these problems by means of the MR system. Thus, recourse to the principle of mutual recognition has allowed supervision measures alternative to remand detention to be applied also to defendants who are resident in a country other than that of the proceedings.[70] After the coming into force of the Lisbon Treaty, EU institutions engaged in the implementation of the Roadmap for strengthening the procedural rights of suspected and accused persons in criminal proceedings,[71] meanwhile incorporated into the Stockholm Programme of 11 December 2009,[72] thus introducing minimum rules on the right to translation and interpretation in criminal proceedings.[73] Nevertheless, the adequacy of such legislative interventions depend, in a great part, on the reasonableness of the logic of mutual recognition, called upon to provide tools to reduce the negative repercussions on the individuals involved in transnational procedures of the choice to leave the assignment of the prosecutorial power to the chance and preferably to the territorial jurisdiction. Yet these legislative instruments do not wholly prevent the defendant's isolation from their environment, a result that may paradoxically be enhanced by the adoption of supervision means, due to the more extensive possibility for the issuing authority than in ordinary cases to obtain the defendant's surrender by means of a European arrest warrant even beyond the sentencing limits laid down by Article 2(1) FD EAW.[74]

Against this background, the solution of choosing the forum of the country the defendant substantially and regularly belongs to seems to provide unquestionable advantages. Especially, it would allow the defendant to face the criminal process in their own cultural context, thus enjoying the best conditions to properly understand procedural activities and effectively exercise defence rights. Furthermore, in cases of coercive means, it would not isolate defendants from their environment, thus making it unnecessary to invoke mutual recognition to render them to their *own* country.

Despite these advantages, two main problems must be faced from a procedural viewpoint. The first concerns how we can deal with the possible concurrence of competing jurisdictions. The second regards how criminal inquiries into different offences and/or offenders in complex transborder cases can be efficiently prosecuted and ascertained. The first question poses the need to solve *conflicts of jurisdiction*, whereas the second raises the problem of *coordination among prosecutorial powers*. For the sake of clarity I shall analyse the two questions separately on the basis of the distinction between crimes committed by a single offender and crimes committed by several accomplices. In both cases we cannot, however,

---

[70] Framework Decision 2009/829/JHA. See, among others, Rafaraci (2012), pp. 67ff.

[71] Resolution of the Council of 30 November 2009 (2009/295/01).

[72] The Stockholm Programme—An open and secure Europe serving and protecting citizens (2010/C 115/01), point 2.4.

[73] Directive 2010/64/EU.

[74] See Article 21(2) Framework Decision 2009/829/JHA. For some criticism in this regard, cf. Ruggeri (2012), pp. 66f.

overlook the need to respect the multicultural character of transborder offences, which should lead to a change in the approach used in purely national criminal affairs.

3.2.1 Concurrence of National Jurisdictions and the Choice of the Forum. The Need to Supplement Substantive Criminal Laws

The problem of assigning the power to prosecute transnational cases can be solved by starting with the adequacy of the substantive law of the country the offender substantially and regularly belongs to. This assumption does not in itself rule out the possibility of concurrence among several jurisdictions arising in the concrete case, a situation that can emerge from at least two situations. The first is when the criterion of substantial and regular belonging does not lead to a clear, unequivocal assignment since the alleged offender can be deemed as belonging to more than one country. Such an eventuality is realistic in the current European scenario, such as in cases in which the offender, although formally residing in one country, lives in two, or works outside his country of residence (*e.g.*, a surgeon operating regularly in clinics or hospitals in different countries). In this case concurrence arises from jurisdictions claiming prosecutorial power on the basis of the same criterion. But concurrence can also occur among jurisdictions claiming prosecutorial power on the basis of heterogeneous criteria. In my view, the forum may not be chosen flexibly among jurisdictions claiming the prosecutorial power on the basis of *any* criterion,[75] since this would lead to solutions that may not comply with the aforementioned need to respect the *nullum crimen sine lege* and *nulla pena sine culpa* principles. As has been observed, concurrence may only arise among jurisdictions claiming the power to prosecute on a legitimate basis, thus ensuring respect for the requirements of a human rights-oriented criminal law.

This is surely the case in which the defendant is proved to belong substantially to more than one country. In this case, between two concurring jurisdictions, preference might be given to territorial law when the conduct was committed in one of the two States involved. The issue of territoriality would, however, play a subsidiary role, thus supporting the jurisdiction of the country the defendant belongs to, not *vice versa*.[76] The problem becomes more complicated where States other than that the defendant substantially and regularly belongs to, no matter whether the conduct or its consequences took place there, claim their jurisdiction and the application of their criminal law. Indeed, the appropriateness of the substantive criminal law of

---

[75] For a flexible solution concerning the choice of the jurisdiction to enforce, see, instead, Böse (2013), pp. 85f., who, moreover, requires respect for the dual criminality requirement in the event of the choice of derivative jurisdiction.

[76] In the "statutory determination model," proposed by the research project coordinated by *Arndt Sinn*, the law of residence plays instead a subsidiary role in cases in which criminal conduct spans multiple Member States, but none of the conduct took place in a jurisdiction where the consequences of the conduct were also felt. See Article 1(3) of the proposed Directive on the avoidance of jurisdictional conflicts in criminal proceedings. In: Sinn (2012b), pp. 609f.

the defendant's *own* country does not mean that the jurisdiction thereof is the most adequate to prosecute the alleged crime. Whereas only jurisdictions claiming a legitimate *Strafanspruch* can concur with the jurisdiction of the defendant's *own* country, this does not mean that any legitimate *Strafanspruch* can prevail. The cases falling within the universality principle would be insolvable, since the universally recognised character of these crimes would in principle justify the assignment to *any* jurisdiction, including the territorial one. Also in these cases, however, the recourse to the criterion of the country the defendant is proved to substantially belong to, can be of much help.[77]

Upon closer analysis, it appears to me that the assignment of the prosecutorial power to a jurisdiction other than that of the offender's own country, rather than the extraterritorial exercise jurisdiction, needs be justified and that the sole justification lies in the State's need to protect its essential interests, i.e. the values which are essential to ensure its existence and survival. These values can be viewed not only in light of the protection of the State's interests such as in cases of offences against the State's personality but furthermore from a human rights perspective, i.e. in terms of the protection of victims' rights.[78] Also here, however, the assignment of prosecutorial power to this jurisdiction cannot lead us to overlook human rights requirements which are inherent in the *nullum crimen sine lege* and *nulla pena sine culpa* principles. The risk that these end up being purely formal guarantees is particularly accentuated in cases of *Strafansprüche* based on the passive personality principle, since the defendant is often unaware not only of the victim's citizenship but also of their identity, and consequently is hardly likely to know the relevant legal provision beforehand.[79] In general terms, jurisdictional power may be assigned to the State affected in its essential interests on two conditions: (a) that the offender was in a position to have access to its criminal law and can therefore be effectively deemed as criminally liable according to the *nulla pena sine culpa* principle, (b) that the offender's own State does not properly protect the essential values of the other State.

The combination of these conditions can lead to practical problems. Firstly it can be extremely difficult for the competing State to demonstrate the inadequacy of the solutions provided by the criminal law system of the defendant's own country. If this is to be meant in terms of a *less* adequate criminal law response than that of the country whose essential interest are touched upon, the competition for jurisdiction would clearly lead to insolvable situations. Therefore, in light of the need for legal

---

[77] In this regard, *Brazil* provides an interesting model as to the criteria of activation of national jurisdiction to fight international crimes such as genocide. In this case, albeit being a universally recognised crime, the Brazilian *Strafanpruch* is only apparently unconditioned, since it is mitigated by the recourse to the principle of active personality in terms of Brazilian citizenship or the offender's domicile in Brazil. See D'Avila (2013), § 1.7.

[78] In *Hungary* the new criminal code (Btk.), which came into force in July 2013, has strengthened the role of the passive personality principle in light of a conception of criminal law aimed at protecting either natural or legal persons if they have links with Hungary. See Karsai (2013), § 5.

[79] Böse and Meyer (2011), p. 341.

certainty, this inadequacy may seem to occur only where the defendant's own country does not provide any criminal law protection of the affected country's legal interest. Nevertheless, in the first case it would be extremely difficult to punish, on the basis of the affected country's criminal law provisions, offenders who have legitimately trusted their own law by engaging in what is considered licit conduct under their own legal system. The same seems to apply to the case in which the offender's own country makes punishment dependent on a condition the affected State does not allow for.

In the light of this, it seems that prosecutorial power may be assigned to a State other than the offender's own country on the strict condition that this provides criminal law solutions similar to those of the State the offender substantially belongs to.[80] Significantly, in countries such as *Germany*, the extraterritorial prosecution of crimes on the basis of the passive personality principle requires, as a general rule, that the conduct should constitute a criminal offence under *lex loci*.[81] Neither could the affected State's criminal law be applied without this fundamental condition by demonstrating that the offender was in the position to have access to it, since this would give rise to a clear infringement of the ban on discrimination among EU citizens. The identity of the relevant criminal law provision should ensure the fulfilment of the requirement of legal certainty, i.e., the foreseeability and accessibility of the affected country's criminal law.

On the other hand, requiring the identity of the criminal law provision considerably reduces the risk of inadequacy of the law of the offender's own country. To be sure, the possibility of assigning prosecutorial power to a jurisdiction other than the one of the defendant's own country should progressively decrease in a common area of freedom, security and justice. It has been observed that the condition under which the other State may claim its right to prosecute the offence is that this demonstrates that it has been affected in the interests which are essential to its existence and survival. And there is no doubt that, as long as the country with primary jurisdiction protects these interests, there is no need for the other States to intervene.[82] This result could certainly be achieved by extending the principle of assimilation, aimed at protecting EU legal interests, to the protection of the national interests of other EU member States.[83] At any rate, the requirement of the identical criminal law provision undoubtedly allows us to question the assumption that national criminal law does not aim to protect other States' legal interests. But then, when could the affected country claim its right to prosecute? In my opinion, derivative jurisdiction might be exercised only in the cases in which the defendant's own country, albeit providing the same criminal law protection as the offender's

---

[80] As seen above (fn. 76), also models based on the primacy of territorial jurisdiction, such as that elaborated by *Martin Böse* and *Frank Mayer*, require an identical criminal law provision in *lex loci* for the exercise of derivative jurisdiction.

[81] In this regard, see Wörner (2013), § 2.4.

[82] Böse and Meyer (2011), p. 342.

[83] Böse and Meyer (2011), pp. 342f.

own country, does not intend to prosecute the alleged offence. A useful way would therefore be to construe the right to prosecute of the State whose essential interests are affected by following the requirements of the principle of so-called "representative prosecution" (*stellvertretende Strafrechtspflege*). Also in these cases, furthermore, the exercise of foreign jurisdiction should presuppose the demonstration that an essential interest for this country has been affected. The risk that negative proof can give rise to negative conflicts of jurisdiction might be prevented by strengthening the role of Eurojust in binding national authorities to prosecute cross-border crimes to avoid impunity, unlike what happens in the provisions regarding the current regulation on Eurojust.[84]

The assignment of the prosecutorial power to a State other than the country the defendant substantially belongs to would not, furthermore, imply overlooking the need to preserve the guarantees provided for adjudication by the defendant's own law. Upon close examination, the comparison between transnational and national conflicts of jurisdiction appears to be misleading in that at a domestic level the settlement of jurisdictional conflicts leads to assigning the prosecutorial power to a jurisdiction, which will follow its *own* procedural and substantive regulation. Nevertheless, we have noted that the development in international cooperation and the need to prosecute efficiently crimes with a transborder dimension have led to overcoming the traditional application of the *lex loci* alone. And one might argue that the same needs should nowadays require an in-depth reflection on the traditional tie existing at a transnational level between criminal enquiry, the prosecution of cross-border crimes and the application of a single national criminal law. To be sure, in the case of complex crimes, as we will see, one should perhaps maintain the assumption that *one* offence must be prosecuted by *one* jurisdiction,[85] but also that *one* jurisdiction must apply *one* (i.e., only its own) criminal law.[86]

The comparative analysis of national laws shows, moreover, that this perfect one-to-one-correspondence has widely been broken. Thus, in *Switzerland* the IRG provides, while establishing the conditions under which Switzerland may claim its right to representative prosecution, that Swiss criminal law must be applied within the mitigating limits laid down by foreign law. Thus, foreign law will be applied whenever more lenient than the Swiss system and provided that Swiss authorities may not apply foreign sanctions which are not envisaged under national law [Art. 86(2)].[87] In *Austria*, the StGB contains an even more completed regulation, which

---

[84] The concerns relating to the infringement of the principle of the judge established in advance *by the law* do not have the same weight by means of the enhancement of the role of Eurojust in cases of positive and negative conflicts of jurisdiction. In the former, Eurojust should, by solving a jurisdictional concurrence, oblige a national authority to waive prosecution in favour of another. In the latter, taking into account what has been noted in the text, Eurojust should, by solving a negative conflict, ask the authority with primary jurisdiction, by means of a binding opinion, to prosecute the crime.

[85] Lagodny (2002), p. 263.

[86] Di Martino (2006), pp. 29ff.

[87] See Gleß (2011), p. 59.

in cases of extraterritorial jurisdiction offloads to the Austrian judge the difficult task of ascertaining, while defining the defendant's punishment, that, considering their overall position (*Gesamtauswirkung*), they are not dealt with less favourably than they would be by applying the territorial law (§ 65). Also in *Denmark*, foreign law must be always taken into account, in light of the need for legal certainty, in all cases of extraterritorial jurisdiction. Significantly, in cases of application of the dual criminality requirement, Danish law requires its national authorities to respect the foreign *lex mitior*,[88] a task that entails respect not only for the maximum penalty established by the territorial law [Art. 10(2) Criminal law] but also for the foreign case law for sentencing purposes.[89]

These solutions give clear examples of the application of foreign *substantive* criminal law,[90] thus posing new challenges for a new criminal justice system at a European level. These challenges have already been accepted by the aforementioned research projects coordinated by *Arndt Sinn*, and *Martin Böse* and *Frank Meyer*, who have especially focused on the dual criminality requirement and the respect for *lex mitior* in cases of the exercise of derivative jurisdiction as preventive mechanisms to avoid the risk of forum shopping. In my view, similar solutions provide suggestions of great interest in light of the creation of a model of fair multicultural criminal justice, which from the human rights perspective of this study should not give rise to concerns as to the hybridisation of criminal law systems, albeit only with reference to the single case.[91] Since the State affected in its essential interests should intervene in representation not of the territorial jurisdiction but of the jurisdiction of the country the offender substantially belongs to, the sentence will be established within the limits set by the criminal of *this* country, i.e., by the criminal law to which the offender could have access and has legitimately trusted.[92]

---

[88] Cornils and Greve (2012), p. 186.

[89] Greve (2005), pp. 753ff.

[90] On the application of foreign criminal law, see Cornils (1978), *passim*. Concerning cases such as those set forth in the text, it is widely assumed that foreign law is not to be applied but only taken into consideration. See, for example, Sinn (2012a), p. 538. I cannot share this opinion, since if national law is applied within the limits established by foreign law, these limits are to be applied, not just taken into consideration. Significantly, although some national legislation explicitly states that the case is to be adjudicated according to national law [*e.g.*, Art. 86(1) of the Swiss IRG], the same provision concerning the applicable law allows for the *application* of foreign law, whenever more lenient.

[91] Alongside with *Bernd Schünemann*, several scholars look at the application of foreign law with concern. See, in German literature, Ambos (2011), pp. 128f.

[92] To be sure, where the affected country is not the State in whose territory the conduct took place, also the territorial criminal law should be applied as *lex mitior* to avoid discriminations among EU citizens. Upon closer examination, this solution is excessive and unnecessary. Indeed, where neither the offender substantially belongs to the State in which the conduct took place nor this State's essential interests have been touched upon, nothing seems to justify intervention of the territorial criminal law.

3.2.2 Prosecution of Complex Crimes and the Need to Coordinate Criminal Inquiries

The proposed approach seems to provide a proper solution in relation to forms of micro-criminality and, at any rate, in relation to transborder criminal affairs with a fairly simple structure, i.e., consisting of single offences committed by single offenders.[93] But in cases of complex cross-border criminal affairs (or even criminal phenomena) consisting of several offences committed in the territories of several countries and committed by several accomplices residing in different countries and often with different citizenship, the recourse to the law of the country to which the *single* offender substantially and regularly belongs can give rise to a plethora of competing jurisdictions claiming their right to prosecute the *entire* criminal affair. To be sure, it has been observed that such concurrence derives from the adoption of the so-called "*Gesamtlösung*" by almost all countries despite the considerable differences existing in ways of conceiving complicity, participation, etc., as well as organised forms of crime. And we have seen that this solution has increasingly widened the notion of territoriality for the purposes of allowing the single national jurisdiction to prosecute the entire complex crime.

Against this background, a possible solution might be to adopt a restrictive interpretation of the accessorial action, by ruling out that the right to prosecute might be claimed by the State in which a marginal contribution to the global action took place[94] and by thus breaking the necessary link between main and accessorial action. Nevertheless, such a solution would not apply to those legal systems, such as *Italy*, where the law does not distinguish among the different roles of the accomplices. Moreover it would not help in all those cases in which the criminal action consisted in several acts of equal seriousness, committed in the territories of several countries and by several accomplices. But at a closer look the main limit of this approach seems to be inherent in the *Akzessorietätsthese*.

Certainly the *Gesamtlösung* has the benefit of satisfying the need to grasp the complexity of the most serious and, from a criminological viewpoint, most relevant forms of transborder crimes and the need to ensure their prosecution by means of a unified action. This does not, however, mean that the prosecution by a single national authority is the only way to achieve this result and therefore to avoid fragmentation of the unified character of such criminal phenomena. Nor can the need for a unified action involve overlooking the need to respect the fundamental

---

[93] For a similar conclusion in relation to the solution provided by the law of residence, cf. Wörner (2012), § 4.1.

[94] Along these lines, see Böse and Meyer (2011), p. 343. To be sure, in *Germany*, although the StGB, following the *Gesamtlösung*, provides for the application of German law to the accomplice's contribution, which took place in German territory, to a criminal action mainly committed abroad [§ 9(2)], the StPO considerably attenuates the severity of this regulation, thus empowering the Public Prosecutor to waive prosecution where the accomplice's conduct in Germany has contributed to a criminal action that mainly took place overseas [§ 153c(1)(1)].

criminal law guarantees of the alleged offender. In this regard, we have noted that the territorial solution has several shortcomings, which are not only concerned with organised crimes. Serious problems emerge also from the field of medical responsibility, since an extensive interpretation of the criminal liability for criminal participation by means of omission entails the risk of excessively widening the duty of any specialist doctor to control the conducts of all his colleagues who intervene *abroad* in subsequent moments of the patient's treatment.[95]

In light of this, the solution of submitting the entire criminal action, irrespective of the different forms of complicity and participation, to the territorial jurisdiction and the *lex loci* does not appear to be a suitable model. Not to mention the repercussions of procedural concentration on the defence rights of accused persons, who are thus obliged to face a criminal process in a country they could not substantially belong to.[96] But, as noted above, the main shortcoming of this approach perhaps lies in the way of dealing with complex criminal affairs that precisely because of the multiplicity of crimes they encompass, cannot be treated properly by a single jurisdiction in the same way as happens for single offences. Thus, the complex features of these criminal affairs reveal the need for a *transcultural, multilevel prosecution*, which does not seem to lead to a fragmentation of the criminal inquiry. Both in cases of criminal participation and organised crimes, therefore, we should consider the advantages of the so-called "*Einzellösung*,"[97] which in light of the solutions proposed in this study would, however, entail the distribution of powers not among territorial jurisdictions but among the jurisdictions of the countries the accused substantially belong to.

This solution would clearly not jeopardise the defendant's right not to be prosecuted twice, since the national proceedings would be conducted against different defendants. As long as a concerted action of the national authorities is ensured, complex criminal phenomena will be properly prosecuted by means of *coordination*. Moreover, insofar as cooperation is ensured at the pre-trial stages in the investigation of complex criminal affairs consisting of several criminal actions spread throughout Europe, coordination will be of fundamental importance to prevent the occurrence of conflicts through a proper distribution of resources (and crimes) among the cooperating authorities.

---

[95] De Francesco (2013), pp. 137s.

[96] This shortcoming also relates to the model of transnational procedural unity. See Satzger (2006), p. 148.

[97] Along these lines, meanwhile, see Oehler (1983), para. 361. More recently, see also Böse and Meyer (2011), p. 343. Criticism against the *Einzellösung* has been raised, with regard to criminal complicity, by many scholars. See, among others, Satzger (2011), p. 51.

3.3 Cross-Border Investigations and Transnational Evidence Gathering

It has been noted that one of the main methodological deficiencies of the traditional approaches is that the issue of *transborder* inquiries and the gathering of evidence *overseas* is often dealt with as a matter of evidence law and is therefore analysed irrespective of the assignment of the power to prosecute, which remains regulated under national law and can lead to different solutions in actual cases. However, the establishment of clear rules for the assignment of jurisdiction does not only satisfy the need for legal certainty but is also a crucial question to solve properly the problem of how to investigate with authorities of *other* nations and to gather evidence in *other* countries.

As noted above, the model of transnational procedural unity is unique among the models outlined above in that it provides a strict link between investigations and the assignment of the prosecutorial power, a link based on the territorial extension of the investigative powers of the competent authority. However, since considerable flexibility is provided in the choice of jurisdiction, this system does not make it possible to know with certainty what national jurisdiction will have competence to investigate throughout Europe. Concerning the MR and MLA models, it has been observed that, whereas neither of the two systems generally provides for rules on the assignment of jurisdiction, both have always relied, albeit in different fashions, on the prevalence of territorial procedural criminal law as the basis of investigative cooperation. Procedural territoriality constitutes, furthermore, the main criterion for gathering evidence by means of joint investigation teams. On the other hand, in some of the models proposed so far, the choice of the forum has been mainly construed with a view to satisfying the needs of the transborder inquiry. The choice of the territorial jurisdiction as a starting point certainly takes into account that as a rule most of the evidence is available in the country where the offence was committed.[98] Both the "statutory determination model"[99] and the model of "transnational procedural unity"[100] provide for a cut-off rule allowing the assignment of prosecutorial power, in cases of several defendants with different citizenships, to the country where the greatest amount of important evidence or simply most of the evidence is located. Also in this regard, furthermore, the model of "transnational procedural unity" gives great importance to the practical problem of ensuring that the enquiry be conducted on a harmonised basis.

The approach of this study attaches prime importance to the need for legal certainty in the assignment of jurisdiction in a manner that preserves the defendants' right to be prosecuted in their own country and adjudicated pursuant to a criminal law they could know and have access to. However, this does not mean that

---

[98] Böse (2013), p. 85.

[99] Art. 2. See Sinn (2012b), p. 611.

[100] Art. 2(2). See Schünemann (2006b), pp. 5f.

the problems concerned with the conduction of cross-border inquiries should be overlooked. Furthermore, the same human rights perspective that has been adopted in the choice of jurisdiction must lead to construing transnational criminal inquiries in such a way that the requirements of a fair procedure can be respected.

The first question concerns the *form* of conducting cross-border investigations and collecting evidence overseas. Certainly a deficiency of the current EU legislation is that national authorities have too much leeway in choosing whether to collect evidence pursuant to the assistance model or pursuant to the model of transborder evidence gathering by means of joint investigations.[101] Some federalist models, such as the former Swiss one, have a similar defect in that they do not lay down clear rules on the choice of the form of the enquiry, which can manifestly give rise to solutions detrimental to the accused and third parties.[102] This uncertainty must be avoided and the simplest way of doing so is, in my view, to establish the form of evidence gathering depending on *which countries* are involved in the transnational enquiry. Thus, recourse to the assistance model should be restricted to those cases in which the State in which the sought evidence is located neither has primary jurisdiction nor can compete for the prosecution of the alleged crime since it has not been affected in its essential interests. An exception might be the case in which the power to prosecute has been assigned to a State other than the defendant's own country and the State to which the defendant substantially belongs is not interested in prosecuting the crime. But where the State in which the sought evidence is located, even if it has not been chosen as the forum State, can *legitimately* compete for prosecution, because more than one State has primary jurisdiction or evidence is placed in a State that needs to defend its own essential interests, the model of joint investigation seems to provide the most adequate form of conducting an enquiry of common interest.

This distinction, which clearly reflects the cooperating State's involvement in the transnational inquiry, should also impinge on the establishment of the applicable procedural law. We have seen that the model of "transnational procedural unity" widened not only the territorial competence of the prosecuting authorities but also the scope of application of *lex fori* in light of the need for coherence of the investigation. The need for coherence is clearly of fundamental importance also in transnational inquiries. Also here, however, it does not seem to me that an integration of procedural laws *according to the needs of the concrete case* can jeopardise the uniformity of the investigation or entails the risk of dangerous procedural hybridisations for the individuals involved. To be sure, the need for coherence must be balanced with the multicultural challenges posed by transborder inquiries. From a human rights perspective, all the combination models both of the MR and the MLA systems reflect not only the need to satisfy the interests of the cooperating countries—i.e., respectively, the interest of the requested State to meet

---

[101] For an analysis of evidence-gathering models, see Gleß (2006), respectively, pp. 109ff. and 121ff.

[102] Schünemann, Part IV, Sect. 3.

the requirements of its own procedural law and the interest of the forum State to preserve the admissibility of the collected evidence with a view to the needs of the ongoing prosecution—but furthermore the need to provide proper protection of the defence rights respectively of the addressees of the transborder inquiry during the investigative activities and of the defendant with regard to their adjudication. In the light of this, both the competence of the territorial authority and the application of *lex loci*, albeit mixed in different fashions with *lex fori*, offer solution models which still appear to be valid *insofar as* they preserve the right of the addressee of the transborder inquiry to be investigated according to the procedural law of the country they belong to and by the investigative authorities that are the most qualified to apply it properly.

Of course, this is not always the case, and it cannot therefore be ruled out that the addressee of the investigation substantially belongs neither to the forum State nor to the country where they are at the time of the investigations. In these cases the forum State should seek the cooperation of the country to which the addressee of the investigative activity also substantially belongs, rather than of the country where they (temporarily) are.

In a nutshell, the choice of the authority with which to cooperate and the establishment of the applicable *procedural* criminal law in the context of cross-border inquiries should follow the same logic of respect for individual rights that has been proposed for the choice of the forum. The different nature of procedural law and the fact that it generally follows the *tempus regit actum* rule does not imply that the fundamental requirement of legal certainty should not be fulfilled here.[103] Furthermore, procedural scholarship has in great part questioned the different regulation on the temporal application of criminal law,[104] thus paving the way for overcoming the rigid distinction between substantive and criminal law. This applies especially to some procedural provisions, which contain a sort of procedural projection of substantive law rules for the purposes of the prosecution investigation. These requirements, known in German literature as *Sachgestaltungsvoraussetzungen*,[105] make it possible to draw a distinction between purely procedural rules and procedural rules that are to be deemed as structurally similar to substantive law provisions.[106] This phenomenon is particularly evident in cases of interferences with fundamental rights that, no matter whether by means of coercion or not, are always based on a *fumus delicti*, i.e., on a suspicion of guilt, albeit differently construed. Significantly, also the ECtHR has extended the requirement of foreseeability to procedural law based on the characteristics of the common-law system.[107]

---

[103] See Böse (2013), p. 80, with extensive reference to ECtHR case law.

[104] Nobili (1982), p. 2138.

[105] See, among others, Volk (1978), pp. 147f.

[106] Along these lines, see Negri (2004), pp. 51ff.

[107] ECtHR, Decision of 5 October 2004, *H.L. v United Kingdom*, Application No. 45508/99, § 114.

In the context of transborder inquiries, interference with individual rights is so frequent that one might doubt that investigative means neutral to fundamental rights exist at all. This confirms the need for a multilevel approach, which takes into due account the exigency of balancing the protection of the accused in the forum State and the individuals' trust for the specific *legal* system of their *own* country. However, this balance may have different features according to the form of cooperation. At a closer look, combination models still offer an appropriate solution in cases of assistance requested from a country which either cannot legitimately compete for prosecution or is not interested in prosecuting the alleged crime, provided the fundamental principles of procedural law of the requested country are preserved and both authorities of the requesting State and private parties are granted the right to take part in the investigative activities supporting national authorities to apply properly foreign formalities. Instead, combination solutions seem to be insufficient to fulfil the needs of transnational inquiries involving the forum State and other countries with a legitimate right to prosecute the alleged offence, and even more inadequate to satisfy the need for a concerted action against complex (often organised) crimes. In these cases, the *combination of single national procedures* should be replaced by the *mutual integration of national laws* in order to establish a procedure of gathering evidence on a balanced, common basis, which fits the requirements of a fair transnational criminal inquiry.

But how could this integration be achieved? One of the main shortcomings both of the MR and the MLA system is that they are aimed at combining *single* procedures of both laws, as if they could be dealt with outside the legal context they belong to. On the other hand, any procedure reflects specific balances between often-conflicting interests against a constitutional framework. A mixture of single procedural forms can alter this scheme and lead to different constitutional balances colliding with each other, which is perhaps the main reason behind the alternative model of "transnational procedural unity." But, as we have noted, conducting transborder investigations, which pose difficult transcultural challenges, does not seem to be the only way of ensuring coherence. Nor can balanced integration be achieved by requiring that the forms of *lex fori* perfectly comply with the requirements of *lex loci*, an approach that, albeit followed by some national legislation,[108] gives rise to a somewhat unbalanced procedure in favour of *lex loci*. A useful alternative—as *Richard Vogler* has outlined in this research from the perspective of the relationship between supranational and national case laws—would be to establish a dialogue[109] between the authorities involved in the joint investigation (as well as, whenever possible, among them and the defences of the people involved) to set an *ad hoc* investigative procedure, reflecting a *new* balance among colliding interests according to the human rights needs of the concrete case.[110] In this

---

[108] See, for example, Art. 65(2) of the Swiss IRG. Cf. Gleß (2011), p. 89.

[109] Vogler, Part IV, *passim*.

[110] Indeed, the awareness has grown today that human rights requirements must be assessed on the basis of the actual case in hand. Sanders et al. (2012), pp. 29f.

context, however, each of the domestic laws must cease to be part of its legal system[111] and cannot therefore be applied *as such*. Neither needs any procedural formality to be applied. Furthermore, dialogue could be of great help to detect the *constitutional requirements* of the countries concerned with the investigation at stake, which will allow the legal requirements essential from a human rights perspective to be laid down.[112] To be sure, even the idea of *closed Constitutions* has for the most part been overcome by the constitutional doctrine in favour of the more modern conception of *inter-constitutional legal systems*, which open towards *other* charters of human rights either at a supranational or national level.[113] In this regard, the recourse to the so-called "principle of quality" (*Qualitätsprinzip*), proposed in the field of conflict of jurisdiction,[114] would allow an effective balance to be achieved between the values at stake in concrete cases, especially in light of the need to ensure the *highest* protection to the individuals involved in transborder inquiries.

4 Conclusion

The issue of transborder criminal investigations and the gathering of overseas evidence cannot be adequately dealt with independently of the assignment of the power to prosecute and adjudicate cross-border crimes. In the European scenario, characterised by an increasingly transcultural criminal law system, the choice of the forum and of the applicable criminal law cannot be left to a bargaining among the competing authorities on the basis of uncoordinated national laws. The need for legal certainty requires clear rules on the assignment of the prosecutorial power that meet the requirements inherent in the essential principles of criminal law, such as the *nullum crimen sine lege* and *nulla pena sine culpa* principles. The choice of the forum pursuant to these fundamental requirements is of crucial importance for establishing both the *form* of conducting cross-border investigations and collecting evidence overseas, and the applicable procedural criminal law.

---

[111] From a similar perspective, Klip (2012), p. 393, points out that domestic judicial products are no longer products once they go across the border, where different requirements apply.

[112] Outside Europe, the *USA* has developed extensive case law on overseas investigations conducted by foreign officials in a "joint venture" with US authorities. And it is noteworthy that, if US law enforcement officials have "substantially participated" in conducting investigations overseas, US courts require US constitutional law governing the gathering of evidence to be applied. This doctrine has allowed for the application of the Fourth Amendment to overseas searches, the "Miranda warnings" to extraterritorial interrogations and the Sixth Amendment to depositions of witnesses abroad. See extensively Thaman (2013), pp. 518ff.

[113] Ruggeri (2001), pp. 544ff.

[114] Lagodny (2002), pp. 264ff.

References[115]

Ambos K (2003) §§ 3–4 StGB. In: von Heintschel-Heinegg B, Joecks W, Miebach K (eds) Münchner Kommentar zum Strafgesetzbuch, vol I. C.F. Beck, München

Ambos K (2011) Internationales Strafrecht, 3rd edn. C.F. Beck, München

American Law Institute (ed) (1988) Third restatement of the law – the foreign relations of the United States, vol 1. West, St. Paul

Basile F (2009) Localismo e non-neutralità culturale del giudice penale "sotto tensione" per effetto dell'immigrazione. In: Risicato L, La Rosa E (eds) Laicità e multiculturalismo. Profili penali ed extrapenali. Giappichelli, Torino, pp 206ff.

Biehler A, Kniebühler R, Lelieur-Fischer J, Stein S (2003) Freiburg proposal on concurrent jurisdictions and the prohibition of multiple prosecutions in the European Union. Max-Planck-Institut für ausländisches und internationals Strafrecht, Freiburg i. Br.

Bitzilekis N, Kaiafa-Gbandi M, Symeonidou-Kastanidou E (2006) Alternativüberlegungen zur Regelung transnationaler Strafverfahren in der EU. In: Schünemann B (ed) Ein Gesamtkonzept für die europäische Strafrechtspflege/A programme for European criminal justice. Carl Heymanns, Köln, pp 250–253

Böse M (2012) Vor § 3. In: Kindhäuser U, Neumann U, Paeffgen H-U (eds) Nomos Kommentar – Strafgesetzbuch, vol I, 3rd edn. Nomos, Baden-Baden

Böse M (2013) Choice of the forum and jurisdiction. In: Luchtman M (ed) Choice of the forum in cooperation against EU financial crime. Freedom security and justice and the protection of specific EU-interests. Eleven International Publishing, The Hague, pp 73–87

Böse M, Meyer F (2011) Die Beschränkung nationaler Strafgewalten als Möglichkeit zur Vermeidung von Jurisdiktionskonflikten in der Europäischen Union. Zeitschrift für internationale Strafrechtsdogmatik 336–344

Böse M, Meyer F, Schneider A (eds) (2013) Conflicts of jurisdiction in criminal matters in the European Union. National reports and comparative analysis, vol I. Nomos, Baden-Baden

Caprioli F (2013) Report on Italy. In: Ruggeri S (ed) Transnational inquiries and the protection of fundamental rights in criminal proceedings. A study in Memory of Vittorio Grevi and Giovanni Tranchina. Springer, Heidelberg, pp 439–455

Cornils K (1978) Die Fremdrechtsanwendung im Strafrecht. De Gruyter, Berlin

Cornils K, Greve V (2012) Dänemark. In: Sinn A (ed) Jurisdiktionskonflikte bei grenzübers-chreitend organisierter Kriminalität. Ein Rechtsvergleich zum internationalen Strafrecht/Conflicts of jurisdiction in cross-border crime situations. A comparative law study of international criminal law. V&R Unipress, Osnabrück, pp 181ff.

D'Avila FR (2013) Normativa e giurisprudenza brasiliane in tema di conflitti transnazionali di giurisdizione in materia penale. La legislazione penale (in press)

De Francesco G (2013) Diritto penale, vol II, Forme del reato. Giappichelli, Torino

Di Martino A (2006) La frontiera e il diritto penale. Natura e contesto delle norme di "diritto penale transnazionale." Giappichelli, Torino

Gascón Inchausti F (2007) El decomiso transfronterizo de bienes. Colex, Madrid

Gleß S (2006) Beweisrechtsgrundsätze einer grenzüberschreitenden Strafverfolgung. Nomos, Baden-Baden

Gleß S (2011) Internationales Strafrecht – Grundriss für Studium und Praxis. Helbing Lichtenhahn, Basel

Greve V (2005) Strafzumessung im internationalen Strafrecht. In: Arnold J, Burkhardt B, Gropp W, Heine G, Koch H-G, Lagodny O, Perron W, Walther S (eds) Menschengerechtes Strafrecht. Festschrift für Albin Eser zum 70. Geburtstag. C.F. Beck, München, pp 751ff.

---

[115] The chapter contributions contained in this book have been quoted with the only reference to the Author's surname, the Part in which the contribution is contained and the number of the paragraph concerned.

Gropp W (2012) Kollision nationaler Strafgewalten – nulla prosecutio transnationalis sine lege. In: Sinn A (ed) Jurisdiktionskonflikte bei grenzüberschreitend organisierter Kriminalität. V&R Unipress, Göttingen, pp 41–63

Karsai K (2013) La via ungherese alla risoluzione dei conflitti: più paternalismo, meno flessibilità. La legislazione penale (in press)

Klip A (2012) European criminal law, 2nd edn. Intersentia, Antwerp

Lagodny O (2002) Viele Strafgewalten und nur ein transnationales ne-bis-in-idem? In: Donatsch A, Forster M, Schwarzenegger C (eds) Strafrecht, Strafprozessrecht und Menschenrechte. Festschrift für Stefan Trechsel zum 65. Geburtstag. Schulthess, Zürich, pp 253–267

Lagodny O (2005) Überlegungen zu einem menschengerechten transnationalen Straf- und Strafverfahrensrecht. In: Arnold J, Burkhardt B, Gropp W, Heine G, Koch H-G, Lagodny O, Perron W, Walther S (eds) Menschengerechtes Strafrecht. Festschrift für Albin Eser zum 70. Geburtstag. C.F. Beck, München, pp 777–795

Lelieur J (2013) Report on France. In: Ruggeri S (ed) Transnational inquiries and the protection of fundamental rights in criminal proceedings. A study in Memory of Vittorio Grevi and Giovanni Tranchina. Springer, Heidelberg, pp 309–407

Negri D (2004) Fumus commissi delicti. La prova per le fattispecie cautelari. Giappichelli, Torino

Nobili M (1982) Successione nel tempo di norme sui termini massimi della custodia preventiva e principi costituzionali. Foro italiano I

Oehler D (1983) Internationales Strafrecht, 2nd edn. Carl Heymanns, Köln

Padovani T (2012) Diritto penale, 10th edn. Giuffrè, Milano

Panebianco G (2010) L'esercizio di un diritto. In: de Vero G (ed) La legge penale, il reato, il reo, la persona offesa. Trattato teorico-pratico di diritto penale, coordinated by Palazzo F, Paliero CE, vol I. Giappichelli, Torino, pp 329ff.

Peers S (2010) The proposed European Investigation Order. Assault on human rights and national sovereignty, www.statewatch.org

Rafaraci T (2012) The application of the principle of mutual recognition to decisions on supervision measures as an alternative to provisional detention. In: Ruggeri S (ed) Liberty and security in Europe. A comparative analysis of pre-trial precautionary measures in criminal proceedings. V&R Unipress, Göttingen, pp 67–83

Risicato L (2004) Gli elementi normativi della fattispecie penale. Profili generali e problemi applicative. Giuffrè, Milano

Ruggeri A (2001) Sovranità dello Stato e sovranità sovranazionale, attraverso i diritti umani, e le prospettive di un diritto europeo "intercostituzionale". Diritto pubblico comparato ed europeo 2:544ff.

Ruggeri S (2012) Libertà personale e procedimento penale nel diritto comparato: tutela del processo e tutela della persona in Europa. Revista de Estudos Criminais 9–69

Ruggeri S (2013a) Horizontal cooperation, obtaining evidence overseas and the respect for fundamental rights in the EU. From the European Commission's proposal to the proposal for a directive on a European Investigation Order: towards a single tool of evidence gathering in the EU? In: Ruggeri S (ed) Transnational inquiries and the protection of fundamental rights in criminal proceedings. A study in memory of Vittorio Grevi and Giovanni Tranchina. Springer, Heidelberg, pp 279–310

Ruggeri S (2013b) Concorrenza tra potestà punitive, conflitti transnationali di giurisdizione. Il contributo della comparazione giuridica al diritto penale transnationale orientato ai diritti della persona. La legislazione penale (in press)

Ruggieri F (ed) (2013) Criminal proceedings, language and the European Union. Linguistic and legal issues. Springer, Heidelberg

Sanders A, Young R, Burton M (2012) Criminal justice, 4th edn. Oxford University Press, New York

Satzger H (2006) Die europäische Vollstreckungsübernahme. In: Schünemann B (ed) Ein Gesamtkonzept für die europäische Strafrechtspflege/A programme for European criminal justice. Carl Heymanns, Köln, pp 146–159

Satzger H (2011) Internationales und Europäisches Strafrecht, 5th edn. Nomos, Baden-Baden

Schünemann B (2003) Europäischer Haftbefehl und EU-Verfassungsentwurf auf schiefer Ebene – Die Schranken des Grundgesetztes. Zeitschrift für Rechtspolitik 185–480

Schünemann B (2006a) Die Grundlagen eines transnationalen Strafverfahrens. In: Schünemann B (ed) Ein Gesamtkonzept für die europäische Strafrechtspflege/A programme for European criminal justice. Carl Heymanns, Köln, pp 93–111

Schünemann B (ed) (2006b) Ein Gesamtkonzept für die europäische Strafrechtspflege/A programme for European criminal justice. Carl Heymanns, Köln

Sinn A (2007) Rechtsvergleichende Beobachtungen zu organisierter Kriminalität/kriminellen Organisationen und Terrorismus. In: Gropp W, Sinn A (eds) Organisierte Kriminalität und kriminelle Organisationen. Präventive und repressive Maßnahmen vor dem Hintergrund des 11. September 2001. Nomos, Baden-Baden, pp 641ff.

Sinn A (2012a) Jurisdictional law as the key to solving conflicts: comparative law observations. In: Sinn A (ed) Jurisdiktionskonflikte bei grenzüberschreitend organisierter Kriminalität. Ein Rechtsvergleich zum internationalen Strafrecht/Conflicts of jurisdiction in cross-border crime situations. A comparative law study of international criminal law. V&R Unipress, Osnabrück, pp 531–554

Sinn A (2012b) Draft models of a regulatory mechanism for the avoidance of jurisdictional conflicts. In: Sinn A (ed) Jurisdiktionskonflikte bei grenzüberschreitend organisierter Kriminalität. Ein Rechtsvergleich zum internationalen Strafrecht/Conflicts of jurisdiction in cross-border crime situations. A comparative law study of international criminal law. V&R Unipress, Osnabrück, pp 597–615

Sinn A (ed) (2012c) Jurisdiktionskonflikte bei grenzüberschreitend organisierter Kriminalität. Ein Rechtsvergleich zum internationalen Strafrecht/Conflicts of jurisdiction in cross-border crime situations. A comparative law study of international criminal law. V&R Unipress, Osnabrück

Thaman SC (2013) Report on USA. In: Ruggeri S (ed) Transnational inquiries and the protection of fundamental rights in criminal proceedings. A study in memory of Vittorio Grevi and Giovanni Tranchina. Springer, Heidelberg, pp 509–529

Vallines García E (2006) Los equipos conjuntos de investigación penal. Ed. Colex, Madrid

Vervaele JAE (2009) Il progetto di decisione quadro sul mandato di ricerca della prova. In: Illuminati G (ed) Prova penale e Unione europea. Bononia University Press, Bologna, pp 153–160

Visconti C (2003) Contiguità alla mafia e responsabilità penale. Giappichelli, Torino

Vogel J (2010) Transkulturelles Strafrecht. Goltdammer's Archiv für Strafrecht 1:1–13

Volk K (1978) Prozeßvoraussetzungen im Strafrecht. Zum Verhältnis von materiellem Recht und Prozessrecht. Gremer, Ebelsbach am Main

Wörner L (2013) Conflitti transnazionali di giurisdizione in materia penale. La prospettiva del diritto tedesco. La legislazione penale (in press)

Wörner L, Wörner M (2012) Landesbericht Deutschland. In: Sinn A (ed), Jurisdiktionskonflikte bei grenzüberschreitend organisierter Kriminalität. Ein Rechtsvergleich zum internationalen Strafrecht/Conflicts of jurisdiction in cross-border crime situations. A comparative law study of international criminal law. V&R Unipress, Osnabrück, pp. 203–261

Annex

Format for the Analysis on the Proposal for a Directive on the European Investigation Order

Stefano Ruggeri

General Issues

1. Subject of the new instrument: a new legislative action aimed at providing a single instrument of gathering evidence overseas

    1.1. The aim of replacing all the existing instruments with an EIO with a global scope: similarities and differences between the proposed approach and the FD EAW

    1.2. The *need* for replacing all the existing instruments with an EIO with a global scope: practical and theoretical justification

2. Approach of the new instrument: mutual recognition as basis for the collection of overseas evidence

    2.1. A new way of providing mutual recognition

    2.2. The complex nature of the new proposed instrument: from MR *instead of* MLA to MR *combined with* (the flexibility of) MLA

3. Cross-border investigations under the new instrument

    3.1. The widening of the notion of "transnational investigations" in the new instrument

    3.2. The co-existence of three models of obtaining evidence overseas: (a) ordering an investigative activity overseas, (b) obtaining the results of investigative activities already in possession of the executing authority and (c) conducting extraterritorial investigations

S. Ruggeri (ed.), *Transnational Evidence and Multicultural Inquiries in Europe*,
DOI 10.1007/978-3-319-02570-4, © Springer International Publishing Switzerland 2014

  3.2.1. The application of the new approach of mutual recognition to extra-territorial investigations
  3.2.2. The relationship between the EIO and the JIT

4. Aims of the proposed directive: the complex functional approach of the EIO

  4.1. Simplifying and speeding up the procedure
  4.2. Ensuring the admissibility of evidence
  4.3. Maintaining a high level of protection of fundamental rights (especially procedural rights)
  4.4. Reducing the financial costs
  4.5. Increasing mutual trust and cooperation between the member states
  4.6. Preserving the specificities of the national systems and their legal culture

Specific Issues

1. Defining the investigative activity to be conducted

  1.1. Focussing on the measure to be executed rather than on the evidence to be collected
  1.2. The possibility for the executing authority to use a different investigative measure

2. The preventive controls on overseas investigations

  2.1. The test of proportionality and necessity
  2.2. The check of availability of the measure in a similar national case

3. Recognition and execution: combining *lex loci* and *lex fori*

  3.1. Integration of procedural laws
  3.2. From mutual trust to mutual knowledge of procedural and evidentiary systems
  3.3. Similarities and differences between the EIO and the EEW

4. Joint inquiries and the collection of overseas evidence

  4.1. The role of authorities from the home state
  4.2. The role of private parties

    4.2.1. The right to defence in the execution of overseas investigations
    4.2.2. The right to defence while obtaining the evidence already gathered abroad
    4.2.3. The protection of the rights of third parties

5. Non recognition and non-execution: the protection of national sovereignty and individual rights

5.1. The two-level catalogue of grounds for non-recognition
5.2. Measures of coercion

    5.2.1. Need for a definition of "coercive measures" under the PD EIO
    5.2.2. The principles applying to coercive measures
    5.2.3. Investigative measures impinging on fundamental rights without coercion
    5.2.4. Carrying out non-coercive measures by coercive means

6. The protection of personal data
7. Challenging investigations overseas

    7.1. Legal remedies
    7.2. Preventive remedies

        7.2.1. Preventive means by the host authorities
        7.2.2. Preventive means by private parties

8. Special investigative measures
9. Alternative proposals

Printed by Printforce, the Netherlands